Lab Manual

to accompany A+ Guide to PC Operating Systems

Michael W. Graves

THOMSON
DELMAR LEARNING

Australia • Canada • Mexico • Singapore • Spain • United Kingdom • United States

Lab Manual to accompany A+ Guide to PC Operating Systems

by Michael W. Graves

Vice President, Technology and Trades SBU:
Alar Elken

Editorial Director:
Sandy Clark

Senior Acquistions Editor:
Stephen Helba

Senior Channel Manager:
Dennis Williams

Senior Development Editor:
Michelle Ruelos Cannistraci

Marketing Director:
Dave Garza

Marketing Coordinator:
Stacey Wiktorek

Production Director:
Mary Ellen Black

Production Manager:
Larry Main

Senior Project Editor:
Christopher Chien

Art/Design Coordinator:
Francis Hogan

Senior Editorial Assistant:
Dawn Daugherty

Printed in Canada
1 2 3 4 5 6 XXX 07 06 05

For more information contact Thomson/Delmar Learning
5 Maxwell Drive
Clifton Park, N.Y. 12065

Or find us on the World Wide Web at
www.delmarlearning.com

Library of Congress Card Number: 2005920436

Lab Manual to accompany A+ Guide to PC Operating Systems/
Michael W. Graves

ISBN: 1401852513

NOTICE TO THE READER

TABLE OF CONTENTS

INTRODUCTION

Welcome to the Lab Manual for *The A+ Guide to PC Operating Systems*. The labs included in this manual have been specifically designed to provide the student with some hands-on experience in the installation, configuration, and troubleshooting of Microsoft operating systems. In addition, there is going to be a bit of exposure to the system hardware as well, so it wouldn't hurt to have a basic understanding in that area of expertise.

In order to accomplish the exercises in these labs the classrooms will have to be equipped with some basic necessities. These include a PC for each of the students with the following minimum specifications:

- 700MHz CPU
- 128MB RAM
- 2GB hard disk drive
- Floppy diskette drive
- CD-ROM drive
- Keyboard
- Mouse
- SVGA monitor
- One available PCI slot

A network interface card will also be required. However, it is best that this not be integrated onto the motherboard. One of the exercises deals with installing that device, so the card should not already be installed into the system.

Other materials needed to complete these labs include:

- One copy each of the following operating systems:
  - MS-DOS version 5 or later (optional)
  - Windows 98 or Windows 98SE
  - Windows 2000
  - Windows XP
- A box of floppy disks
- Tapes for the drive
- A printer (or even better, one printer for each computer)
- Device drivers for the printer
- A tape drive (optional)
- A patch cord long enough to reach from the computer to the wall jack or hub
- Writing materials
- A good sense of humor

The classroom should be set up in such a way that each student will have sufficient space to work. In one lab this will involve installing a network interface card and another will involve building a peer to peer network. For those labs, a little extra workspace is in order as well.

These labs are going to provide students an opportunity to get their hands a bit dirty as they encounter a large number of the CompTIA objectives for the Core Exam. Unfortunately, since the exam is theoretical as well as practical, some objectives won't be covered. For those, you'll need to rely on your textbook. Objectives that are covered include the following:

1.1 Identify the major desktop components and interfaces and their functions. Differentiate the characteristics of Windows 9x/Me, Windows NT 4.0 Workstation, Windows 2000 Professional, and Windows XP.

1.2 Identify the names, locations, purposes, and contents of major system files.

1.3 Demonstrate the ability to use command-line functions and utilities to manage the operating system, including the proper syntax and switches.

1.4 Identify basic concepts and procedures for creating, viewing, and managing disks, directories, and files. This includes procedures for changing file attributes and the ramifications of those changes (for example, security issues).

1.5 Identify the major operating system utilities, their purpose, location, and available switches.

2.1 Identify the procedures for installing Windows 9x/Me, Windows NT 4.0 Workstation, Windows 2000 Professional, and Windows XP, and bringing the operating system to a basic operational level.

2.3 Identify the basic system boot sequences and boot methods, including the steps to create an emergency boot disk with utilities installed for Windows 9x/Me, Windows NT 4.0 Workstation, Windows 2000 Professional, and Windows XP.

2.4 Identify procedures for installing/adding a device, including loading, adding, and configuring device drivers, and required software.

3.1 Recognize and interpret the meaning of common error codes and startup messages from the boot sequence and identify steps to correct the problems.

3.2 Recognize when to use common diagnostic utilities and tools. Given a diagnostic scenario involving one of these utilities or tools, select the appropriate steps needed to resolve the problem.

3.3 Recognize common operational and usability problems and determine how to resolve them.

4.1 Identify the networking capabilities of Windows. Given configuration parameters, configure the operating system to connect to a network.

4.2 Identify the basic Internet protocols and terminologies. Identify procedures for establishing Internet connectivity. In a given scenario, configure the operating system to connect to and use Internet resources.

You will notice as you go through the labs that the same objectives will appear in different labs, again and again. This shouldn't come as much of a surprise since each of these objectives includes a number of subcomponents. So don't get tied up in the details to the point that you don't have fun and *learn!*

LAB 1

MS-DOS, CONFIG.SYS, AND AUTOEXEC.BAT

For many of you, this is not likely to be a hands-on lab. It's been a few years since MS-DOS has been available for purchase. If your school has copies available, then I highly recommend that the installation portion of this lab be completed as described. A hands-on installation will demonstrate just how far OS technology has come in two decades. It will also provide a more solid foundation for understanding the concepts and importance of CONFIG.SYS and AUTOEXEC.BAT.

In the event that this is not possible, skip to the sections that discuss various commands issued from the command prompt. Regardless of whether you ever see another system running DOS, you will still need a solid understanding of the command prompt in order to be a successful computer technician. *NOTE: This lab cannot be successfully completed using the command prompt of Windows XP without errors.*

The only materials you'll need for this lab are your lab computer systems and a copy of any version of MS-DOS later than 5.0.

The CompTIA objectives covered in this lab include the following:

1.1 Identify the *major* desktop components and interfaces and their functions. Differentiate the characteristics of Windows 9x/Me, Windows NT 4.0 Workstation, Windows 2000 Professional, and Windows XP.

1.2 Identify the names, locations, purposes, and contents of major system files.

1.3 Demonstrate the ability to use command-line functions and utilities to manage the operating system, including the proper syntax and switches.

EXERCISE 1: INSTALLING MS-DOS (OPTIONAL)

As much as I hate to do this, I have no choice but to make this an optional lab. If the software is available for installation, then by all means proceed. Unfortunately, this won't be an option for many. Therefore, the best you'll be able to do is follow along with the screen shots and read the instructions.

MS-DOS did not ship on CDs as do the OSs to which you've grown accustomed today. Depending on the version, DOS shipped on three to four high-density 3.5" floppy diskettes. DOS 6.22 was a short-lived version that shipped on four floppies. All other versions shipped on three. The first diskette is bootable. To install the OS, you place this first installation diskette into the floppy drive and start the machine. This diskette is configured with a default AUTOEXEC.BAT and CONFIG.SYS that first do a system check, as you see in **Figure L1.1** and then boot the computer to the initial installation screen shown in **Figure L1.2**.

From this screen, the user has several options. Pressing <Enter> causes the installation process to continue. Pressing F1 brings up a very limited help menu. F3 allows the boot process to continue—a skeleton OS is loaded to RAM, and the user can boot the machine to an A: prompt. This is useful as a troubleshooting tool in a few instances. Pressing F5 converts the display to monochrome, and F7 allows the user to set up an installation of MS-DOS that runs exclusively from floppy disks. (Yes, as amazing as it may seem, there was a time when computers did not ship with hard drives.)

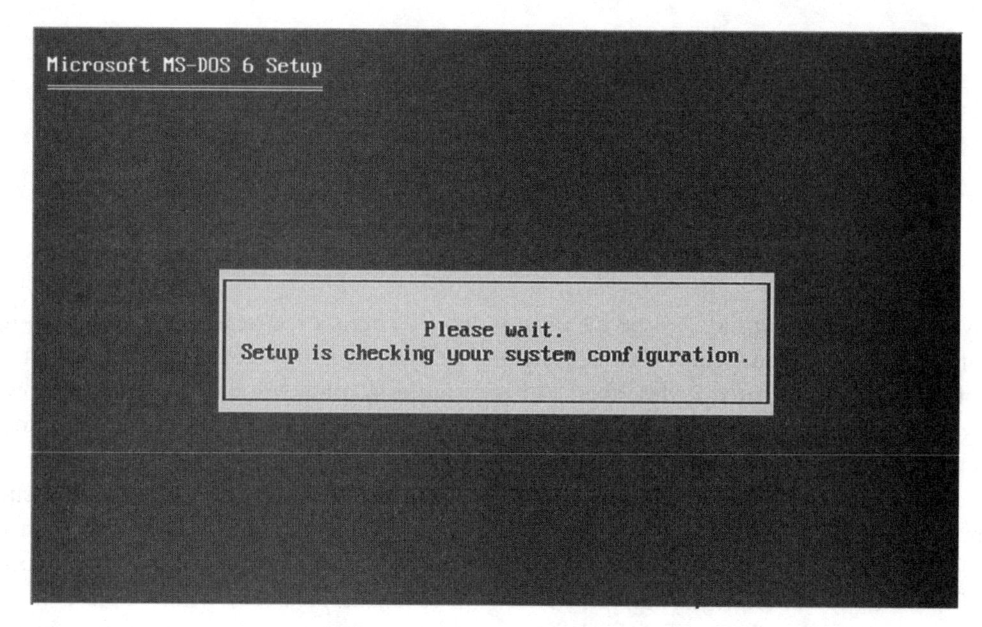

Figure L1.1 First DOS does a system check to see how much horsepower you're running.

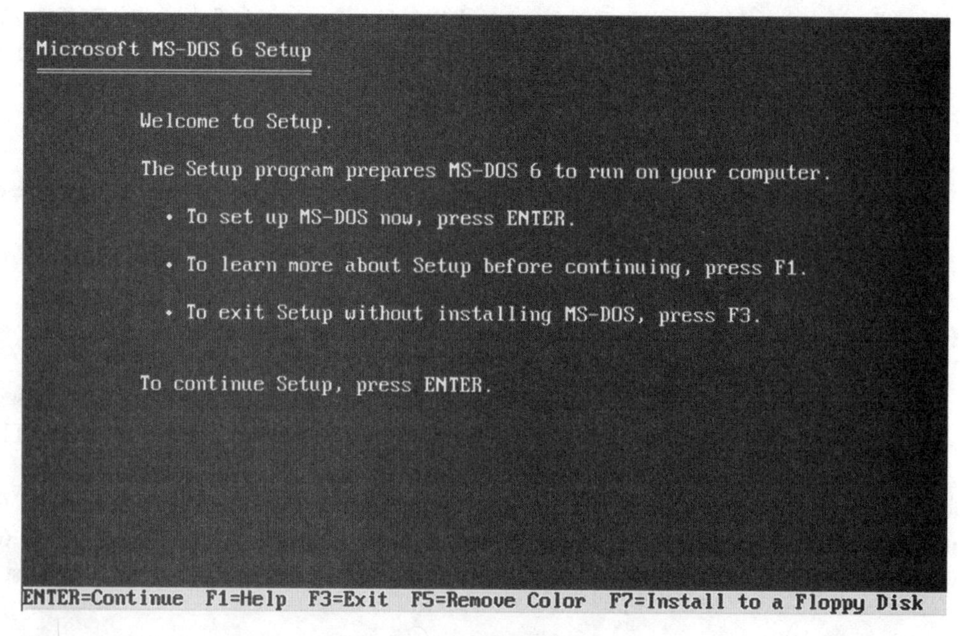

Figure L1.2 The initial installation screen of MS-DOS

Obviously, since this lab concerns the installation of DOS, you'll press <Enter>. If the hard disk onto which you are installing DOS has not been partitioned and formatted, as in the case of a brand new system or hard disk, the next screen to appear is the one shown in **Figure L1.3**. Select the option Configure unallocated disk space (recommended) and press <Enter>. By the way, if you are actually performing this installation, by now you've noticed that your mouse doesn't work. You have to make all of these selections using the arrows on your keyboard. How quaint!

This step doesn't take long at all. What is happening is that, in the background of the splash screen, the DOS installation program is using the FDISK utility to create an active partition and is writing the master boot record (MBR) to the hard drive. Next the screen shown in **Figure L1.4** tells you that your

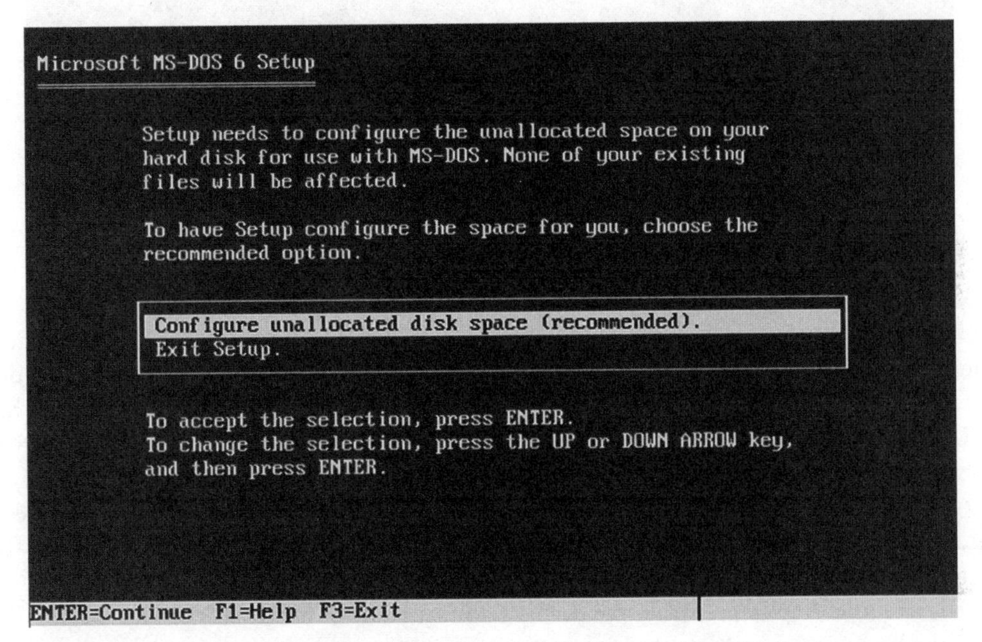

Figure L1.3 Before a new hard disk can accept a DOS installation, it must be configured.

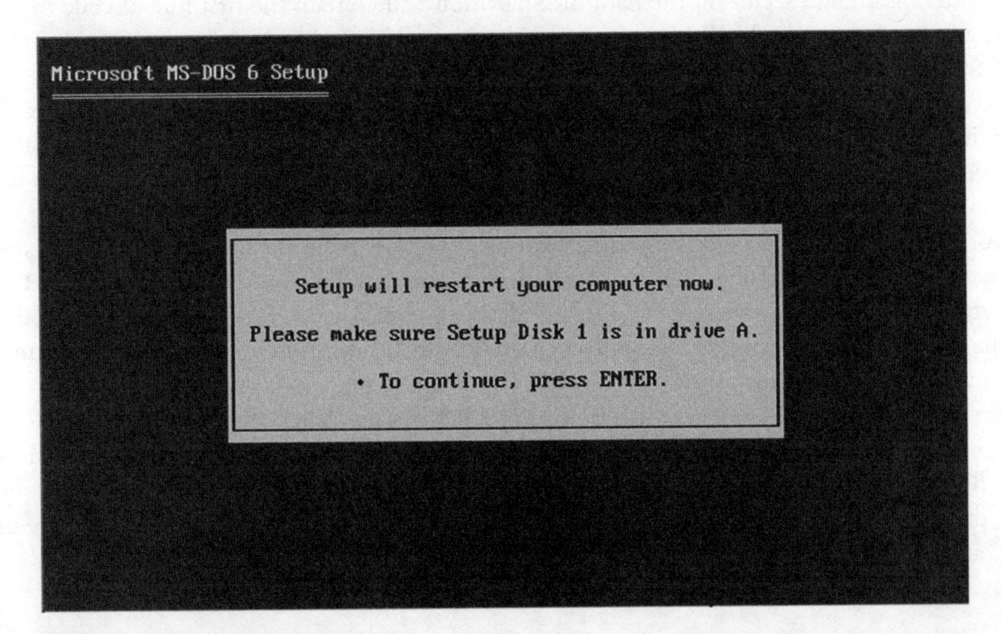

Figure L1.4 The first reboot

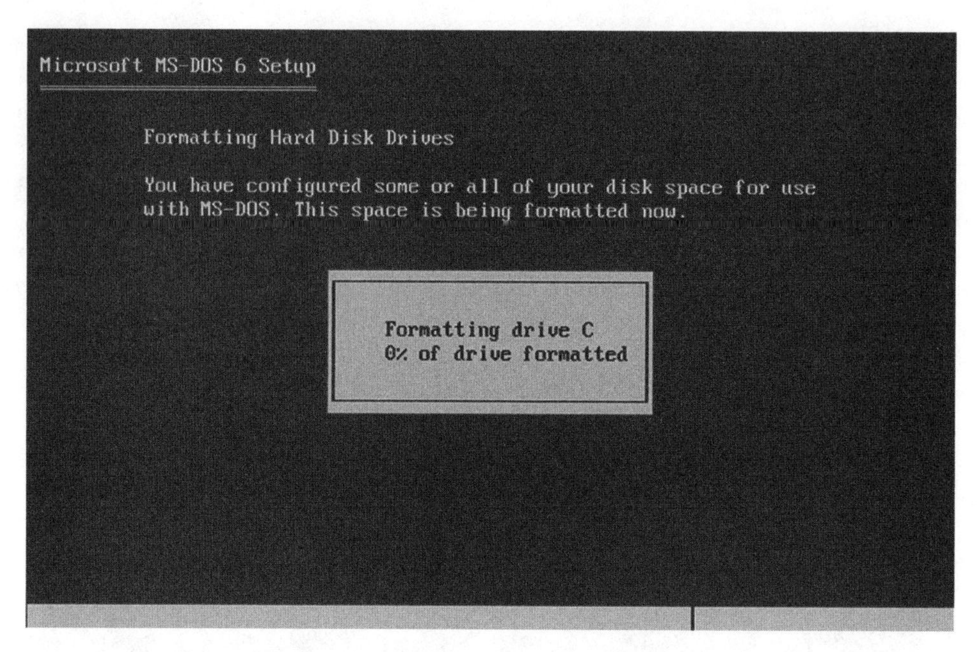

Figure L1.5 Formatting the hard disk

machine is about to reboot and that you need to leave Setup Disk One in the drive. Without that diskette in the floppy disk drive, the machine will not yet boot. There's still a lot more work left to do.

After the reboot is completed, the next step for the installation program is to format your hard disk (**Figure L1.5**). Something to keep in the back of your head throughout this lab is that MS-DOS knew no file system more complex than FAT16. (See Chapter One: An Introduction to Operating Systems in your text for a detailed discussion of file systems.) As such, the largest partition it can create is 2GB. Therefore, even if you're installing DOS onto an 80GB hard drive, the format procedure at this stage is going to give you a maximum of 2GB.

There is one final step in preparing the drive that must be done before this process begins. This step is done in the background and is completely transparent to the end user, but as a technician, you need to be aware of what is going on. During the formatting procedure, the file allocation tables (FAT) are being written to the hard disk. After the FAT is completed, the DOS installation program knows exactly what cylinder, head, and sector on the hard disk partition will contain the first line of code for the OS. It writes a short entry to the MBR identifying that location. This is the OS pointer discussed in Chapter One of the text.

Next you have the option of changing the default configuration for the DOS installation (**Figure L1.6**). There isn't a whole lot involved in this process. You can set the date and time, the country where you reside, and your choice of keyboard layout. Any other configuration changes have to wait until the installation is completed.

Before the actual copying of files begins, you are going to be given the opportunity to select the directory where the DOS system files will be stored (**Figure L1.7**). The default directory is C:\DOS. Unless you have some overpowering need to install to another directory, it is generally a good idea to select the default. Some programs look only to C:\DOS for critical system files and don't run if they aren't found in the first place they look.

After that the file copy process shown in **Figure L1.8** begins. When the File Copy process is about 20 percent complete, you will be prompted to insert Setup Disk Two by a screen like the one in **Figure L1.9**. This will happen yet again when the copying is about 56 percent done. Just insert the disks requested. If you accidentally insert the wrong diskette, Installation will tell you. The floppies are digitally labeled, and Setup reads the label to make sure it has the correct file source.

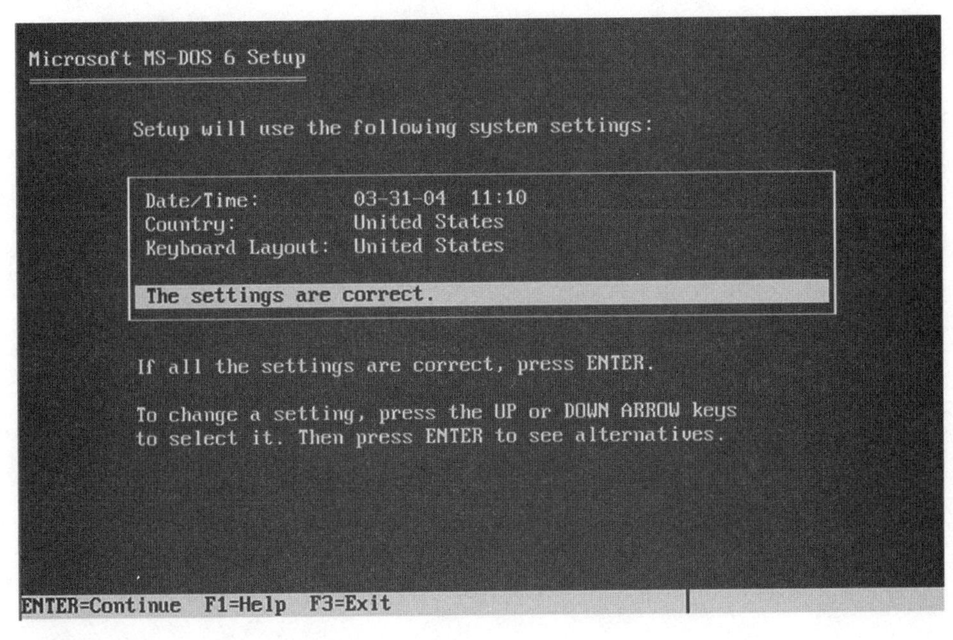

Figure L1.6 Configuring DOS

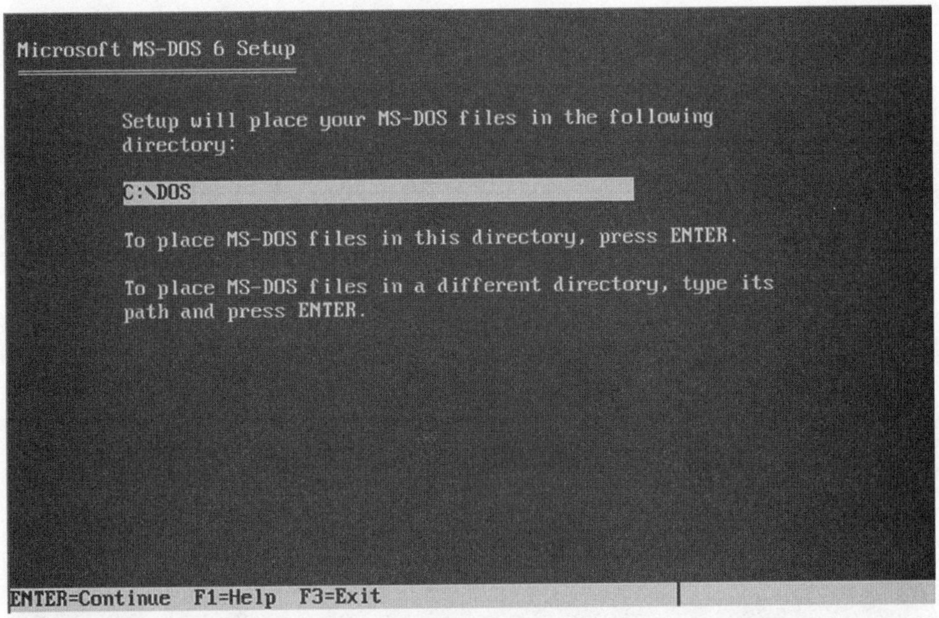

Microsoft MS-DOS 6 Setup

Setup will place your MS-DOS files in the following directory:

C:\DOS

To place MS-DOS files in this directory, press ENTER.

To place MS-DOS files in a different directory, type its path and press ENTER.

ENTER=Continue F1=Help F3=Exit

Figure L1.7 Selecting the DOS directory

When the last file has been copied to your hard drive, you've reached the final stage of the DOS installation. You must reboot the system one more time. You want it to boot to the hard disk, so, as the Setup program tells you in **Figure L1.10**, you need to remove the last floppy diskette from the drive and press the <Enter> key to continue.

MS-DOS is now installed on your computer. It will now boot to the lovely command prompt each and every time your start your computer.

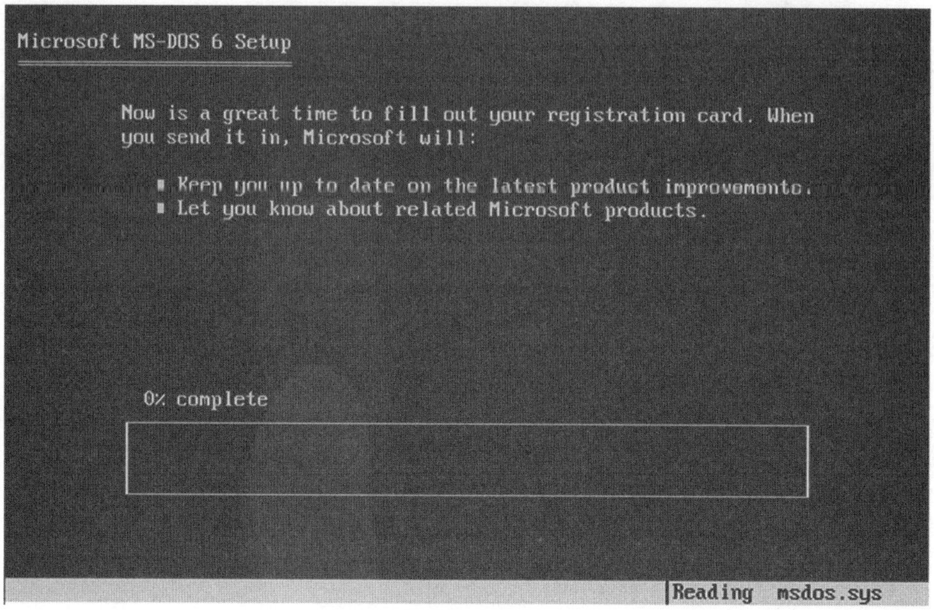

Microsoft MS-DOS 6 Setup
Now is a great time to fill out your registration card. When you send it in, Microsoft will:
Keep you up to date on the latest product improvements.
Let you know about related Microsoft products.
0% complete
Reading msdos.sys

Figure L1.8 Throughout the file copy process, you'll be bombarded by advertisements for a product you already bought.

Microsoft MS-DOS 6 Setup
Double your hard disk with DoubleSpace. MS-DOS 6 gives you a safe, easy way to increase your disk capacity by integrating data compression into the operating system.
Please insert the following disk in drive A:
Setup Disk #2
When you are ready to continue, press ENTER.
ENTER=Continue F3=Exit

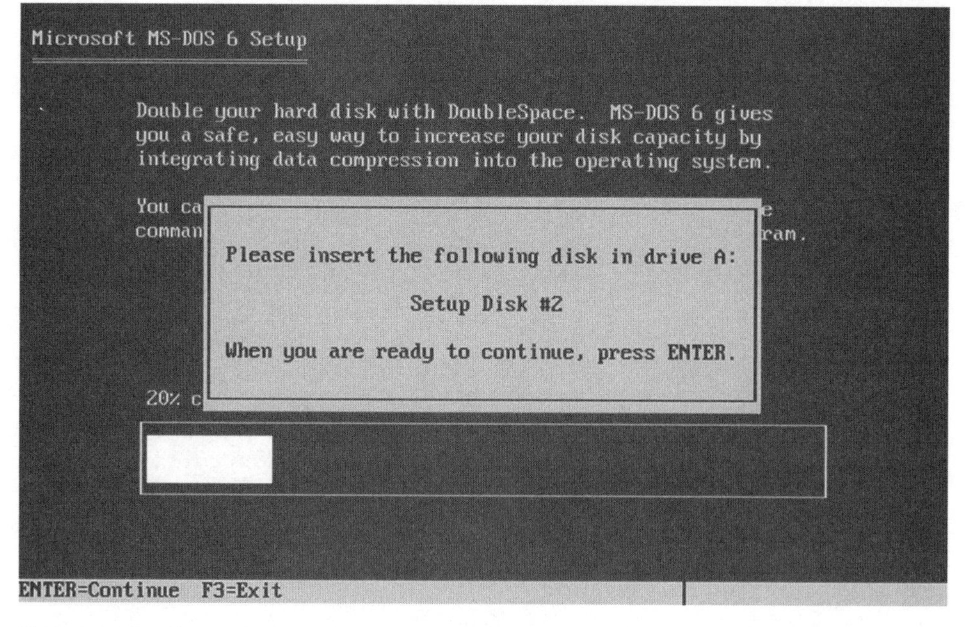

Figure L1.9 When the File Copy process is about 20 percent complete, and once again when it is about 56 percent complete, you will be prompted to change the diskette in the drive.

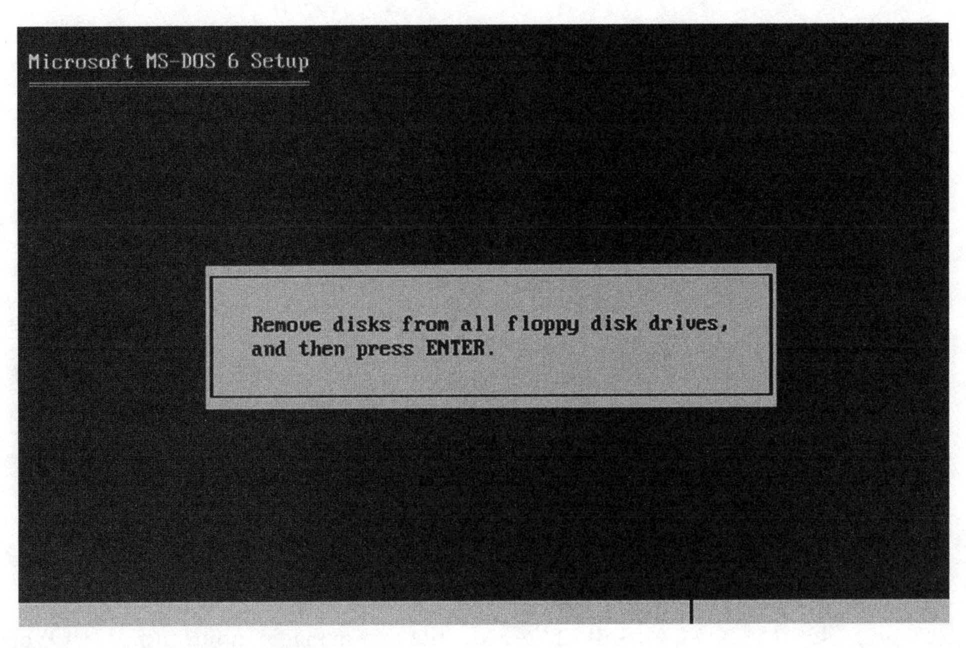

Figure L1.10 The final reboot

Exercise 1 Review

1. How many diskettes did MS-DOS 6.22 ship on? How about the other versions?
2. How many times does the computer reboot during the installation process?

Exercise 2: CONFIG.SYS and AUTOEXEC.BAT

Two files that were almost always necessary to the MS-DOS configuration were CONFIG.SYS and AUTOEXEC.BAT. CONFIG.SYS, as its name implies, is a file that defines the system configuration. AUTOEXEC.BAT defined what programs would launch automatically each time the machine started, and then remain RAM-resident the entire time, even if for any reason the program was shut down. Programs of this nature were called Terminate and Stay Resident (TSR) applications. Both of these files could be used to fine-tune the system configuration.

If you recall from Exercise 1, I mentioned that the configuration allowed during installation was rather minimal. CONFIG.SYS and AUTOEXEC.BAT allow third-party device drivers, configuration parameters, and TSRs to be selected and tweaked by the user. Both of these files load in advance of any user applications, although AUTOEXEC.BAT can be used to automatically order user applications to be loaded.

If you didn't have the luxury of installing MS-DOS onto computer systems in Exercise 1, the following exercises can be done from any Microsoft-based computer using the command prompt. On a Windows 98 computer, you can either click Start→Programs→MS-DOS Prompt or you can click Start→Run and type `command` in the run line. On Win2K or WINXP machines, select Start→Run and type `CMD` into the field.

Exercise 2A: CONFIG.SYS

If you recall from Chapter Two: MS-DOS and the Command Prompt from your text book, DOS has a strict order in which it loads. Three files constitute the core of the OS. These files are IO.SYS,

Figure L1.11 The XP incarnation of the old DOS Editor

MSDOS.SYS, and COMMAND.COM. IO.SYS is the file that manages input/output (I/O) operations. You probably already figured that out from its name. A key task of I/O for any computer system is talking to peripherals installed on the system. This includes devices that were installed after the fact, such as sound cards, modems, SCSI adapters, and a host of other devices that didn't come equipped on the original computer. During the boot process, before anything else can happen, I/O control must be established. Therefore, IO.SYS is the first file to load. It locates and loads CONFIG.SYS. CONFIG.SYS is where device drivers, both real and virtual, are loaded, as well as a number of configuration parameters. In this section I'll cover some typical commands to be loaded into CONFIG.SYS.

In the old days of DOS these files were edited using the MS-DOS Editor. This was launched by typing **`Edit`** at the command prompt. Oddly enough, that little utility has never gone away. **Figure L1.11** shows the Edit utility for WINXP. For editing CONFIG.SYS and AUTOEXEC.BAT, either the DOS editor or the Notepad utility in Windows should always be used. They do not add extraneous formatting characters, as do Wordpad or MS Word.

For the rest of this exercise and throughout the next, I'll be having you use the command prompt editor for creating these files. If you are performing these exercises on working machines, you might want to save any pre-existing CONFIG.SYS files on the system. From the command prompt, type **`CD\`** to get to the root directory. Next, type **`REN CONFIG.SYS CONFIG.BAK`** in order to rename the file. Type **`REN AUTOEXEC.BAT AUTOEXEC.BAK`** to rename AUTOEXEC.BAT.

To start, simply type the first line I provide into the Editor and then save the file as C:\CONFIG.SYS. When you're finished, make sure you save the final version. Now let's look at some of the commands typically found in CONFIG.SYS. In order to emphasize where spaces belong and where they don't in the next few pages, I will be placing three spaces in place of a single space. This is not recommended in real practice.

FILES= This statement specifies the maximum number of individual file handles DOS will generate. Since DOS can only open a file if there is a file handle available, this dictates how many files can be open. With no entry, the default setting is 8. The maximum number allowable is 255. Frequently the default number of files DOS could open was far too small. Some applications adjusted this value for the end user during installation, increasing it to the necessary level. If not, a minimum value of 32 was recommended. It was important not to get carried away. Increasing the number in the FILES= statement increased the amount of conventional memory used. **Table L1.1** lists the amount of memory used for some common values.

The proper syntax for the FILES= statement is

```
FILES=32
```

Type that into CONFIG.SYS and save your file.

BUFFERS= DOS needs an area of reserved memory it can use for storing data that is in transit. I/O operations rarely occur in a single clock cycle. Therefore, a stream of data can only flow as fast as the receiving device can take it. This is true of commands as well as data. If a system is configured to use high memory, 512 bytes of conventional memory will be allocated as a "window" for buffered data as it moves from conventional to high memory. If high memory is not used, each buffer will allocate 532 bytes of conventional memory. By default, the number of buffers allocated by DOS varies with system configuration. **Table L1.2** shows the default allocation of buffers by MS-DOS.

The proper syntax for loading buffers is

```
BUFFERS=20
```

Type that line into CONFIG.SYS and save the file.

Table L1.1 Conventional Memory Used by the FILES= Statement

Files Value	Bytes Consumed
8 (Default)	192
10	496
15	608
20	896
25	1200
30	1488
35	1776
40	2080
45	2368
50	2672
55	2960
60	3260
65	3552
70	3856
75	4144

Increasing the number of files open in CONFIG.SYS consumed additional conventional memory.

STACKS= Hardware interrupts require a certain amount of conventional memory for their interrupt drivers. The STACKS= statement is going to contain two values, separated by a comma. The first value dictates the number of stacks, and the second determines the size of each stack in bytes. A valid range for the number of stacks is from 8 to 64. Stacks can be a maximum of 512 bytes. If MS-DOS detects a CPU more recent than a 80286, it assigns a default value of 9,128, or nine stacks of 128 bytes. Most systems are more stable with nine stacks of 256 bytes. The correct syntax for the line is

```
STACKS=9,256
```

Table L1.2 Default Buffers and Memory Usage in MS-DOS

Configuration	Default Buffers	Bytes Used
<128K of RAM, 360K disk	2	1064
<128K of RAM, 720K disk (or larger)	3	1596
128K to 255K of RAM	5	2672
256K to 511K of RAM	10	5328
512K to 640K of RAM	15	7984

When buffers load, increasing the number depletes the supply of available conventional memory.

Add this line to CONFIG.SYS and save the file.

DEVICE= and **DEVICEHIGH=** These are the commands that load third-party device drivers during the boot process of MS-DOS. DEVICE= loads the drivers into conventional memory, while DEVICEHIGH= loads them into high memory. For the latter to work, the first device to be loaded has to be a DOS virtual device called HIMEM.SYS. In order to make use of extended memory, this line has to be followed by another that loads a program called EMM386.EXE. To properly load, the entire path to the file has to be specified in the line. After the name of the device driver, additional parameters specific to the drive can be loaded. This might include bits of information such as what IRQ the device is configured for, a specific I/O address, or a DMA channel. Parameters are preceded by a forward slash. An example used by HIMEM.SYS is the parameter TESTMEM. The options are ON or OFF. Since the vast majority of people using this lab manual will be playing with Windows machines and not DOS, this example is based on the Windows OS. If you were fortunate enough to be able to install DOS, replace \WINDOWS\SYSTEM32 with \DOS. The proper syntax is

```
DEVICE=C:\WINDOWS\SYSTEM32\HIMEM.SYS   /TESTMEM:OFF
```

Add that line to CONFIG.SYS and save your file. Remember that where I used three spaces, you only need one. Since you need EMM386.EXE to be running before you can use expanded or extended memory, also add the line:

```
DEVICE=C:\WINDOWS\EMM386.EXE
```

CAUTION: Do not try this in XP. Add this to CONFIG.SYS and save the file.

LASTDRIVE= By default, DOS looks at the letter of the last hard disk (either physical or logical) installed and adds one more drive, up to drive letter E. By adding a LASTDRIVE statement, drive letters up to Drive Z are possible. The correct syntax is:

```
LASTDRIVE=Z
```

Add this line to CONFIG.SYS and save your file.

NUMLOCK= People who use the number pad on their keyboard for numbers always want this setting to be ON. Gamers who use those keys as arrows for their characters and triggers for their weapons want it OFF. This line in CONFIG.SYS overrides any setting in BIOS. The correct syntax is:

```
NUMLOCK=OFF
```

Or ON, whichever, you prefer. You decide and add the line to your CONFIG.SYS. Save the file.

There are other commands that can be added to CONFIG.SYS, but these are the most common. For a more detailed discussion, refer to Chapter Two in the text book.

EXERCISE 2A REVIEW

1. You've just installed a new DOS program and the first time you run it, you get the message that says "Insufficient File Handles. Application Terminated." What line in CONFIG.SYS would you change to fix this problem?
2. You're running MS-DOS and are frequently getting a message that says "STACK OVERFLOW," and the system shuts down. What line can you change to fix this problem?

EXERCISE 2B: AUTOEXEC.BAT

AUTOEXEC.BAT is kind of a catch-all file that technicians can use to add any number of different things. Device drivers that run as executables can be loaded from here, as can any program or batch file that your little heart desires. There are also some system parameters that load as commands. Here is a look at a few AUTOEXEC.BAT functions.

As with Exercise 2a, open your command prompt editor and create a new file called C:\AUTOEXEC.BAT. As before, if this is a functioning system that you want to put back the way it was, rename the existing AUTOEXEC.BAT to AUTOEXEC.BAK.

@ECHO OFF Many technicians and end users well-versed in MS-DOS frequently place this as the first line in an AUTOEXEC.BAT file. This line prevents commands in AUTOEXEC.BAT from flashing up on the display as they are read and executed. Proper syntax is

```
@ECHO OFF
```

Add this line to your AUTOEXEC.BAT and save the file.

PROMPT This command dictates what the command prompt will look like. There is no equal sign used after this command as in some of the previous examples. There are a number of parameters that define different things, and each of these parameters must be preceded by a dollar sign ($). **Table L1.3** is a list of available PROMPT parameters and what they do.

The proper syntax for a PROMPT command is

```
PROMPT   $P$G$T$D
```

As before, where I've got three spaces for emphasis, you need but one. Add this line to your AUTOEXEC.BAT and save your file.

Table L1.3 Prompt Parameters and Their Results

Parameter	Result
$T	Current time
$D	Current date
$P	Current drive and path
$V	Windows version number
$N	Current drive
$G	> (greater-than sign)
$L	< (less-than sign)
$B	| (pipe)
$H	Backspace (erases previous character)
$E	Escape code (ASCII code 27)
$_	Carriage return and linefeed

In the days of DOS, one of the ways you advertised yourself as a true geek was to make a customized command prompt.

PATH= In the days of DOS, everything was done from a command prompt. Typing a command at the prompt either worked, or it didn't. One of the things that dictated what happened was your path statement. If your prompt looks like C:\DOS\COMMAND, that indicates that you have browsed to the COMMAND subdirectory of the DOS directory. If you type a command at that point and have no PATH statement in AUTOEXEC.BAT, DOS will look in the C:\DOS\COMMAND directory for that command. If the command does not reside in that directory, the user gets the infamous "BAD COMMAND OR FILE NAME" error message. If a PATH statement exists in AUTOEXEC.BAT, after looking in C:\DOS\COMMAND, COMMAND.COM will next search each directory listed in the PATH statement. Most applications are programmed to automatically add themselves to the PATH statement when they install. Each directory in the statement is separated by a semicolon. The correct syntax is

```
PATH=C:\;\DOS;\WINDOWS
```

Add this line to AUTOEXEC.BAT and save your file.

LH This is an acronym for Load High. LH followed by any executable command loads that executable into upper memory, provided there is sufficient space in upper memory to do so and providing that HIMEM.SYS and EMM386.SYS are properly loaded. An example of this command in use, with proper syntax is

```
LH C:\DOS\MOUSE.COM
```

Since it is highly unlikely that you will actually have a DOS directory on the machine you're using, I will *not* have you copy this file to your AUTOEXEC.BAT.

Now that you have both a newly configured CONFIG.SYS and AUTOEXEC.BAT files loaded, reboot your machine and watch for changes. The most noticeable will be your command prompt when you open a command prompt window.

EXERCISE 2B REVIEW

1. What was the purpose of @ECHO OFF?
2. What would be the effect of adding the line PROMPT PG to your AUTOEXEC.BAT?

EXERCISE 3: TROUBLESHOOTING CONFIG.SYS (OPTIONAL)

One of the things about CONFIG.SYS is that, like any other computer code in your system, the system reads the lines in this file quite literally. Any misspelling of a command or device driver will result in errors, and if the path to a particular file isn't correct, you'll get errors. Also, the lines are loaded in the order they appear in the file. If you recall from Exercise 2a, I mentioned that in order to use high memory you have to have a file called HIMEM.SYS loaded. In order for you to use extended memory, EMM386.EXE has to be loaded. They also have to be loaded in the correct order. If you were to reverse lines four and five of the CONFIG.SYS file you created earlier in this lab, the next time you booted your machine you would get an error message during boot up that reads "Error in config.sys, line 4." It won't tell you what the error is, but since it tells you what line the error is in, you should have no difficulty looking at the specific line for errors. Problems to look for include proper spelling, proper syntax, proper placement in the file, and proper use of parameters.

EMM386.EXE requires the services of HIMEM.SYS to properly function. If HIMEM.SYS isn't already loaded when EMM386.EXE attempts to load, it will fail and deliver a message.

Adding any line relating to EMM386.EXE in Windows XP will result in errors. There is no expanded memory support in XP, and this file no longer exists. Let's look at how it works.

1. Open your CONFIG.SYS file in the DOS Editor.
2. Edit line four to read DEVICE=HIMEM.SYS.
3. Restart your machine.

You'll immediately be treated to the Error in CONFIG.SYS, Line X error message. HIMEM.SYS is not located in the root directory and, therefore, could not be located without the full path.

Exercise 3 Review

1. If you are running a Windows machine and you have an error in CONFIG.SYS, how will that error affect your machine? (Note: You'll have to refer to the textbook, Chapter Two, to answer this question.)
2. If the PATH statement in AUTOEXEC.BAT contains the correct path to HIMEM.SYS, will CONFIG.SYS then be able to locate the file even if you haven't typed the full path into the CONFIG.SYS line?

Lab Review

1. You have a device driver located in the C:\TOY directory called TOY.SYS. How would you write a line to load that driver at startup?
2. In what file should you place the above-mentioned line?
3. What utility is used to prepare a hard disk for Microsoft OSs using any version of FAT?
4. You are playing an old DOS game and constantly get STACK OVERFLOW errors the instant the machine crashes. What line might fix this problem and where would you put it?

Lab Summary

For the average Windows user, this entire lab appears on the surface to be about as useful as an ejection seat in a helicopter. Nobody runs DOS anymore, and Windows makes no use of CONFIG.SYS or AUTOEXEC.BAT. So why waste your time?

As of this writing, there are still a number of companies running proprietary DOS applications that for one reason or the other, they can't port to Windows. For those apps to work, a viable CONFIG.SYS and/or AUTOEXEC.BAT file must be present and properly configured. What a wonderful impression you're going to make on your new boss if you have to look him or her right in the eye and say, "I haven't got a clue how to do that."

LAB 2

PREPARING A HARD DISK THE OLD-FASHIONED WAY

Starting with this lab, you're going to begin looking at operating systems that still have a substantial base of installations around the world. An unofficial estimate at the time of this writing is that there are still in excess of 20 million computers out there running some version of Win9x. Although there is a possibility that you may never be called on to install the product, there is an even stronger possibility that you *will* be called on to service it. You might as well get the hang of installing it as long as you're going to all this effort anyway.

The only materials you'll need for this lab are your lab computers, Win98 CD and Startup diskette, and any third-party drivers required for proprietary hardware.

The CompTIA objectives covered in this lab include the following:

1.3 Demonstrate the ability to use command-line functions and utilities to manage the operating system, including the proper syntax and switches.

1.4 Identify basic concepts and procedures for creating, viewing, and managing disks, directories, and files. This includes procedures for changing file attributes and the ramifications of those changes (for example, security issues).

1.5 Identify the major operating system utilities, their purpose, location, and available switches.

PREPARING THE HARD DISK

In the next hour to an hour and a half, you'll be going through an actual installation of Windows 98. I'll take you through the process step by step and explain what's happening along the way. I'll also show you a couple of things you might miss if all you ever do is accept defaults. However, in most cases, before the OS can be installed, the computer's hard disk has to be partitioned and formatted. Exercise 1 covers this aspect of the installation.

EXERCISE 1: THE FDISK UTILITY

For this exercise, each student needs to have access to a lab machine and a boot diskette with CD-ROM support. If you used the Windows 98 Startup Disk utility or downloaded the boot image from www.mwgraves.com, then you have what you need. So let's install Windows. (*Note:* Windows 98 ships on a bootable CD, so if for any reason, a boot diskette is not available, Setup can be started from the CD as long as the machine's CMOS is configured to boot to CD-ROM. The purpose of booting to the floppy in this exercise is to point out a minor difference in the process.)

Insert the boot diskette into the floppy diskette drive and start the machine. If this is the first time you've ever booted to floppy, don't be concerned about the amount of time it takes. That's normal. Using a boot diskette created from Win98, you'll get a Startup menu similar to the one in **Figure L2.1**.

Since you want to configure your hard drive before you do anything else, there's no point in waiting for all those CD-ROM drivers to load. After it boots to the A:\ prompt, perform the following steps:

1. At the A: prompt, type **`fdisk`** and then press the <Enter> key. The opening screen will appear (**Figure L2.2**). All that fancy explanation is simply asking you whether you want to format your drive to FAT16 or FAT32. If you choose Y (yes) when it asks whether you want to use large disk support, you have selected FAT32. If you press N (no), you will select FAT16. If for any reason you need FAT16, you should press N. For the purposes of this (and later) exercises, press Y.
2. The FDISK Options screen appears next (**Figure L2.3**). It is from this screen that the various tasks are selected. Which task you select depends entirely upon what you're trying to do. On a brand new unprepared hard drive, you would choose Option 1: Create DOS partition or Logical DOS Drive. If you are working with a disk that has previously contained data, you would want to start by selecting Option 4: Display partition information. Option 5: Change current fixed disk drive, will appear only in systems that have more than one physical hard disk installed. FDISK can recognize when there is only a single hard disk and, in that case, Option 5 will not appear. For this exercise, select Option 4.

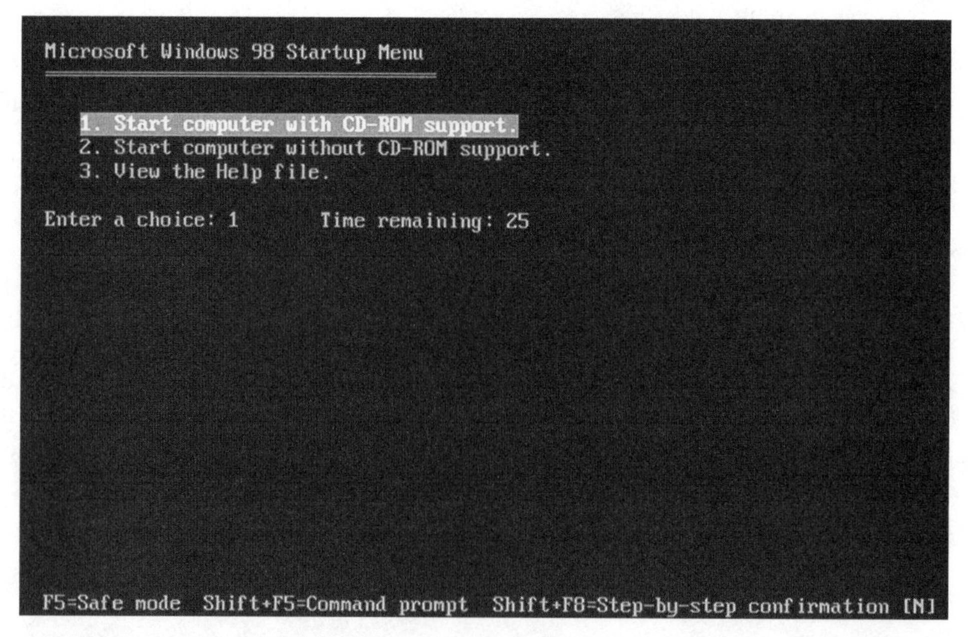

Figure L2.1 Booting a machine to a Startup diskette created by Win98 offers a boot menu with three options.

```
Your computer has a disk larger than 512 MB. This version of Windows
includes improved support for large disks, resulting in more efficient
use of disk space on large drives, and allowing disks over 2 GB to be
formatted as a single drive.

IMPORTANT: If you enable large disk support and create any new drives on this
disk, you will not be able to access the new drive(s) using other operating
systems, including some versions of Windows 95 and Windows NT, as well as
earlier versions of Windows and MS-DOS. In addition, disk utilites that
were not designed explicitly for the FAT32 file system will not be able
to work with this disk. If you need to access this disk with other operating
systems or older disk utilities, do not enable large drive support.

Do you wish to enable large disk support (Y/N)..........? [N]
```

Figure L2.2 The opening screen of FDISK

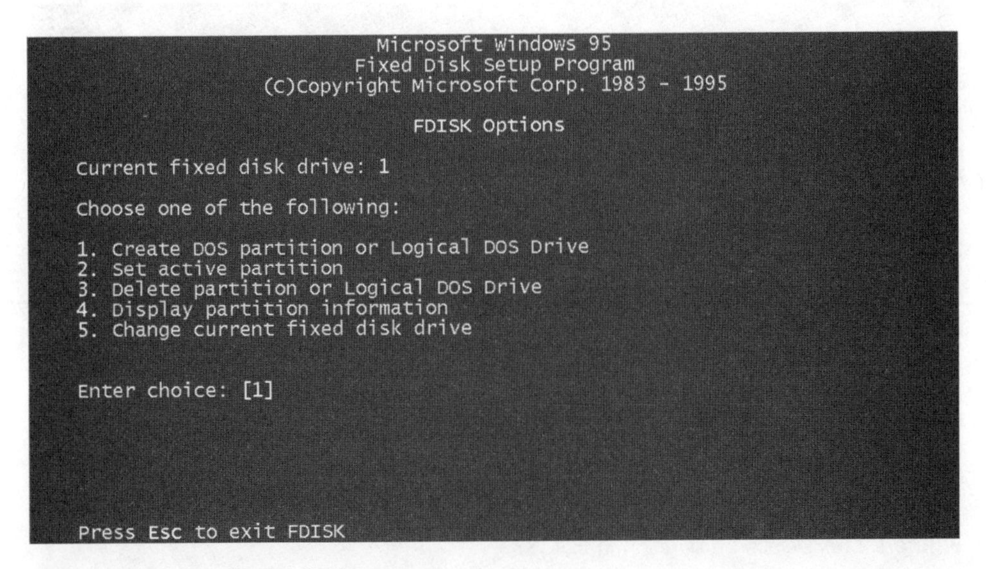

Figure L2.3 The FDISK Options screen

3. The screen shown in **Figure L2.4** will appear. The information contained in that screen may vary from class to class and from computer to computer, depending on what was previously installed on that hard drive. If it's a brand new hard drive, there should be a message telling you that no DOS partitions exist.

4. Press the <Esc> key to return to the FDISK Options screen. If your systems contained previous partitions, you need to delete them. To do so, press Option 3: Delete partition or Logical DOS Drive. This will bring up a screen like the one shown in **Figure L2.5**.

5. If there are extended partitions on your drives, you must first select Option 3: Delete Logical DOS Drive(s) in the Extended DOS Partition and delete each logical drive on the partition. Next you need to delete the extended partition, and finally you can proceed to Option 1: Delete Primary DOS Partition.

```
                    Display Partition Information

Current fixed disk drive: 1

Partition  Status   Type    Volume Label  Mbytes   System   Usage
 C: 1        A     PRI DOS                 12417   FAT32     100%

Total disk space is 12417 Mbytes (1 Mbyte = 1048576 bytes)

Press Esc to continue
```

Figure L2.4 Viewing partitions in FDISK

```
             Delete DOS Partition or Logical DOS Drive

Current fixed disk drive: 1

Choose one of the following:

1.  Delete Primary DOS Partition
2.  Delete Extended DOS Partition
3.  Delete Logical DOS Drive(s) in the Extended DOS Partition
4.  Delete Non-DOS Partition

Enter choice: [ ]

Press Esc to return to FDISK Options
```

Figure L2.5 Deleting a partition in FDISK.

6. This brings up the screen shown in **Figure L2.6**. You are warned that to continue will delete all data on your drive. Select Y and a new field will open up prompting you to enter the Volume Name. If your drive has a volume name, you must enter it exactly as it appears on the screen. You will then be given yet another option to bail out when it asks whether you're really sure. Press Y to delete the partition, and now the previous data on the hard drive is history. This is when far too many technicians scream "**No, wait! That was the wrong drive!!!**"

7. Press <Esc> to return to the FDISK Options menu. Now you want to select Option 1: Create DOS partition or Logical DOS Drive. This will bring up the screen shown in **Figure L2.7**. Before you can create any extended partitions, a primary DOS partition must first be created. Press Option 1: Create Primary DOS Partition. You will be asked whether you want to use all available space and to make the partition active. Select Y.

8. FDISK will then quickly scan the disk for obvious flaws, calculate available space, and create the primary partition. Press <Esc> twice to exit FDISK. You will be prompted that for the changes to take effect, you must restart your machine. Make sure the boot diskette is still in Drive A:, select Y, and let the machine reboot. You are now ready for Exercise 2.

```
                    Delete Primary DOS Partition

Current fixed disk drive: 1

Partition  Status   Type    Volume Label  Mbytes   System   Usage
 C: 1         A    PRI DOS                12417    FAT32     100%


Total disk space is 12417 Mbytes (1 Mbyte = 1048576 bytes)


WARNING! Data in the deleted Primary DOS Partition will be lost.
What primary partition do you want to delete..? [1]


Press Esc to return to FDISK Options
```

Figure L2.6 You get one last chance to bail out!

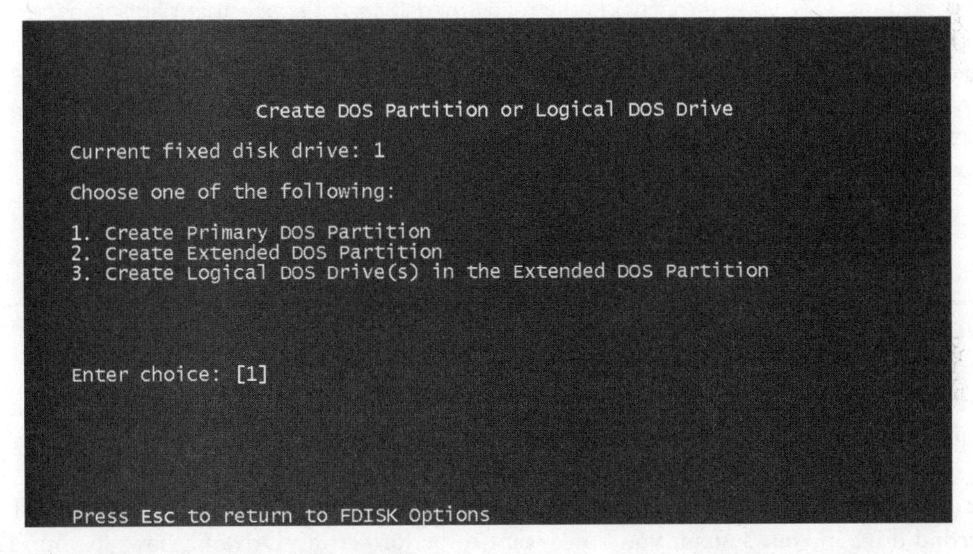

Figure L2.7 Creating a DOS partition

EXERCISE 1 REVIEW

1. Why is it a good idea to view partitions on a previously existing hard disk before making any permanent changes?
2. If you divided your hard disk into multiple partitions using FDISK, what additional step must you complete before you will have a bootable drive?
3. Using FDISK, you want to remove an extended partition, but it won't let you. What does the error message tell you that you must do before removing extended partitions?
4. You created two separate partitions on the same hard disk, using the % Disk Space method of allocating disk space to each partition. Now what must you do before you have a bootable system?
5. In the opening screen of FDISK, you selected N when asked whether you wanted to enable Large Disk Support. Just what did you do to the system when you made that selection?

SOME COMMENTS ON FDISK

Keep in mind that FDISK is an older utility and, as such, is subject to some limitations. For example, a partition created by a non-Microsoft OS such as Linux frequently can't be recognized. When you view partitions, you see a Non DOS Partition listed, but when you try to remove it, you are informed that no Non-DOS partitions exist. It can drive you nuts. Even Microsoft OSs occasionally do something to the MBR that prevents FDISK from being able to work with that disk. I frequently work in classroom environments where the OS of a given system changes from day to day. I discovered that in some cases, Windows 2000 Advanced Server would make the disk unrecognizable after the students had converted the drives to Dynamic Disks. This is an option in Windows 2000 that applies advanced properties to the drive that earlier OSs don't know how to deal with. Oddly enough, I never encountered that problem in classrooms using Windows 2000 Professional.

Along a different line, should you with to create multiple partitions using FDISK, you have two options for dividing your disk into partitions. In Step 8, instead of selecting Y when asked whether you want to use all available space, select N. Now you will be encouraged to enter how much of the drive you want used for the primary partition. If you simply type in a number, such as 150, you are defining how many megabytes of space that partition should contain. A number followed by the percent sign is obviously a percentage. If you type **50%**, it will take exactly half of the available space and assign it to the primary partition. Either way you choose, the result of your actions will be that your primary partition is *not* set as active by default. You'll have to go back to the initial FDISK menu, select Option 2: Set active partition, and select which of the partitions you've created should be the active one.

EXERCISE 2: FORMATTING A HARD DISK

Partitioning the hard disk created a new master boot record, but the disk still isn't usable. You now need to generate the file allocation tables. This is done when you format the hard disk. So let's do it!

1. The first thing you need to do is determine what your new drive letter is going to be. If this is a second drive in your system, you don't want to be formatting Drive C: now do you? That's when the View Partition Information option you saw in the previous exercise comes in handy. If it is the first and/or only drive in the system, then you simply type **format C:** at the command prompt.
2. As you see in **Figure L2.8**, you are warned that continuing will destroy all data on the drive. Do you wish to proceed? Well, as I was preparing this lab, I was using the same computer I'm using to write with. So I chose to press N for no. Go figure. You should press Y for yes and sit back and wait. Depending on the size of the hard drive, your age, and how long it is until lunch, this can take anywhere from several minutes to the rest of your natural life. When it finishes, you're finished with this lab.

EXERCISE 2 REVIEW

1. Why does the drive have to be formatted before you can use it?
2. Referring back to the textbook for reference, why is it possible to retrieve data from a hard disk that has just been formatted?

SOME COMMENTS ON FORMATTING

The format command used by DOS and Windows is known as a high-level format, or sometimes as the operating system format. A low-level format is done at the factory, which maps out the sectors and tracks on each platter. Some older versions of BIOS contain an option for Low Level Format. This is for SCSI or older MFM hard drives **only** and should **never** be used on an IDE drive. Using that utility on an IDE drive will turn it into a paperweight. Some of the better hardware diagnostic utilities include a low-level format for IDE drives. This might be useful in the event that a failed attempt to install an operating system has left Track 0, Sector 1 unreadable. It should, however, be used only as a last resort.

Also, on the initial format of a newly partitioned hard drive, it can take quite some time to format the drive. What the format utility is doing is going out to each file allocation unit (FAU) on the drive, testing its integrity and then going back and writing the FAT entry. Any bad FAUs will be marked as such and will not be reported to the OS. Subsequent formats of that disk can be much quicker. Using the command **`format /q`** will perform a quick format that only rewrites the FAT without doing the surface scan.

Something to keep in mind when reinstalling operating systems is that it is frequently a good idea to FDISK the hard disk before formatting an existing drive. The reason for this is that the operating system owns the FAT. Reinstalling the same OS can result in unpredictable problems.

```
A:\>format c:

WARNING, ALL DATA ON NON-REMOVABLE DISK
DRIVE C: WILL BE LOST!
Proceed with Format (Y/N)?
```

Figure L2.8 Formatting the hard disk.

LAB REVIEW

1. Using information provided in this lab along with information from the text, explain just what is going on during the FDISK routine when you create a primary DOS partition.
2. Using knowledge you gained in this lab as well as from the text book, explain what happened to the MBR when you divided the disk into multiple partitions.

3. Explain what is going on during the format process and just why it takes so much longer to perform an initial format than it does when you select the **`format /q`** option.
4. Using information from this lab and from the text, explain the difference between a low-level format and an operating system format.
5. *For extra credit:* Even after FDISKing and formatting the hard drive, there is still more work that must be done by the OS during its installation. What might that be?

LAB SUMMARY

Well, now you know that either replacing or installing a new hard drive isn't simply a matter of bolting in the new drive and hooking up a couple of cables. There's a certain degree of drive preparation that needs to be done as well. It's all part of the job.

LAB 3

INSTALLING WINDOWS 98

Well, you're finally ready to install the OS. You have a properly FDISKed and formatted hard disk, and you're raring to go. Depending on the speed of your lab computers, the following exercise will take anywhere from 40 minutes to as much as a couple of hours.

The only materials you'll need for this lab are your lab computers, Win98 CD, and any third-party drivers required for proprietary hardware.

The CompTIA objectives covered in this lab include the following:

1.1 Identify the major desktop components and interfaces and their functions. Differentiate the characteristics of Windows 9x/Me, Windows NT 4.0 Workstation, Windows 2000 Professional, and Windows XP.

1.2 Identify the names, locations, purposes, and contents of major system files.

2.1 Identify the procedures for installing Windows 9x/Me, Windows NT 4.0 Workstation, Windows 2000 Professional, and Windows XP and bringing the operating system to a basic operational level.

EXERCISE 1: INSTALLING WINDOWS

For this exercise, each student needs to have access to a lab machine and a boot diskette with CD-ROM support. If you used the Windows 98 Startup Disk utility or downloaded the boot image from www.mwgraves.com, then you have what you need. So let's install Windows. (*Note:* Windows 98 ships on a bootable CD, so if for any reason, a boot diskette is not available, Setup can be started from the CD as long as the machine's CMOS is configured to boot to CD-ROM. The purpose of booting to the floppy in this exercise is to point out a minor difference in the process.)

Insert the boot diskette into the floppy diskette drive and start the machine. If this is the first time you've ever booted to floppy, don't be concerned about the amount of time it takes. That's normal.

The first thing you'll see is a list of the different options for starting the machine. **Figure L3.1** illustrates these options. They include starting the computer with or without CD-ROM support and viewing the help file, which is incredibly useful. Select Option 1: Start computer with CD-ROM support.

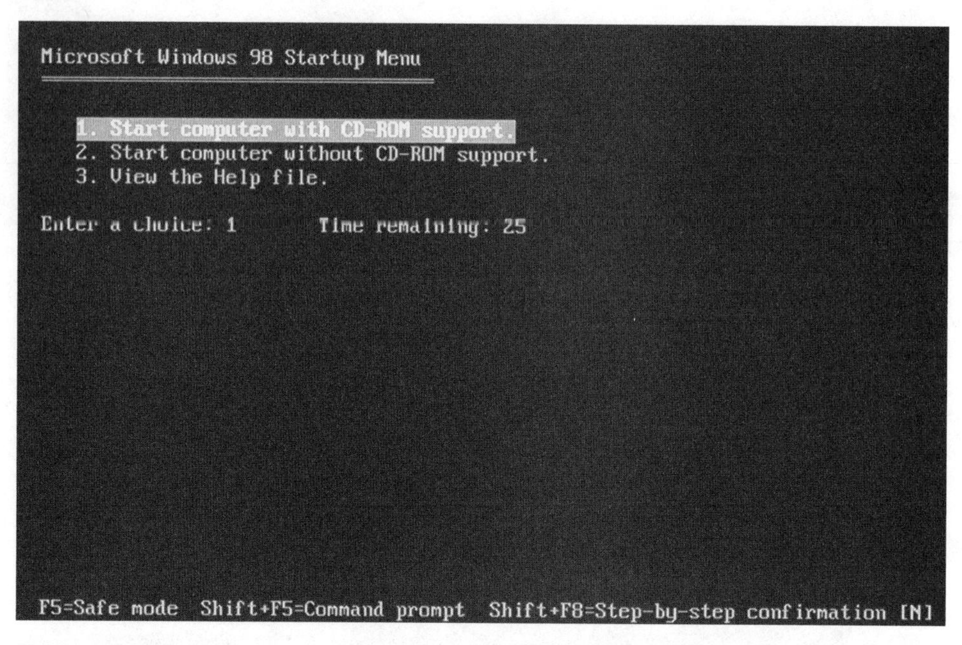

Figure L3.1 The boot menu offered by the Win98 Startup diskette

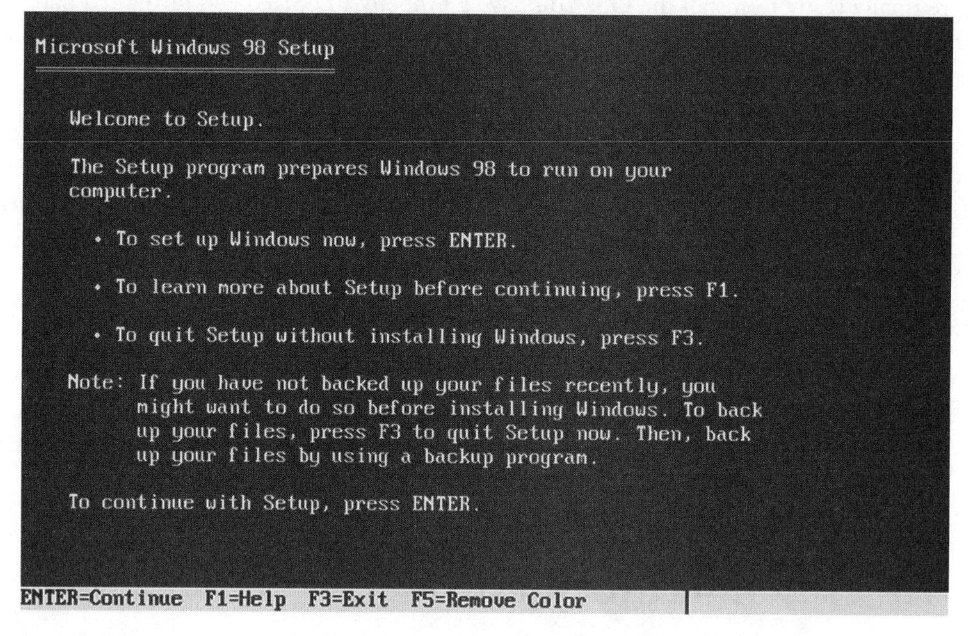

Figure L3.2 Windows Setup

When you boot a computer using the Win98 Startup diskette, a ramdisk will be created. A ramdisk is an area in physical RAM that is treated exactly as if it were a hard disk. It is divided into 512-byte sectors just like a hard disk, and a file allocation table is created for that disk. The Windows Utilities will be loaded to this disk for faster performance. This can throw off the drive letters from what you might be expecting, because the ramdisk will become drive C: until your newly FDISKed hard disk has been formatted. After the hard disk is formatted, the ramdisk will become drive D:, moving your CD-ROM up to Drive E. Therefore, in most cases, your next step is to type **E:\SETUP**. If your lab machines have multiple hard disks, this may vary.

1. This brings up the Windows 98 Setup screen (**Figure L3.2**). You have the option of starting the Windows installation, learning more about Windows setup (but not more than you'll learn

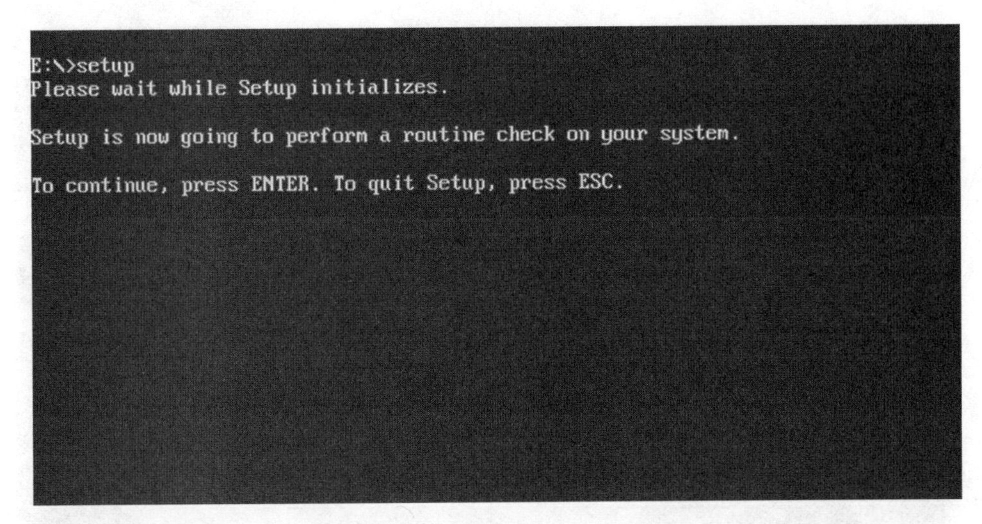

Figure L3.3 Before Setup continues, it performs a routine check on your system to make sure you have sufficient RAM and hard disk space.

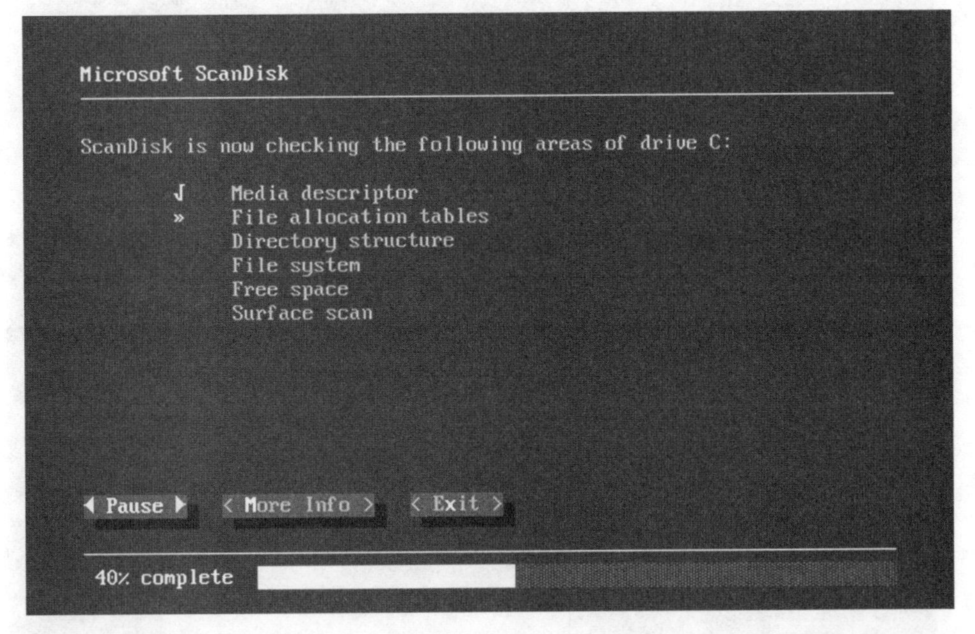

Figure L3.4 The "routine check" includes a ScanDisk of all physical hard drives in the system.

in this lab), or bailing out. The bottom of the screen tells you the press <Enter> to continue, F1 for help, F3 to quit setup, or F5 to remove color. Press <Enter>.

2. You will be notified that Setup is going to perform a routine check on your system, as in **Figure L3.3**. Press <Enter>.

3. Microsoft's ScanDisk utility (**Figure L3.4**) will run an abbreviated check on all hard drives installed in your system. If it discovers any problems, the installation may be aborted. If not, it will tell you that it discovered no problems. Either way, you have either the option of viewing the log or exiting ScanDisk. Press <Tab> to move over to Exit and then press <Enter>.

4. Welcome to Windows 98. Microsoft gives a sales pitch for the OS that you've already purchased (**Figure L3.5**) and over on the left side of the screen tells you that Setup will take

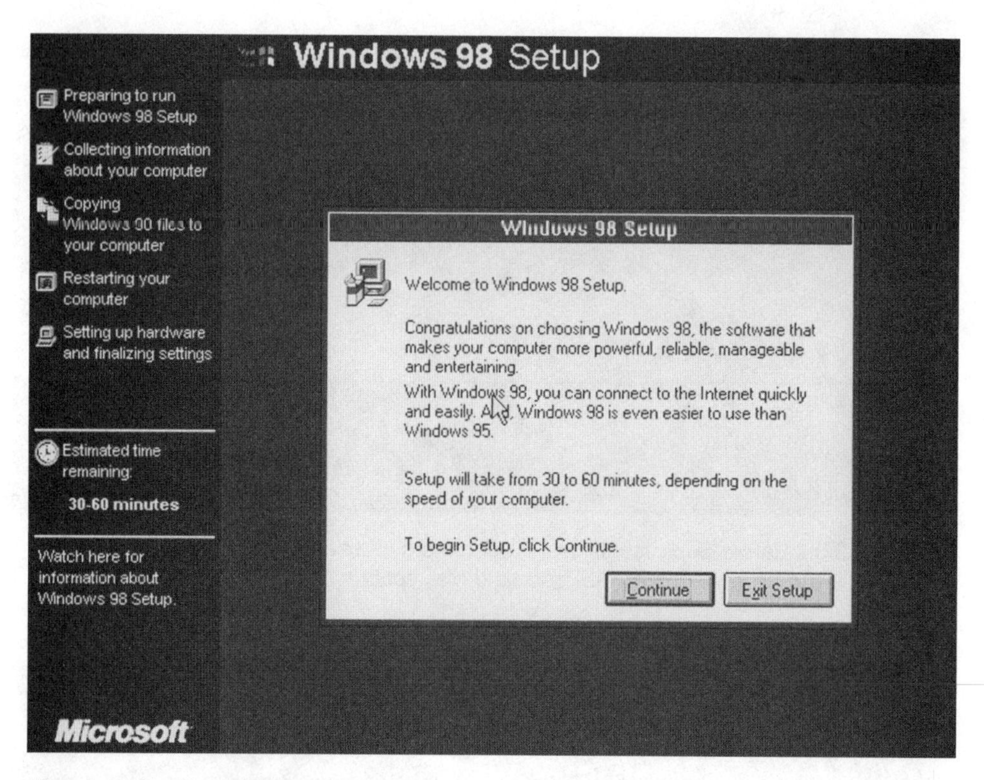

Figure L3.5 The graphical Setup

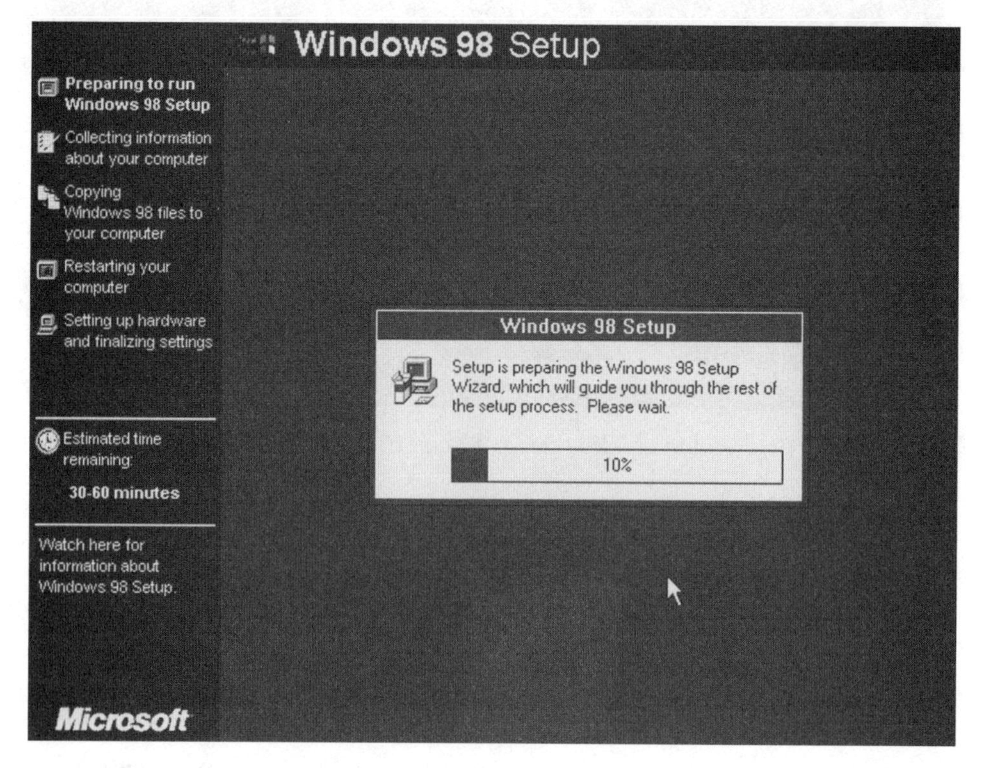

Figure L3.6 Starting the Windows Setup Wizard

anywhere from thirty to sixty minutes. It says the same thing whether you've got a 52x CD-ROM drive that can install it in about twenty minutes or a 4x that will take until your next birthday. Click Continue and Setup begins preparing the Setup Wizard (**Figure L3.6**). This will take several seconds.

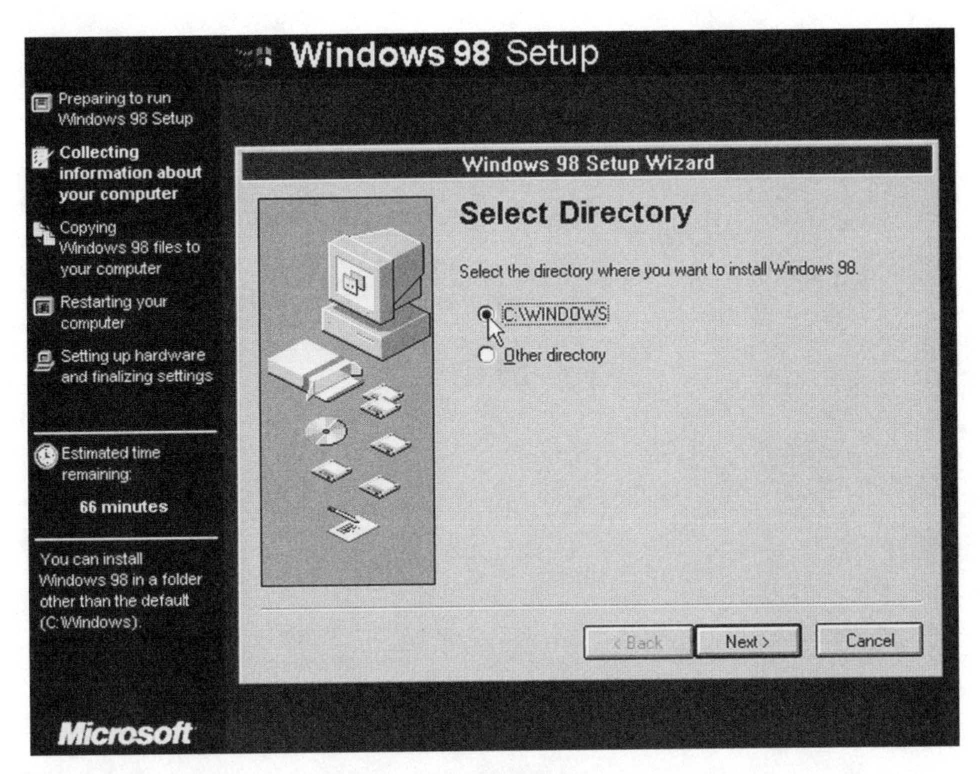

Figure L3.7 You have the option of installing Win98 to the WINDOWS directory (recommended) or to select another directory.

5. Next you will have the option of installing Windows to the C:\Windows directory or to select another directory (**Figure L3.7**). Unless you have a driving need to do otherwise (such as another version of Windows already installed on the system), select the default setting and click Next>.

6. It'll take a few moments for the directory to be prepared. But you have the lovely screen shown in **Figure L3.8** to keep you company.

7. The Setup Options screen appears next. Here, we're going to deviate a bit from a standard installation so that I can point out some interesting and very useful options that don't get installed if you select a Typical installation. Click Custom as in **Figure L3.9** and then click Next>.

8. The Windows Components screen (**Figure L3.10**) will appear. You will note that the checkboxes next to the various options appear three different ways. A clear box with a check indicates that all available options in this category have been selected. A grayed out box with a check indicates that some, but not all options have been selected. You can click the Details button to view the options that have been selected and those that haven't been. A box with no check suggests that none of the options have been selected. Click Details to see what options exist.

9. Select each category in turn to see what options haven't been selected by a Typical installation. In particular, select System Tools (**Figure L3.11**), click Details, and make sure that Backup, System Monitor, and System Resource Meter are installed. You're going to need these later on. Click OK and then Next> in the Components screen.

10. Now you need to identify your computer for the network (**Figure L3.12**). Since a later lab will involve networking these machines, now is as good a time as any to make sure the computers' names are user friendly, rather than the randomly selected collections of letters and numbers

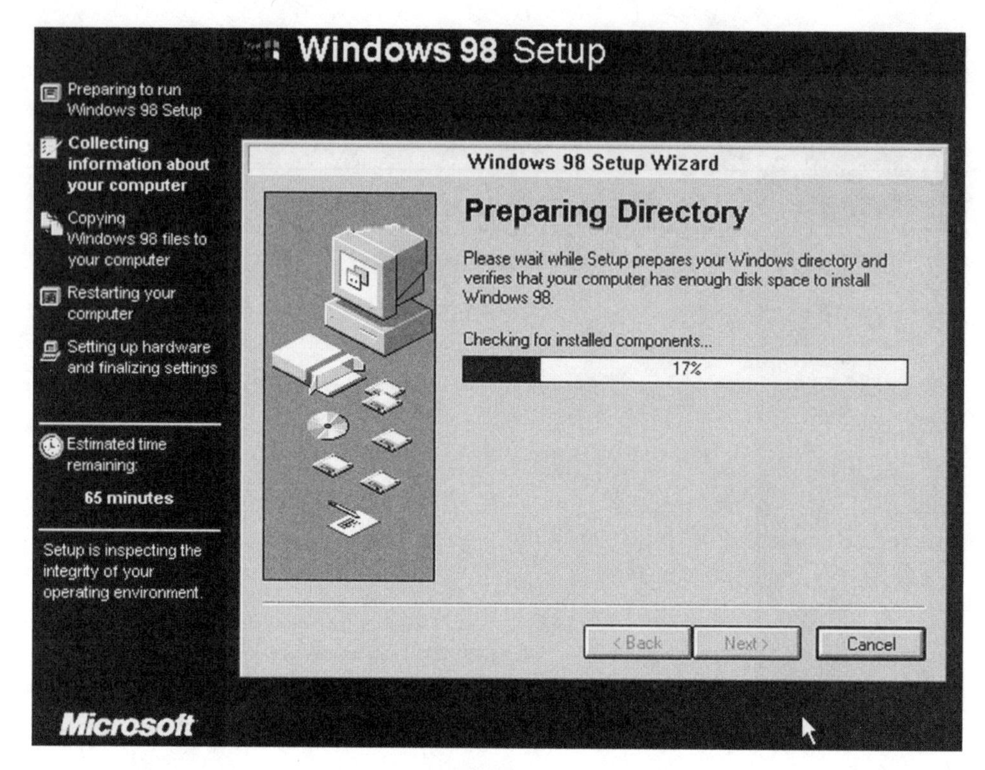

Figure L3.8 Preparing the Windows Directory

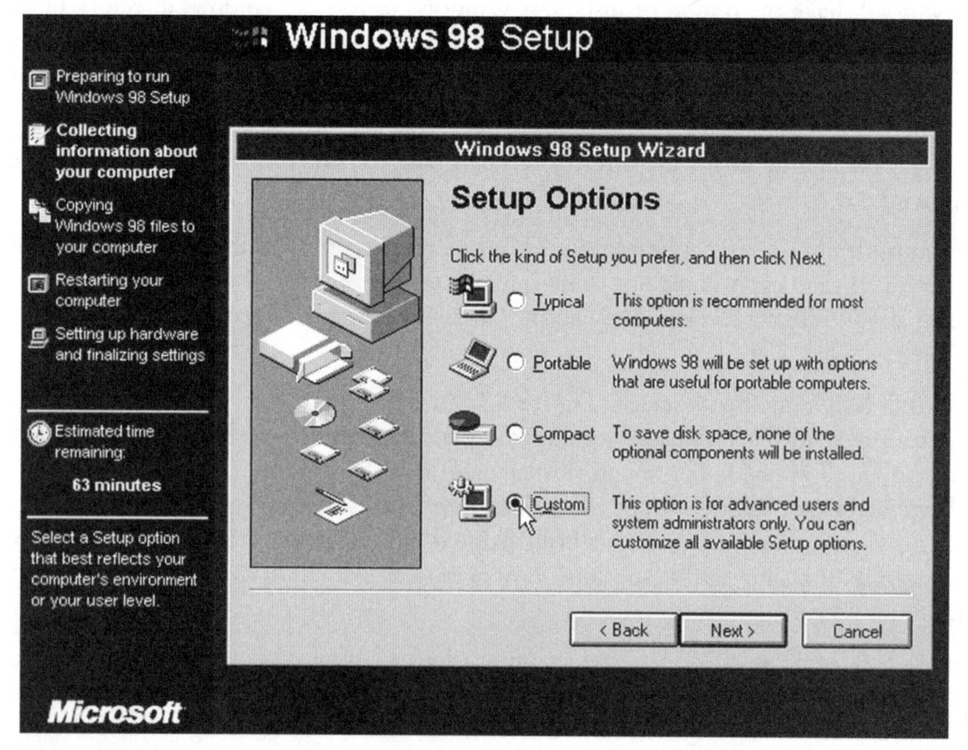

Figure L3.9 For the purposes of this lab, select a Custom installation.

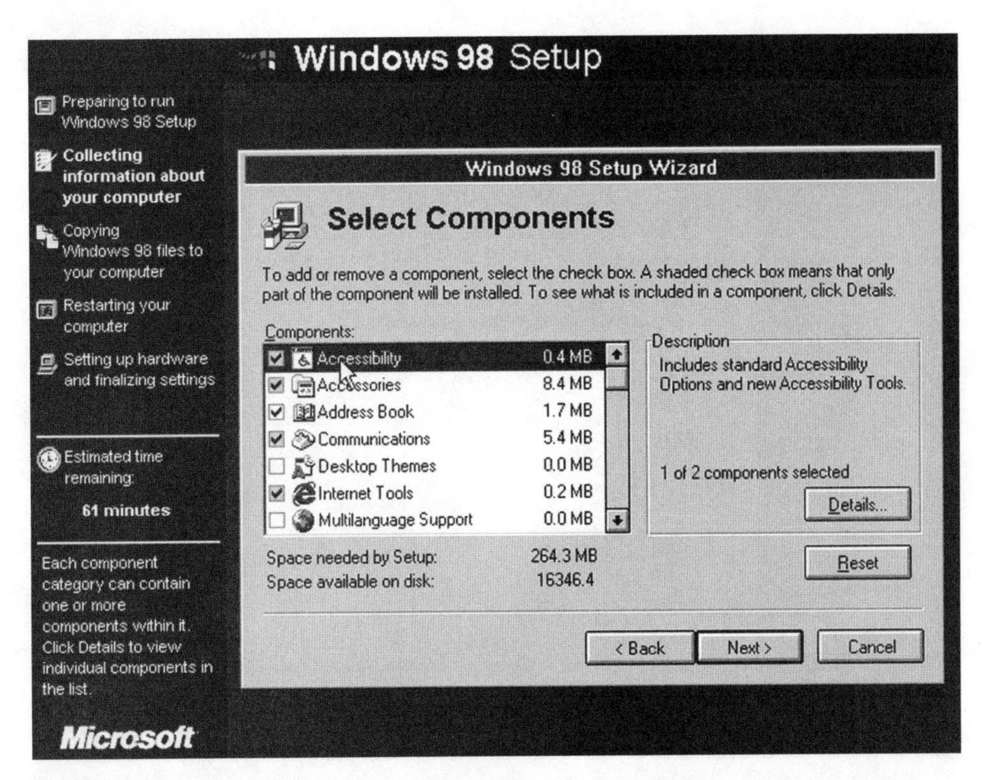

Figure L3.10 There are a number of available options in Windows that do not get installed by default.

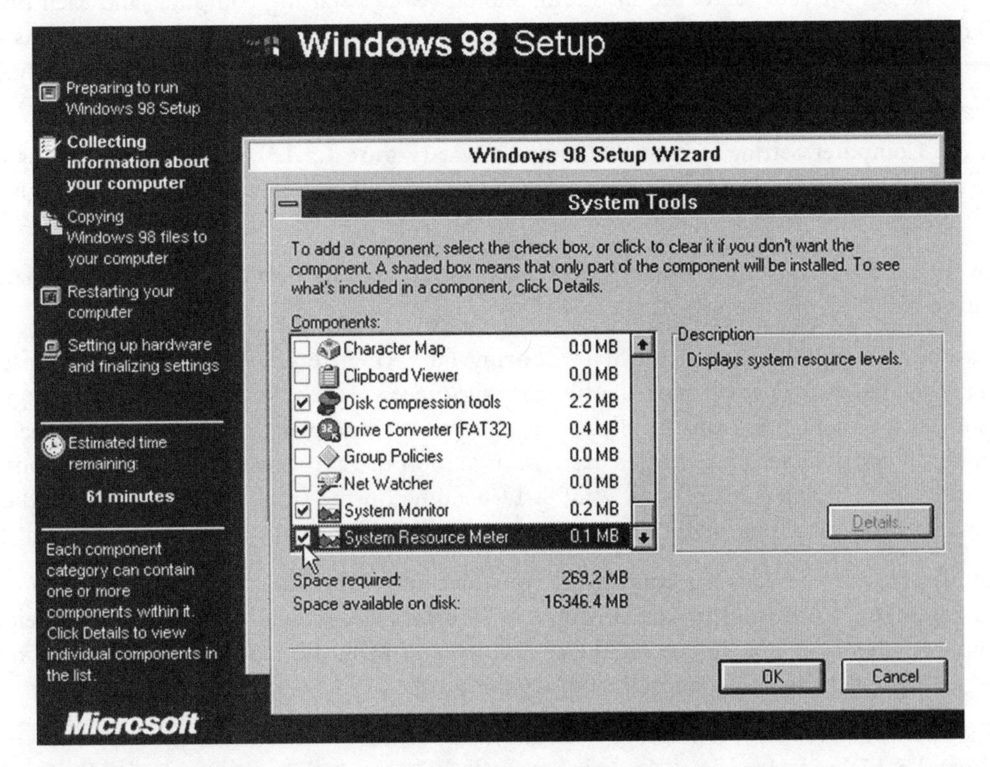

Figure L3.11 Adding new components in Windows Setup

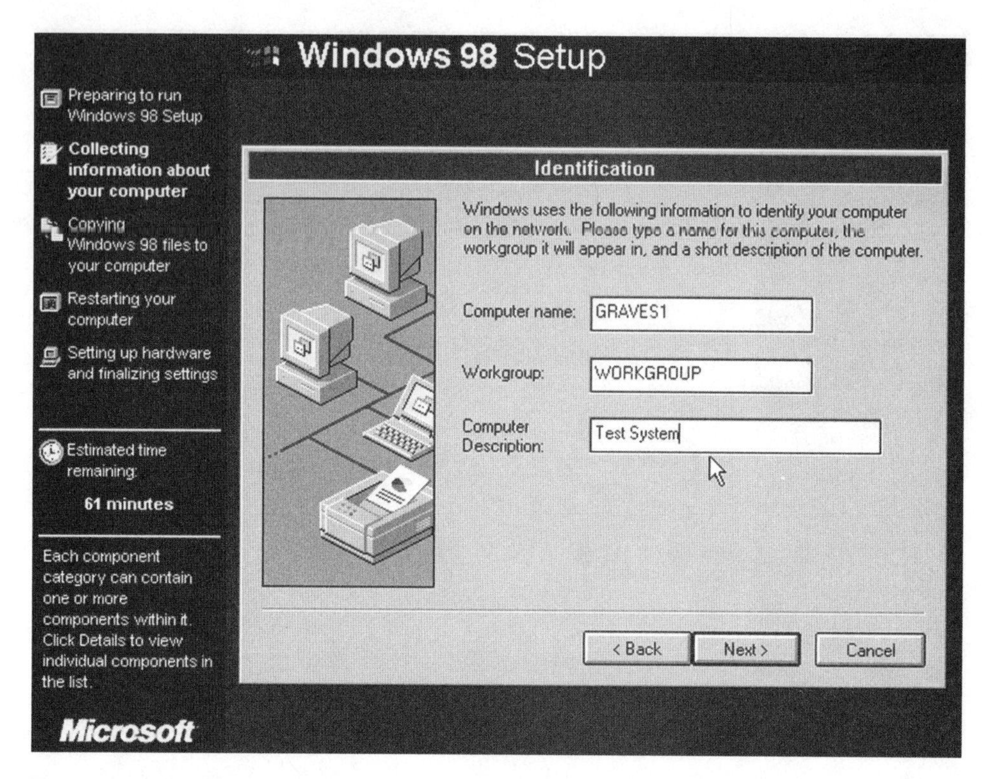

Figure L3.12 Applying computer names for networking should not be random.

Setup chooses for you. Here, the instructor should select a starting computer and each one should be named Student1, Student2, Student3, and so on and so forth until all systems have been given a unique but easily remembered name. The instructor's machine should be named HIZZONNER or HERONNER, whichever is appropriate. Click Next>.

11. On the Computer Settings screen that appears next (**Figure L3.13**), leave the defaults as they are, unless, of course, they aren't correct for your region. If not, change them accordingly and click Next>.

12. The Establishing Your Location (**Figure L3.14**) screen appears next. Select the appropriate location and click Next>.

13. Next you will see the screen titled Start Copying Files. (**Figure L3.15**). As you have most likely already figured out, this will start the file copying process. Click Next> and gather into groups to discuss the football playoffs until the process has been completed. While this is happening a number of different screens, which I have no intention of capturing for this lab, will appear, bragging about the new features of Win98. Depending on the speed of your machine, the estimated time remaining might range anywhere from half an hour to your next birthday.

14. After the file copy process has completed, your machine will reboot automatically, as shown in **Figure L3.16**. If you want to save a couple of seconds, take the CD out of the drive before the computer reboots. If not, just select the option to boot from the hard disk on the boot menu that will appear if there is a bootable CD in the drive.

15. Windows will start with the message "Getting ready to run Windows for the first time" (**Figure L3.17**) embedded in the splash screen. It will eventually move on to the User Information screen.

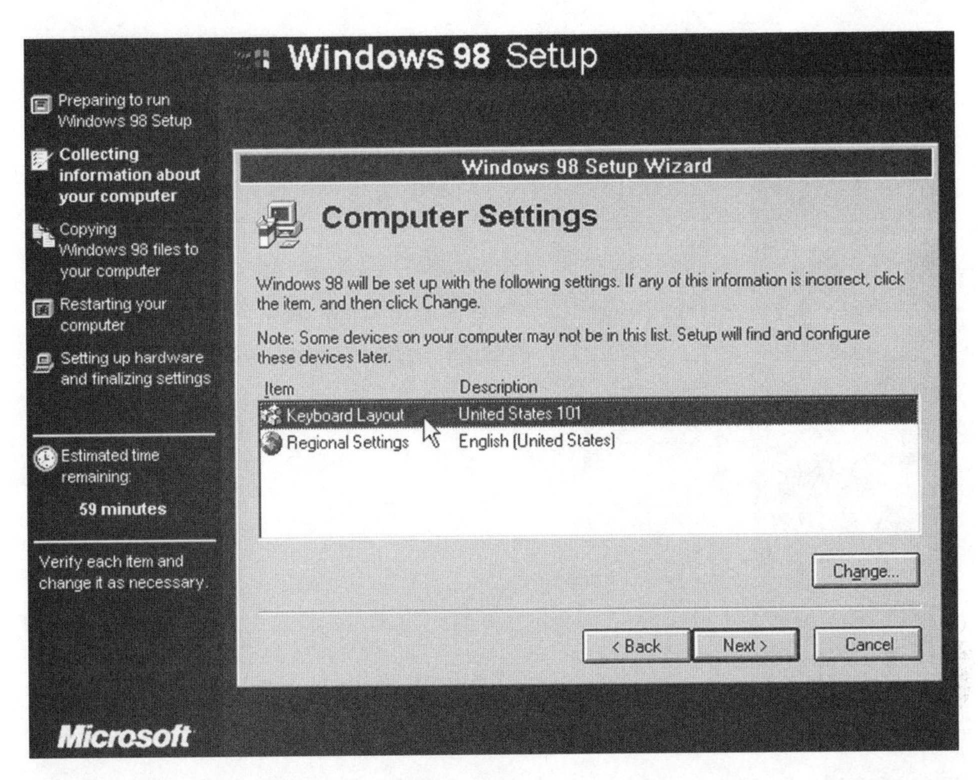

Figure L3.13 The Computer Settings screen

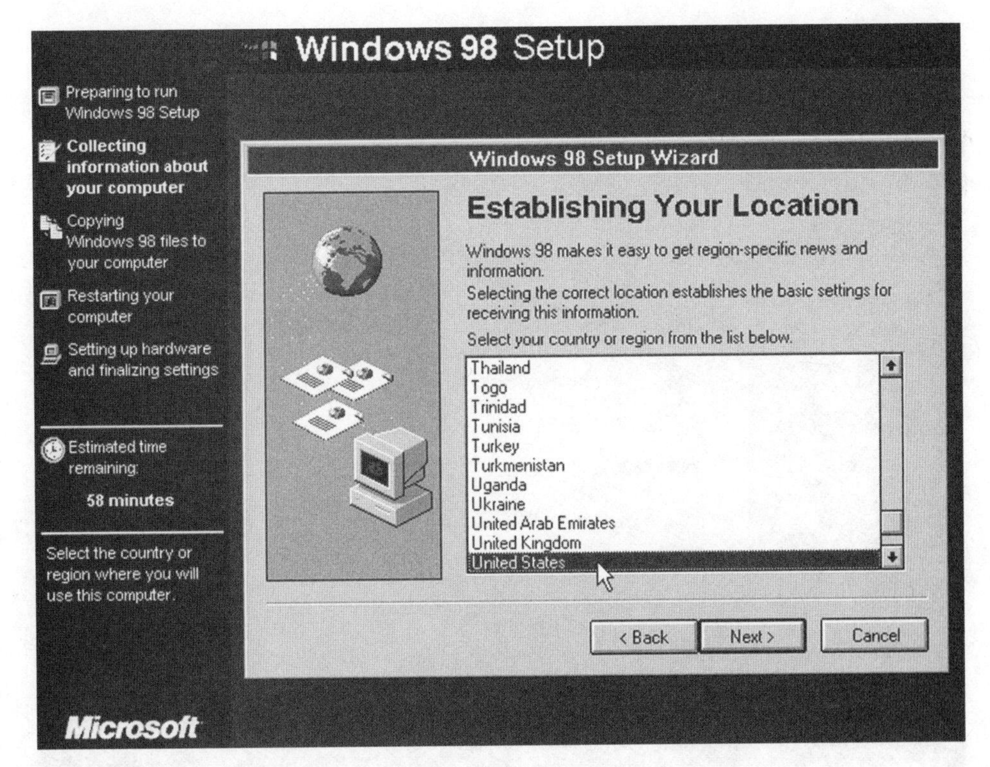

Figure L3.14 Establishing your location

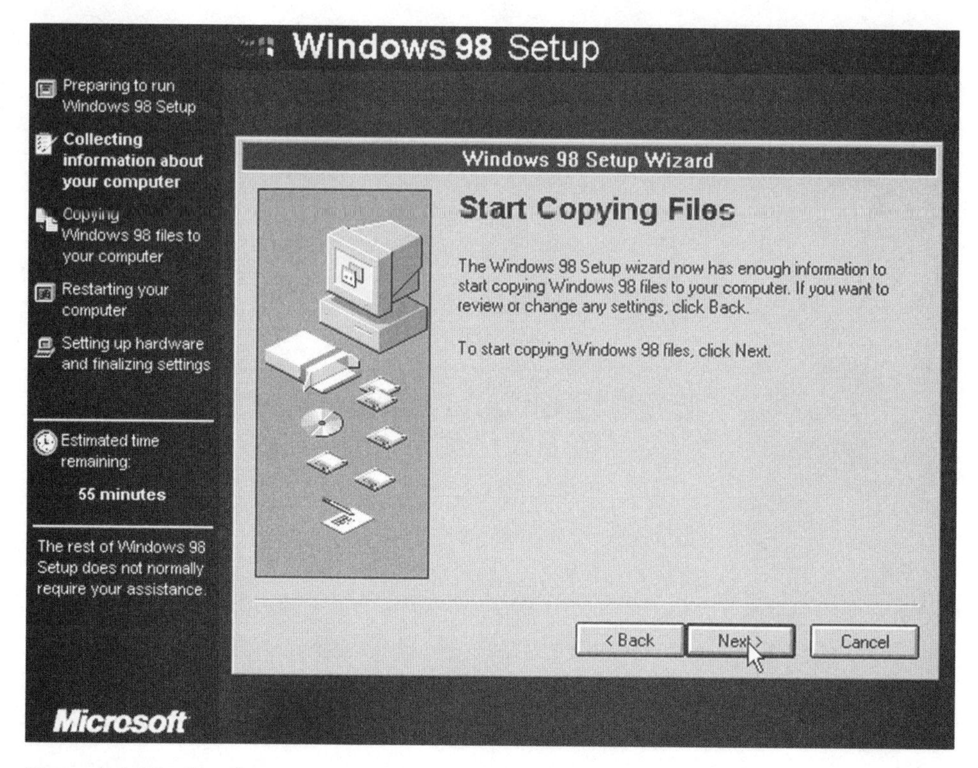

Figure L3.15 The file copy process can take anywhere from thirty minutes to eternity, depending on the speed of your machine and your caffeine level.

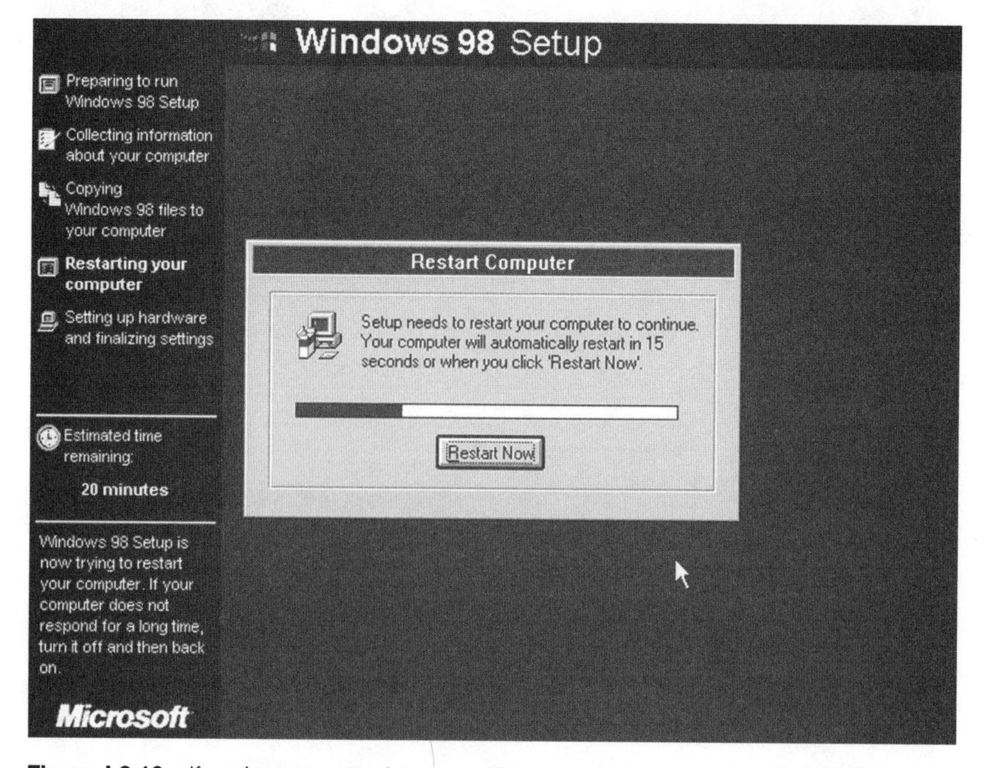

Figure L3.16 If you're not around to manually reboot your computer after the file copy process is complete, Setup will do it for you.

Figure L3.17 Starting Windows for the first time

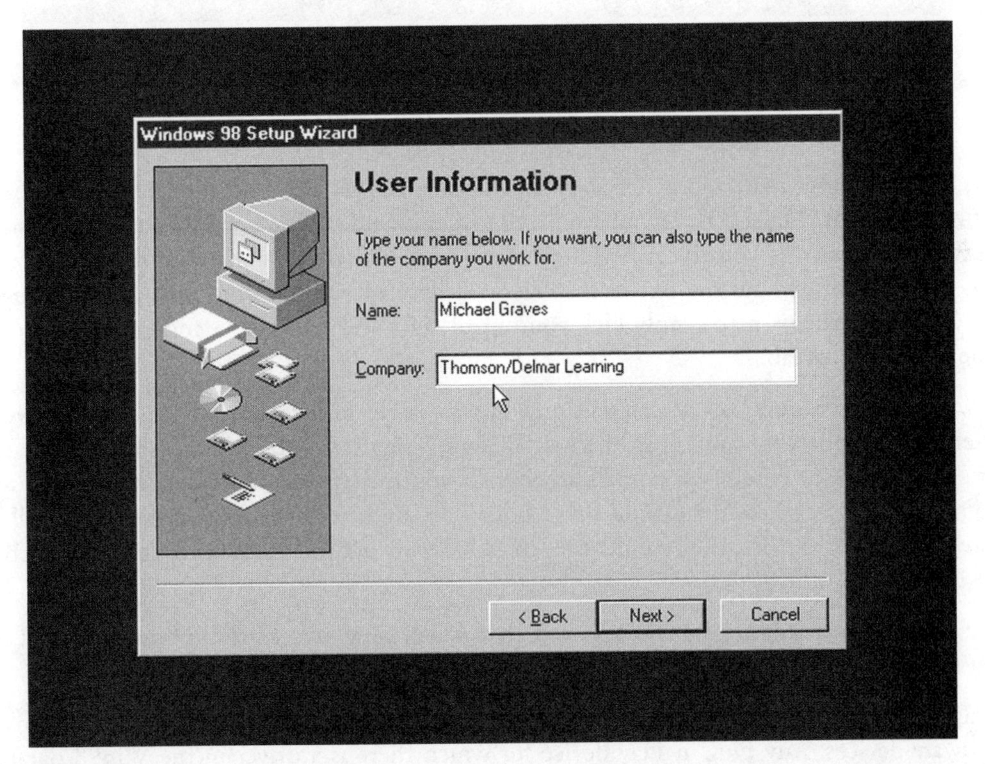

Figure L3.18 The name is mandatory in the User Information Screen. Organization Name is optional.

16. In the window that follows, type your name and organization (**Figure L3.18**). Some sort of name is mandatory. Setup won't let you go on without one. An organization name is optional. You can leave it blank or type in The Bill Gates Fan Club if you so desire. Click Next>.

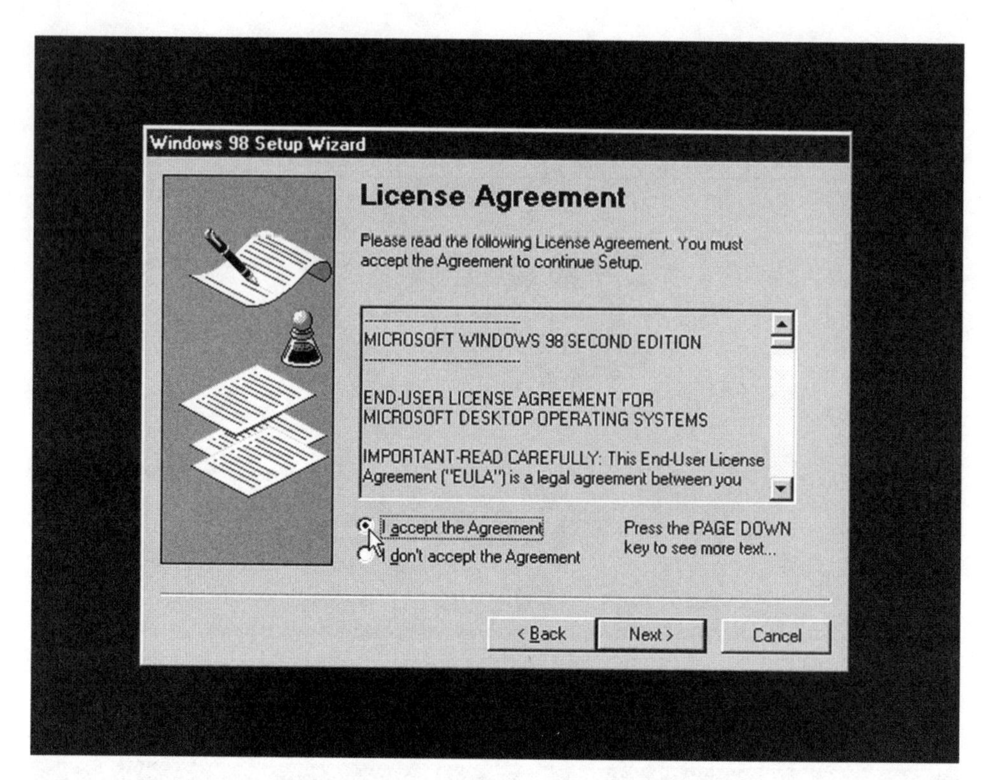

Figure L3.19 The Microsoft License Agreement, Version Win98

17. The licensing agreement appears as shown in **Figure L3.19**. Press Page Down as you read the entire agreement. Make certain you read every single word. Click I accept the Agreement and Next> to continue. If you try to be funny and decline Microsoft's generous terms, the installation will be aborted, and the rest of the class will have to wait for you until you get caught back up. Or the instructor may simply kick you out of class and tell you to come in on your own time to finish this lab.

18. The Windows Product Key screen will now appear, as in **Figure L3.20**. Type in the twenty-five letters and numbers that make up the key. It doesn't matter if you use the shift key for caps or not. Letters will be entered as capitals anyway. If you mistype any character you'll have to try again before you can continue. And don't bother trying to use the product key in the illustration. I didn't think Microsoft would take too kindly to me providing a working key in one of my illustrations. Click Next>.

19. The Start Wizard (**Figure L3.21**) tells you that it will now save all the information and that you should click Finish. That's why it's called the Start Wizard.

20. Setup now initializes the driver database (**Figure L3.22**) and scans your computer for installed hardware devices. Any Plug 'n Play device for which there is a driver in the Win98 database will be automatically installed during the next step (**Figure L3.23**). Those not recognized will need to be manually installed after the installation is completed. When the hardware scan is finished, your computer will restart once again.

21. The Setting Up Hardware screen will be the next thing you see. Setup is now installing the device drivers for the hardware it was able to detect.

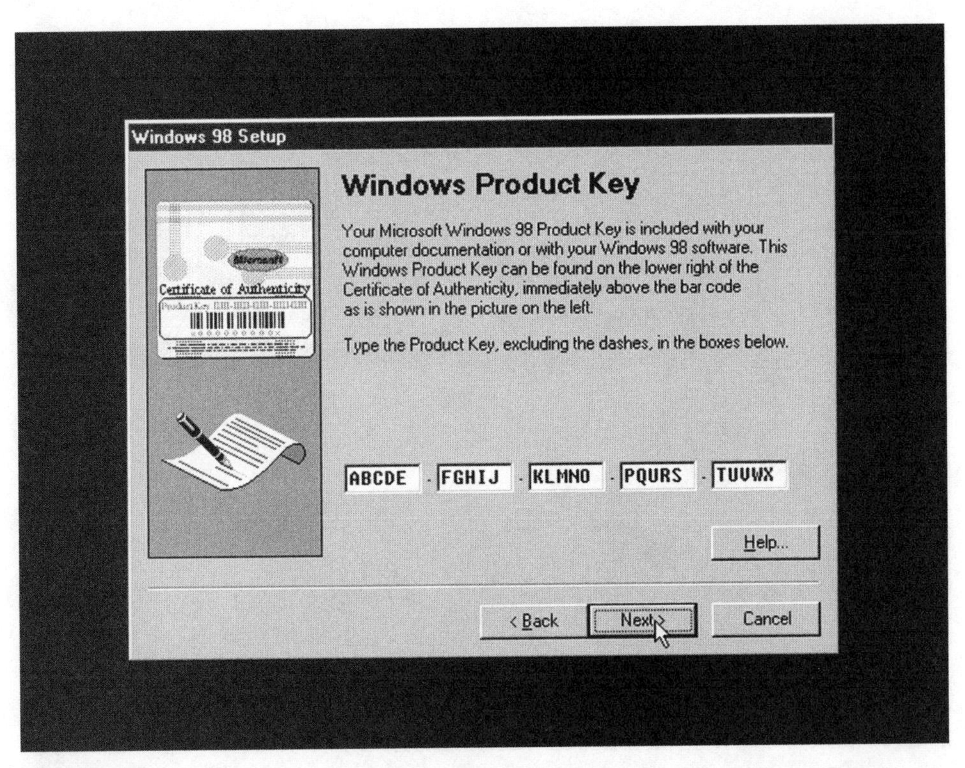

Figure L3.20 Missing even one letter in the Product Key will cause you to have to reenter it.

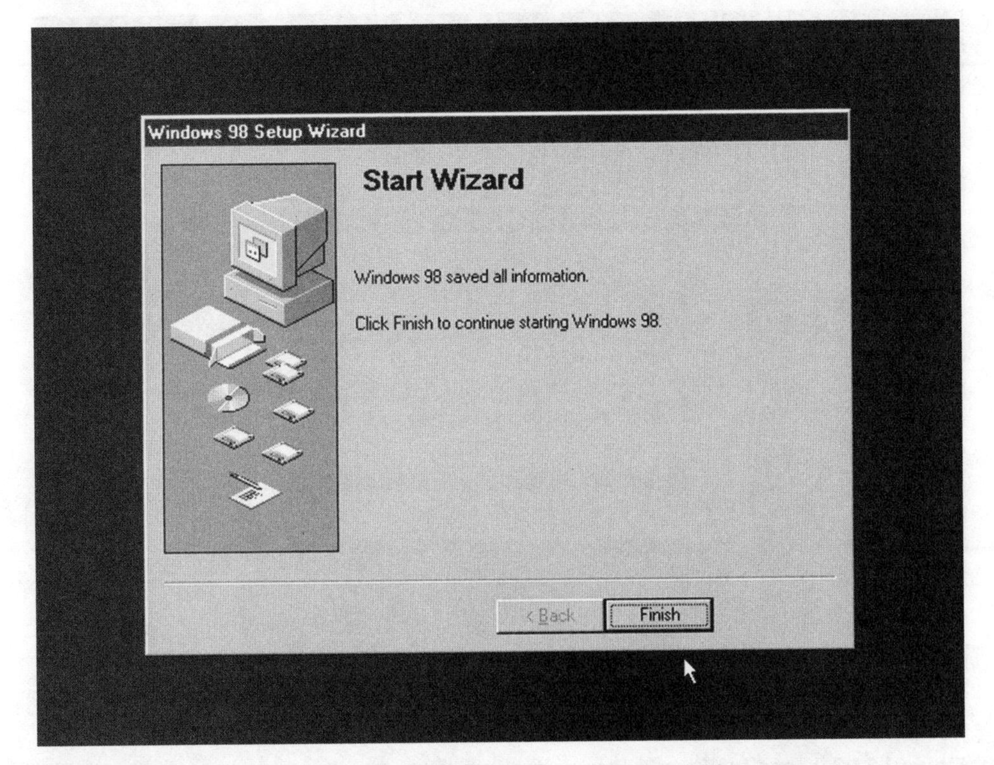

Figure L3.21 Finishing up isn't really finishing up, as you're about to find out.

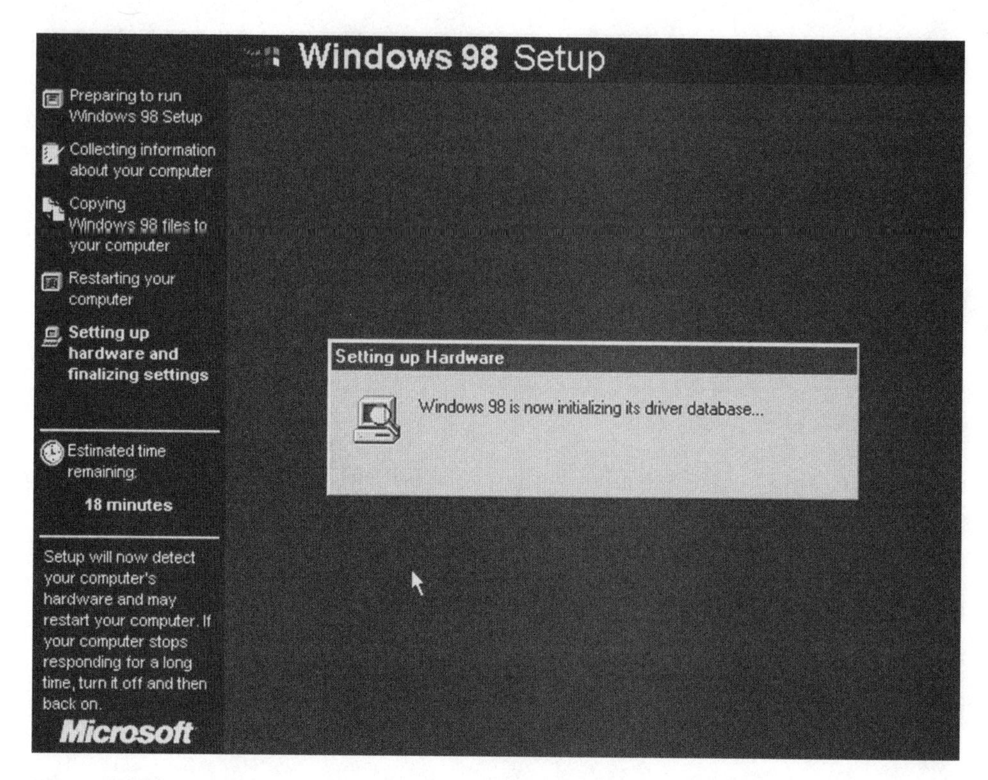

Figure L3.22 First the driver database is opened and read by Setup.

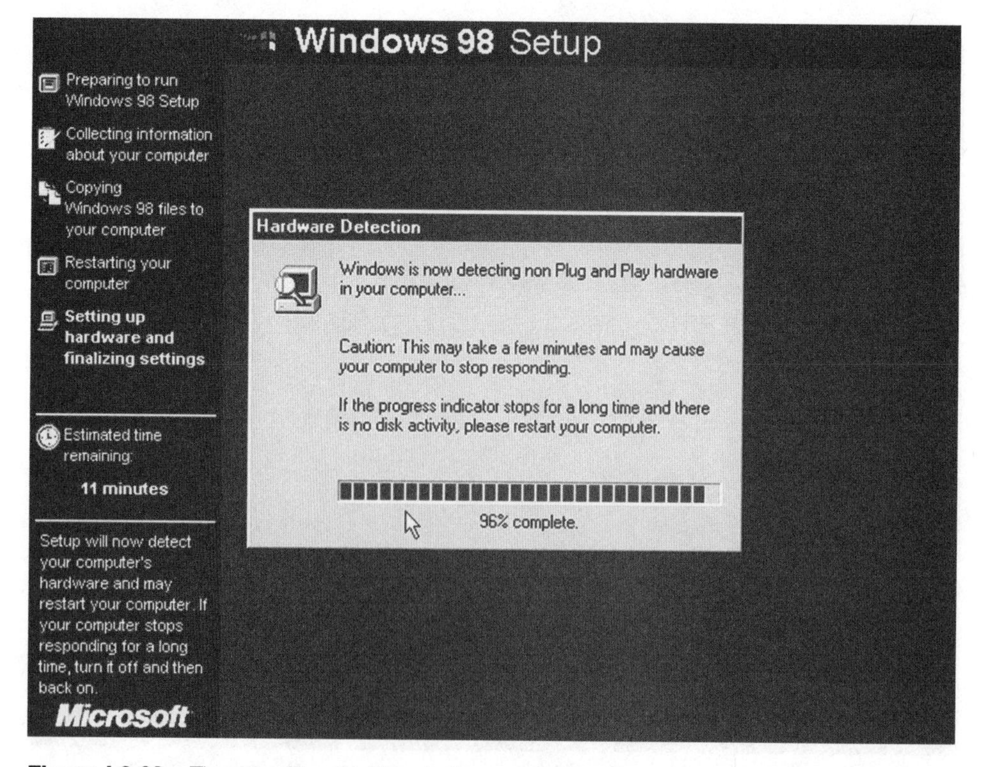

Figure L3.23 Then the Plug 'n Play devices are set up.

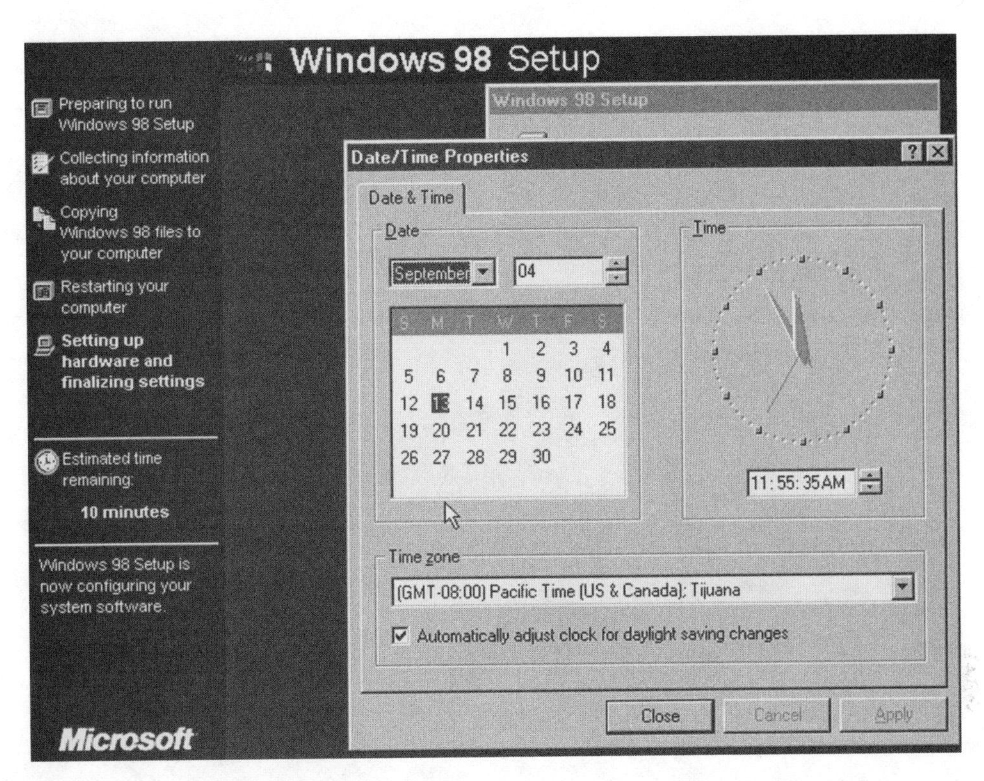

Figure L3.24 Setting the date and time

22. The Date/Time Properties (**Figure L3.24**) screen will eventually appear and you will have the opportunity to set the computer's time and date. By default the selected time zone is Pacific.
23. Now Setup will configure the Control Panel, the Start Menu, Windows Help, how Windows will handle DOS programs, and the configuration settings as shown in **Figure L3.25**.
24. When this is finished, your computer will restart yet again. As Windows starts this time (which may take a bit longer) it will attempt to install devices that weren't installed during the previous hardware installation process. This will include devices hooked up to peripheral ports such as your monitor and non-Plug 'n Play devices. For the latter, in order to successfully install these devices, you will need the device drivers on either floppy diskette or CD-ROM.
25. The Welcome to Windows 98 screen will now appear. In the lower left-hand corner of this screen, deselect the checkbox that says Show this screen each time Windows 98 starts and close the screen.

EXERCISE 1 REVIEW

1. You've just booted your computer to a Windows 98 Startup diskette and now your CD-ROM drive has just been renamed from Drive D: to Drive E:. What happened?
2. What is the first thing the Windows Setup program does after it starts?
3. In the Windows Components screen, some of the boxes are grayed out with check marks inside. What does this indicate?
4. What happens when the first phase of file copying has been completed?

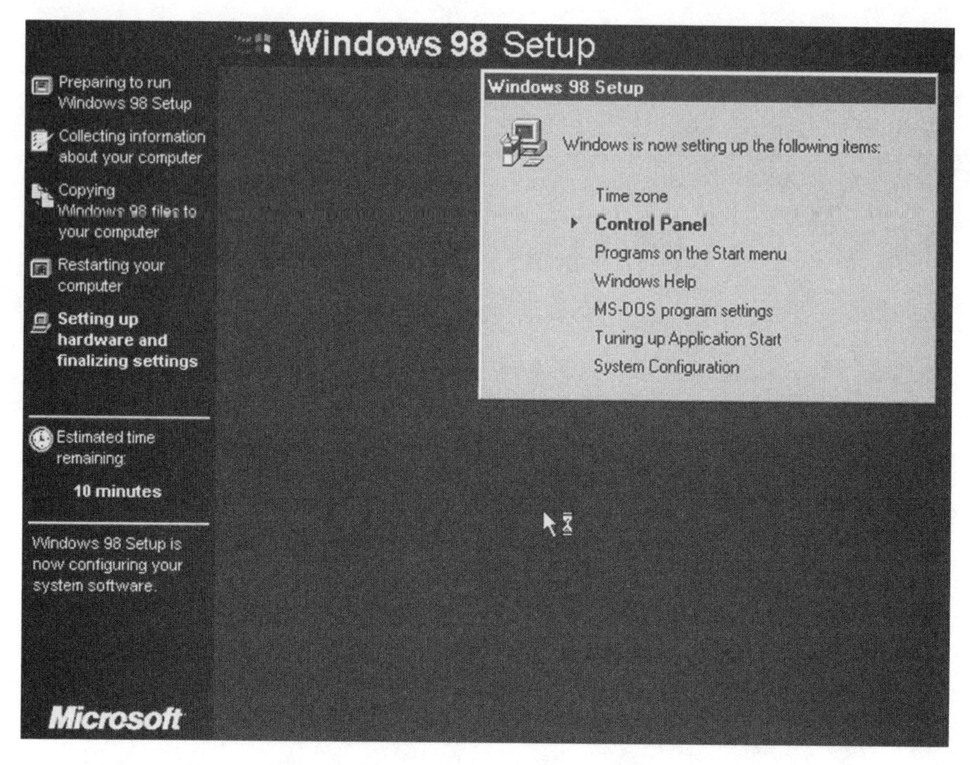

Figure L3.25 Final system configuration (well, almost, anyway).

5. When the Licensing Agreement appears, you say out loud, "What a crock!" and click I Disagree. Now what happens?

EXERCISE 2: CREATING THE TECHNICIAN'S BOOT DISKETTE

The Windows 98 Startup Disk is fine and works quite well. But it carries a lot of excess baggage you don't need for a basic troubleshooting boot disk, and it doesn't include a couple of utilities you'll find useful. In this exercise you'll create the Technician's Boot Diskette.

1. Open a command prompt. To do this, you can either click Start→Programs→MS-DOS Prompt, or you can click Start→Run and type **command** into the command field. If your diskette needs to be formatted before using it, you can type **format a: /s** at the command prompt.
2. Insert a blank, formatted high-density floppy diskette into drive A: and type `sys a:` at the command prompt. Your computer will think about it for a few moments and then copy some files to the floppy and create an MBR on that floppy. The diskette is now bootable, but it isn't finished.
3. To open Windows Explorer, right-click the Start button and select Explore. Browse to the C:\Windows\Command directory, right-click the file MSCDEX.EXE and select copy. Now right-click A: and select Paste.
4. Browse to the C:\Windows directory and locate the files EMM386.EXE and HIMEM.SYS. Copy those file to your floppy.

5. Now, insert the original boot diskette that you used to start your original installation. You're looking for one of two files. I've seen both used from time to time. The file you're looking for on the floppy is either MTMCDAI.SYS or OAKCDROM.SYS. Right-click this file, select copy, and then paste it to the C:\Windows\Temp directory. Put the diskette for your new boot disk back in the drive and cut and paste the file from C:\Windows\Temp to A:.
6. Now, back at the command prompt, type **edit**. The MS-DOS Editor will appear. First you want to create a CONFIG.SYS file. Type the following lines, pressing the <Enter> key after each line.

```
FILES=32

BUFFERS=32

Stacks=9,256

LASTDRIVE=Z

DEVICE=HIMEM.SYS

DEVICE=EMM386.exe

DOS=HIGH

DEVICEHIGH=MTMCDAI.SYS /D:CDROM
```

7. From the Editor menu, select File→Save As and in the file name field, type **config.sys.**
8. Now, select File→New and you'll create an AUTOEXEC.BAT file. In the Editor screen type the following lines:

```
PROMPT $P$G

MSCDEX.EXE /D:CDROM
```

9. Save this file, and you're finished with this part. But there's still more work to do on this disk.
10. From the C:\Windows\Command directory copy the files EDIT.COM, FDISK.EXE, FORMAT.COM, XCOPY.EXE, XCOPY32.EXE, and XCOPY32.MOD.
11. To test your new disk, leave it in the drive and reboot your machine. When you're finished, save the diskette. You'll be using it later to create the Technician's Boot Diskette.

EXERCISE 2 REVIEW

1. What are two different ways to open a command prompt in Windows 98?
2. What is the correct command for making a formatted diskette bootable?
3. You have a diskette that needs to be formatted before you can use it to create a boot diskette. What command can you use to format the diskette and make it bootable at the same time?
4. What files will you copy from the C:\Windows directory of a Windows 98 machine to your Technician's Boot Diskette?
5. What are the two files that you need to create on your boot diskettes?

EXERCISE 3: INSTALLING THE GRAPHICS ADAPTER (OPTIONAL)

The idea of Plug 'n Play is that you're not supposed to have to install and configure any new hardware. It's a great idea when it works. The majority of the time, there are certain devices that have to be installed manually. Later in this manual, you will be installing the NIC for networking, and you'll get another chance to take a look at installing devices. Therefore, if the computers in your lab automatically detected and installed the video card, you can call it quits and move on to the next lab. The video card, on the other hand, is one of the more common culprits for *not* being auto-detected. This is especially true of cards that came out after Win98 was discontinued. If your instructor is hard-core (like me), you'll probably find yourself uninstalling and reinstalling the drivers even if the device was automatically installed. Shall we begin? You're going to love the detailed procedure.

1. Insert the disk that shipped with the graphics adapter.
2. Follow the instructions.

Sorry it isn't more detailed than that. Unfortunately, manufacturers of graphics adapters have more varied methods for installing their drivers than any other device. Fortunately, in this day and age, installation is so automated, they can get away with that.

LAB REVIEW

1. You've just inserted the boot floppy into your drive and started a machine on which you wish to install Win98. You type **D:\SETUP** and get the error message "Bad command or file name." What did you do wrong?
2. What are some of the tools you might not have at your disposal if you accept a factory default installation?
3. What are two devices that are frequent culprits for resisting the charms of PnP?

LAB SUMMARY

Okay, you now have a workable OS on your computers. For many of you this wasn't the first time you've done this. But for those of you who have never installed an OS before, it should have been a satisfying experience. Windows 98 is a bit more cumbersome than some of the more recent Microsoft offerings, but it is a lot easier than other OSs such as Novell or Linux. As you proceed through the remaining labs in this book, you'll see what I mean.

LAB 4

CONFIGURING THE DESKTOP

Now that you have a working OS on your computer, how can you make it *your* OS and not just a clone of everybody else's? Microsoft was fully aware that people were going to want to personalize their computers and provided a number of ways to customize the interface. In this lab, you're going to make your computer unique. If you're working in pairs, try not to get into a fight. You can each set up your own profile so that you both enjoy personal configurations on the same machine.

A couple of short notes about later Windows versions are in order. While Win98 supports profiles, this is something that must be selected. In WIN2K and WINXP, each user account automatically carries its own profile, and no additional steps are necessary. Second, although most of the procedures in this lab are identical in the later versions, there are some minor differences in how things are applied. Rather than set up multiple labs that do basically the same thing, I will merely point out the differences in this lab.

All you need for this lab is the desktop PC onto which you installed Win98 in the previous lab.

There is only one CompTIA objective covered in this lab:

1.1 Identify the major desktop components and interfaces, and their functions. Differentiate the characteristics of Windows 9x/Me, Windows NT 4.0 Workstation, Windows 2000 Professional, and Windows XP.

EXERCISE 1: CUSTOMIZING THE INTERFACE

A number of different display settings allow users to create a computing environment more pleasing to their specific tastes. Among the different tweaks that I'll be examining in this portion of the lab are the following:

- Screen resolution
- Icon size and spacing
- Icon font size

- Desktop wallpaper
- Screen saver
- Active Desktop

EXERCISE 1A: SETTING SCREEN RESOLUTION

1. Right-click the desktop to bring up the menu shown in **Figure L4.1**. Click Properties. Another way to get to this setting is to click Start→Settings→Control Panel and then double-click the Display icon.
2. This will bring up the Display Properties window as shown in **Figure L4.2**. As you can see, there are a number of different tabs at the top of this window. I'll be going over each one in turn in this lab, but this is a situation where I can say with absolute certainty that the last shall come first. Click the Settings tab. The optimal settings for resolution and color depth can vary from one monitor to another, but there are some general rules of thumb you can follow. 15" monitors fare well with 800x600 settings, while 17" monitors can handle 1024x768 (or even higher) resolutions. If your adapter supports a very high resolution along with 32-bit color, select both. In Figure L4.2, I've chosen 1024x768. Make your selections and click Apply and then OK.
3. The next window (**Figure L4.3**) warns you that applying changes without restarting the computer can result in compatibility issues. With video driver settings, this was a fairly rare occurrence, so in this case, I've chosen to make the changes without restarting. Your resolution and color depth settings have now been successfully reconfigured.

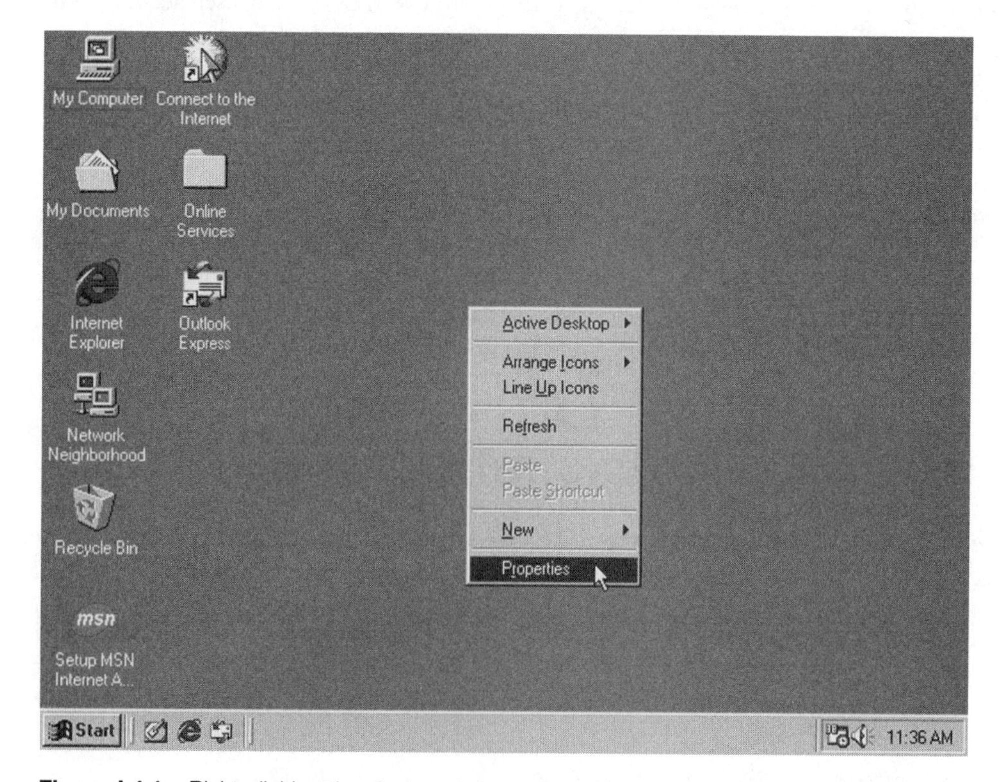

Figure L4.1 Right-clicking the desktop brings up a menu of different options specific to the display settings.

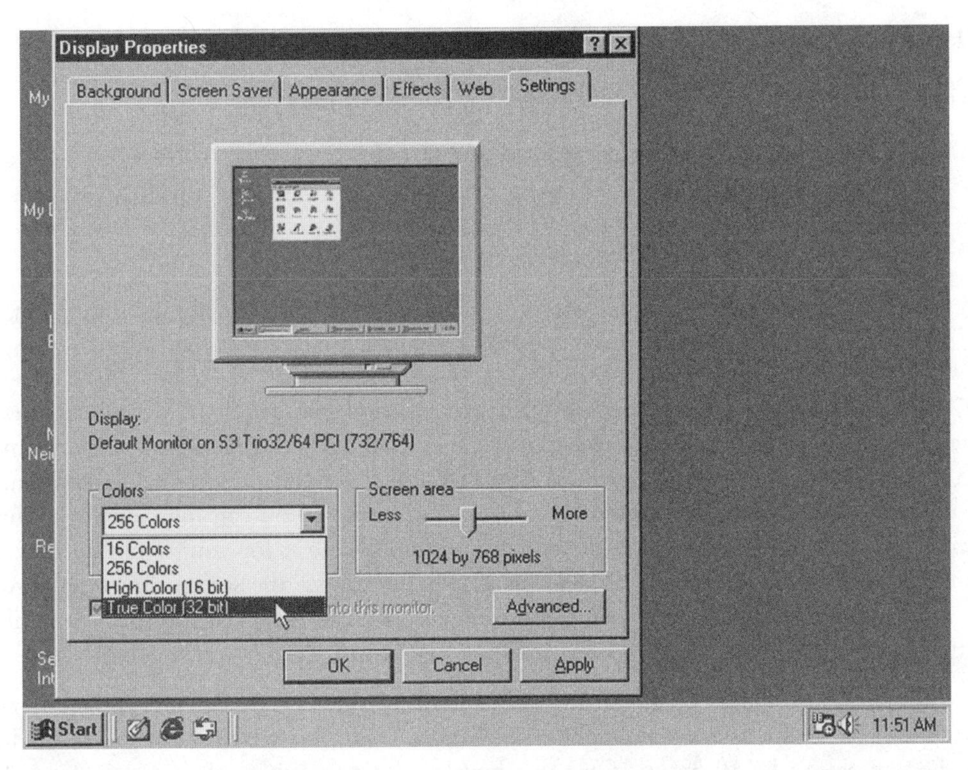

Figure L4.2 The Display Properties window of Win98

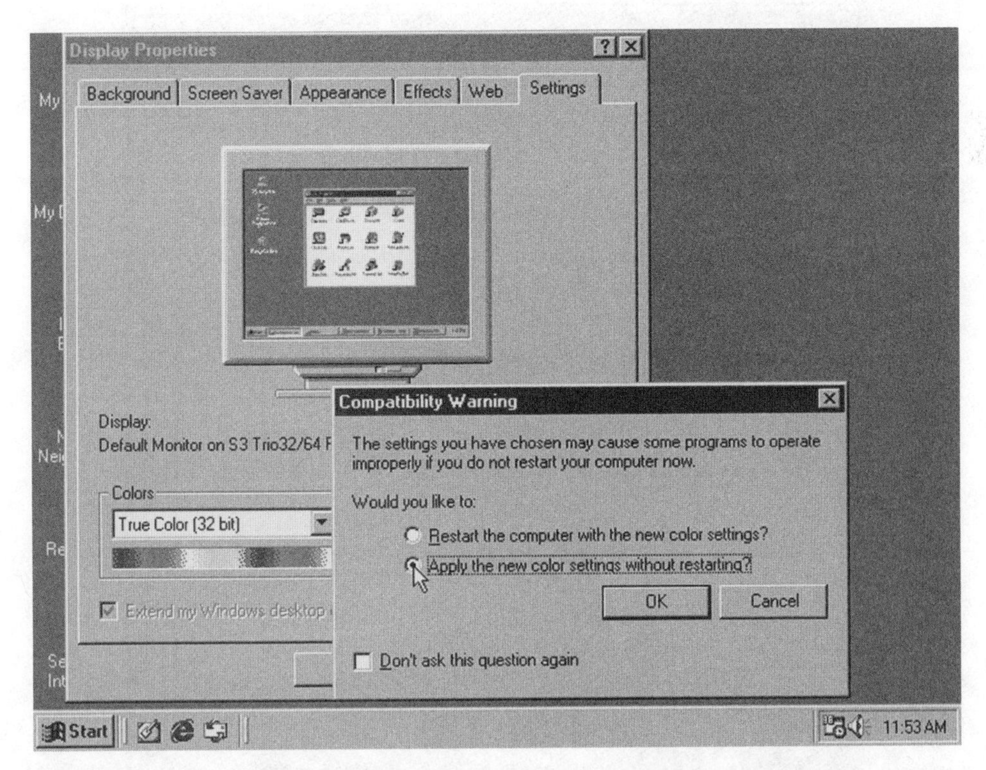

Figure L4.3 If you want to be totally safe, go ahead and restart your system. However, Display Settings rarely cause issues, and it should be safe to accept changes without restarting.

EXERCISE 1A REVIEW

1. What are the two ways to get to the Display Properties window?
2. Is it absolutely necessary to restart your system after adjusting display settings?

EXERCISE 1B: MANAGING ICONS

Okay, now you've got a screen with nice smooth, accurate color and virtually invisible grain. But the icons are so *tiny*! And who can read those captions? Perhaps it might be a good idea to change that.

1. Get back into Display Properties, using whichever method you prefer. Click the Appearance tab. Here is where there is a slight difference between Win98 and later Windows versions. In Win98, you will get the screen shown in **Figure L4.4**. Here you can select a preconfigured scheme that preselects all the settings I'm about to discuss, or you can individually configure specific items. What would be the fun in letting Windows do it for you? What do they know about art? You'll pick your own. In later versions of Windows, the screen shown in **Figure L4.5** appears. To configure individual items, you need to click the Advanced button. This will bring up the screen that allows you to configure individual items.
2. Click the scroll arrow next to the Item list and scroll to the top. By default, you'll enter the list with an item near the bottom highlighted. In **Figure L4.6**, I've set the icon size to be 48 pixels and the font size to be 10 points. On super-high resolutions, you might want to make them

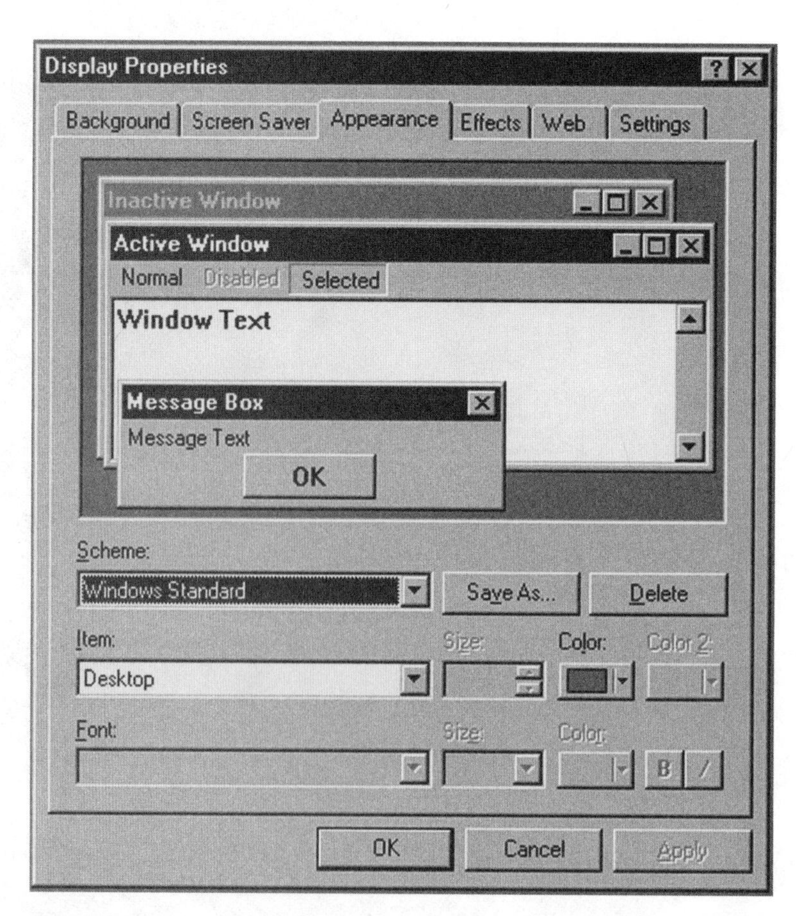

Figure L4.4 Configuring individual desktop items in Win98

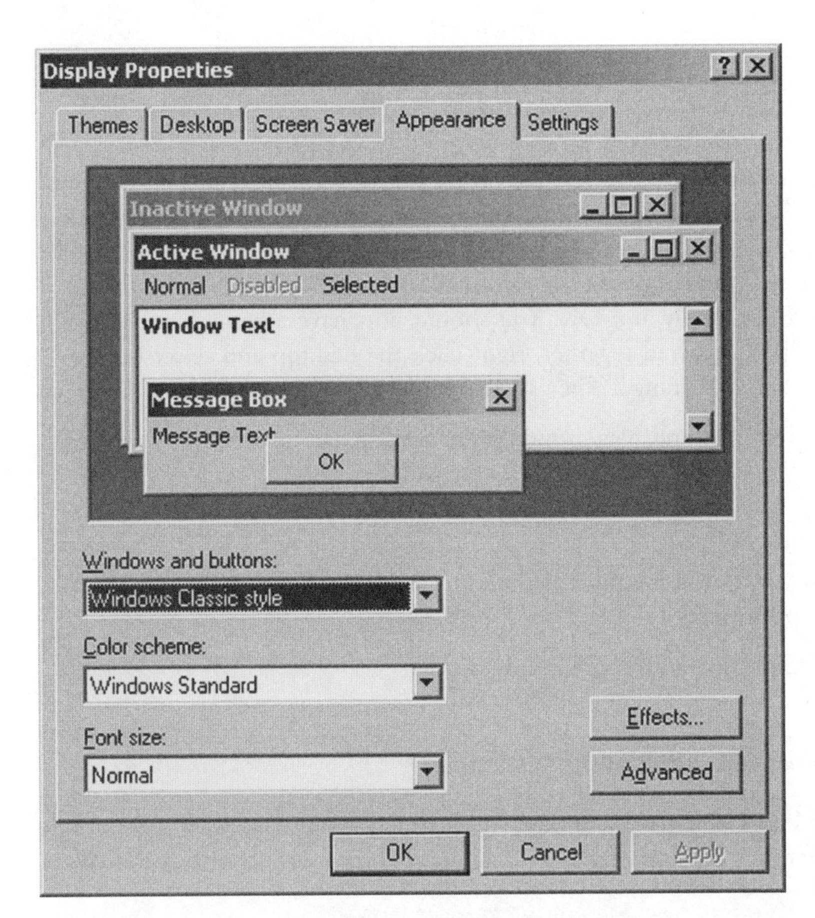

Figure L4.5 Configuring individual desktop items in later Windows versions

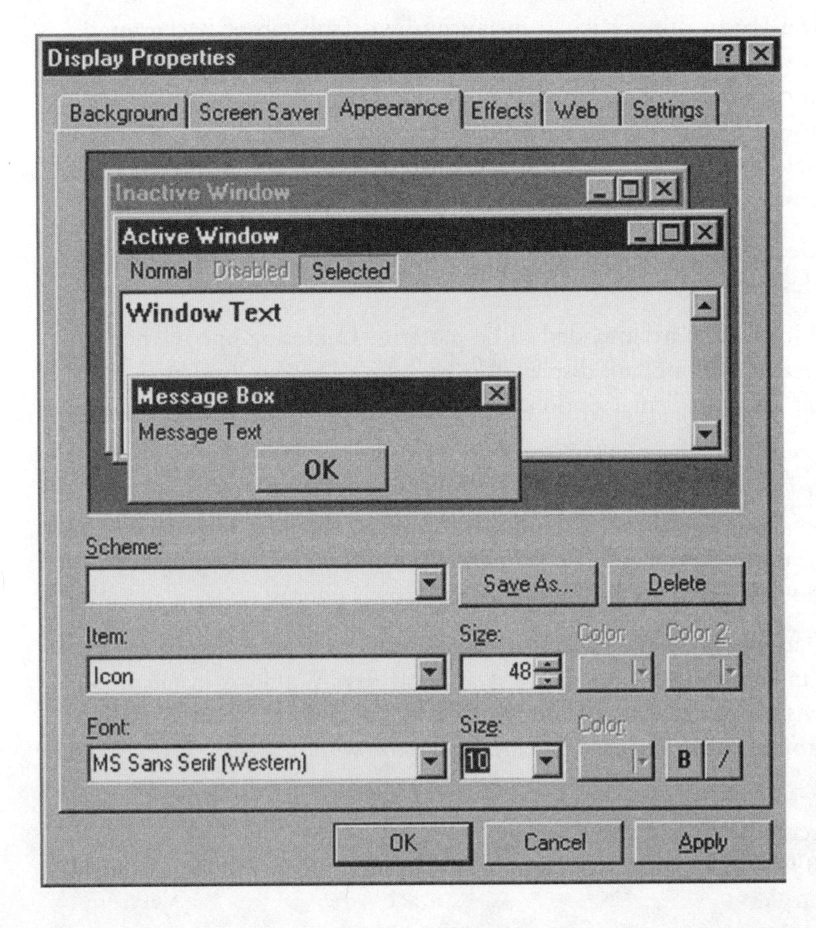

Figure L4.6 Making the icons and the font used in their captions bigger makes a high-resolution screen much easier to read.

even larger than that. If you want, you can even change the font to a different typeface, such as Times New Roman or one of the various script styles, if that is your preference. Click Apply and OK.

3. Wow! Now you've got bigger icons, and the letters are bigger but they're all scrunched together. Whatever are you going to do? You're going to fix it, that's what you're going to do! Go back into the Display Settings and click Appearance once again. This time, in the Item menu, scroll down to Icon Spacing (Horizontal) and increase the value by 50 to 75%. Do the same thing with Icon Spacing (Vertical). Click Apply and OK. You should now have a basic desktop you can live with. If the items are still clustered together, right-click the desktop and select the Arrange Icons option and select Auto-arrange. They should settle into place for you.
4. Go through each item in the Item list and play around with the settings to your heart's desire.

EXERCISE 1B REVIEW

1. Which tab in the Display Properties window houses the options for configuring the size of icons and the fonts used in their captions?
2. Which settings allow you to space the icons more evenly apart?

EXERCISE 1C: THE DESKTOP WALLPAPER

Of course, who wants to stare at a blank blue screen all day? (Even though you're *supposed* to be in one of your applications and working and not fiddling with your desktop!) People want pretty pictures. Want to set the desktop wallpaper?

1. Back to Display Properties you go. In this particular instance, the default tab of Background (**Figure L4.7**) is the one you want. You'll see two fields and two buttons. One of the fields is a list of preselected images you can use as a background, while the other allows you to decide whether you want a single instance of the image centered in the screen, multiple images spliced together and tiled, or the single image stretched across the entire screen. Trust me when I tell you, the last one is not a pleasant option.
2. Better yet, *don't* trust me. Select Bubbles and choose the Stretch option. Now click Apply and OK. Isn't this an attractive desktop?
3. Most of the images available in Win98 are intended to be patterns. Centering one of them on the screen isn't a whole lot better than a blank display. Go back into Display Properties, Background and select Bubble and the Center option. Click Apply and OK. I can see room for improvement here.
4. Go back into Display Properties→Background and select Bubble and Tile. Once more, click Apply and OK. A little better don't you think? The nice thing about the later versions of Windows is that a much larger selection of wallpaper images is available, including some relatively attractive photos. But it's very easy to use one of your own photos.
5. In the Display Properties→Background pane, click Browse. This opens a small Windows Explorer screen like the one in **Figure L4.8**. Since this is a brand new Windows installation, there won't be a lot of options on this machine from which you can choose. Notice that the only file type listed is Background Files. This can be any image file with a .BMP, .GIF, .HTM, or .JPG extension.
6. For the purposes of this exercise, browse to the Windows directory on your hard drive and select the HLPSTEP3.BMP file. Click Open. The Windows Explorer screen will close, and the

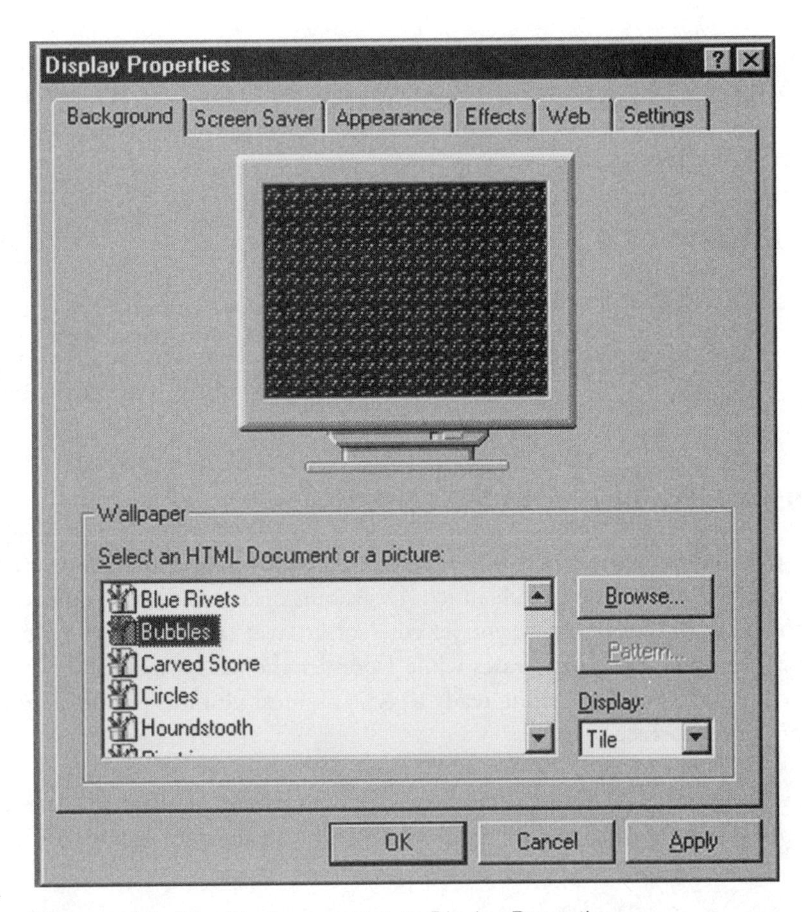

Figure L4.7 The Background tab in Display Properties

Figure L4.8 Browsing for a non-standard image file

file you just selected will be highlighted. Click Apply. You'll be told that this option is only available if Active Desktop is enabled. Do you wish to continue? You do if you want to complete this exercise. This is one of the ways to enable Active Desktop. Another way will be explored later. Click OK.

EXERCISE 1C REVIEW

1. Which tab in Display Properties allows you to configure your wallpaper?
2. How would you choose a picture of your cat to be your wallpaper?
3. Why would you **want** a picture of your cat as wallpaper?

EXERCISE 1D: CONFIGURING THE SCREENSAVER

One of the features of Windows is power management. After so many minutes, your screen will either go blank or a preconfigured screensaver will launch. Decisions, decisions! Which do you want to happen? Also, how long do you want to wait before you let your screensaver take over? As a writer (using the term in its loosest sense), I'm prone to long pauses while I ponder the next passage. The last thing I want is my screensaver kicking in just as I'm getting ready to type my next glorious phrase. Timing is everything. So now you'll configure a screensaver.

1. Yet once again, go back into Display Properties, and this time, select the Screen Saver tab. This will bring up a screen like the one in **Figure L4.9**. There are really only two actions you can

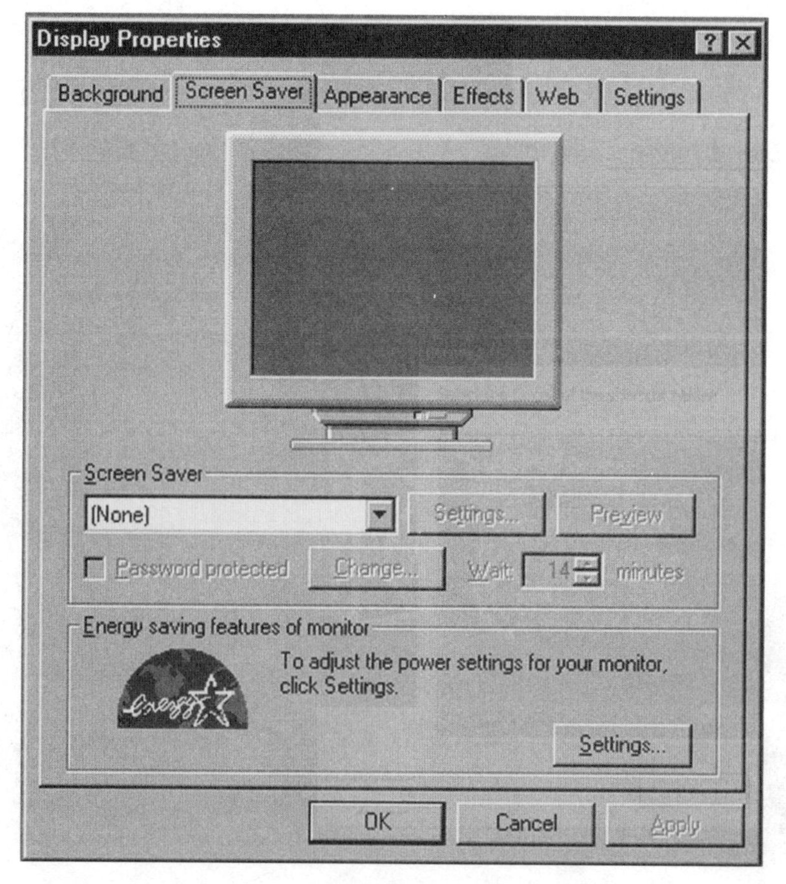

Figure L4.9 The Screen Saver screen in Windows

take here. The rest are all grayed out. One is to select which screensaver you want, and the next is to configure the energy saver settings for your monitor. The Settings, Preview, Password Protect, Change, and Wait buttons are all gray. That's because you have not yet selected a screensaver.

2. Select 3D text. Notice how the grayed out buttons suddenly become active? Click Settings to get the window shown in **Figure L4.10**. You have the option of typing in what text you want displayed or telling the system to display the time. To type in text, overwrite the default text that says OpenGL. You can choose whether you want your letters and numbers to be solidly colored or textured. And you can also select what font to use, the size, resolution, and speed at which the graphic spins. I've chosen "Master Graves" as the text in an effort to soothe my bruised ego, chosen a texture, and adjusted the resolution. The result can be seen in **Figure L4.11**.

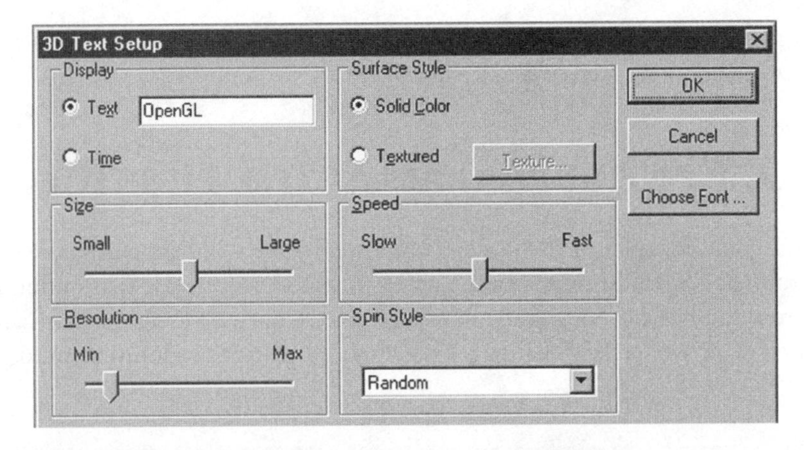

Figure L4.10 Adjusting the settings in your screensaver

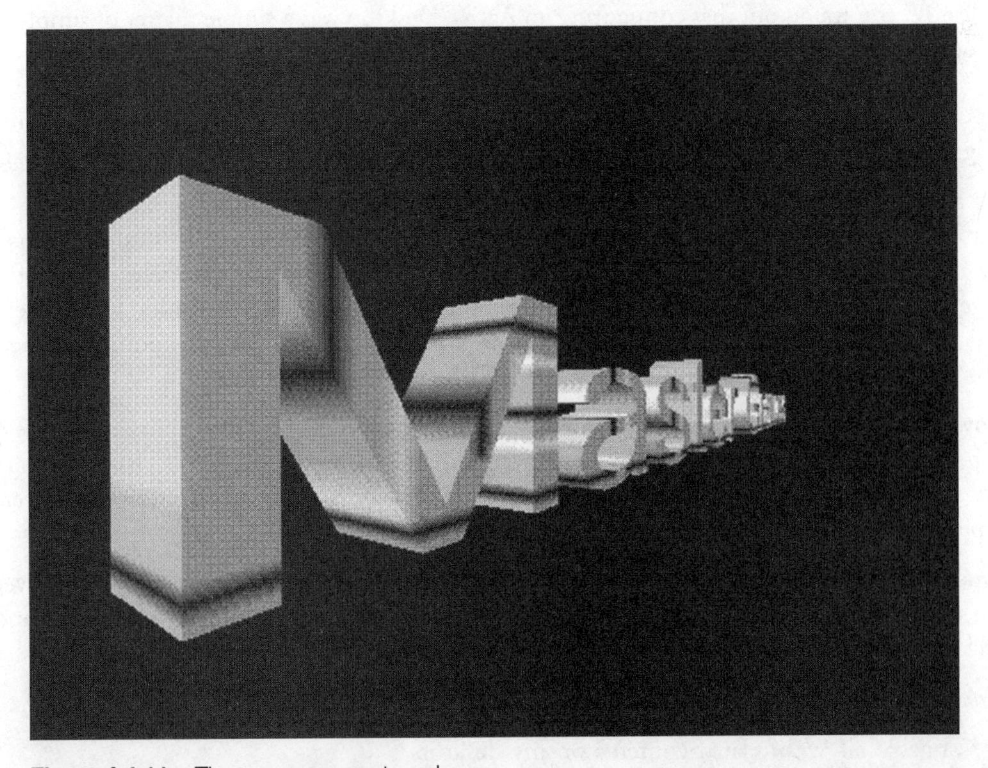

Figure L4.11 The screensaver at work

3. In the Wait field, type the number `1` so that you won't have to wait so long to see the results of your selection. In the real world you might want a setting that is just a trifle longer.
4. If you have materials on your computer that you'd rather other people not see, you can also configure the screensaver in such a way that after it is enabled, you can walk away from your desk. Click the Password Protected box and then click Change. Type in the password you want to use. Now, should unauthorized users come along and hit the spacebar on your keyboard while your screensaver is active, they'll be prompted to enter a password before they can continue. If they don't know your password, they can't browse your machine.

EXERCISE 1D REVIEW

1. Do you have to actually wait for Windows to activate your screensaver before having an idea of what it looks like?
2. Which screensaver option allows the user to put an advertising slogan up on the screen for people to read when the screensaver is engaged?

EXERCISE 2: CONFIGURING AN ACTIVE DESKTOP

Microsoft had this grand idea that if the OS and the Internet were indistinguishable, most users would be happier. After all, double-clicking is such a pain in the neck! So it made that option available. There are two more tabs in the Display Settings window that I have not yet discussed. Both are either directly or indirectly related to Active Desktop settings. Therefore, I've decided to lump them together in separate set of exercises.

EXERCISE 2A: SETTING THE ACTIVE DESKTOP

In Exercise 1c, you found out that configuring an Active Desktop was a simple matter of simply selecting a Desktop wallpaper that required it. There is also another way to get there from here.

1. Open the Display Properties windows and click the Web folder. In the screen that opens (**Figure L4.12**), simply click the checkbox labeled View my Active Desktop as a web page.
2. It's almost as simple as that. But you can get more elaborate than that. By Clicking the New button, you can connect to Microsoft's Web site and browse for Active Desktop options that are not installed from the CD during the initial installation. You can also select a specific Web page you would like displayed. For the latter, you will most likely have to know the user name and password of that site's administrator. Since it is very likely that at this point in time, most labs won't be configured for the Internet, I'll forgo demonstrating this process.
3. Now if you want to activate programs with a single mouse click on an icon there is one more step. Click the Folder Options in the lower right-hand corner. You'll be given a warning that if you continue, Display Properties will close and the Folder Options of Windows Explorer will appear. Continue, and you'll see the screen shown in **Figure L4.13**.
4. Simply clicking the checkbox labeled Web Style allows single click functionality. However, you can do even better by clicking Custom (**Figure L4.13**), based on settings you choose, and then clicking the Settings box. The options available here include the following:

- Active Desktop
  - Enable all Web related contents on my desktop
  - Use Windows Classic desktop

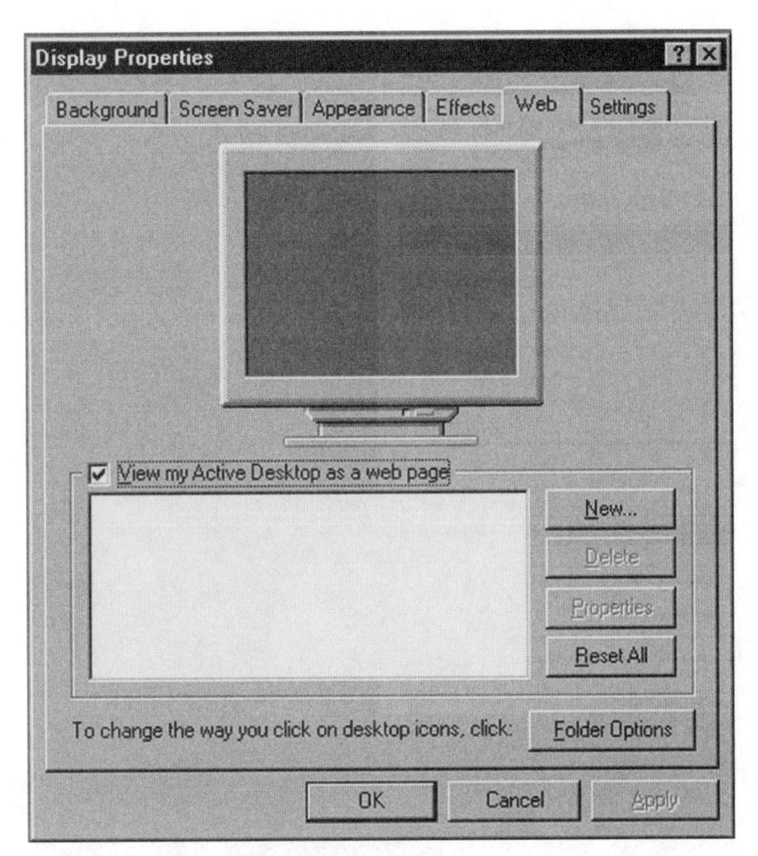

Figure L4.12
Setting the Active Desktop

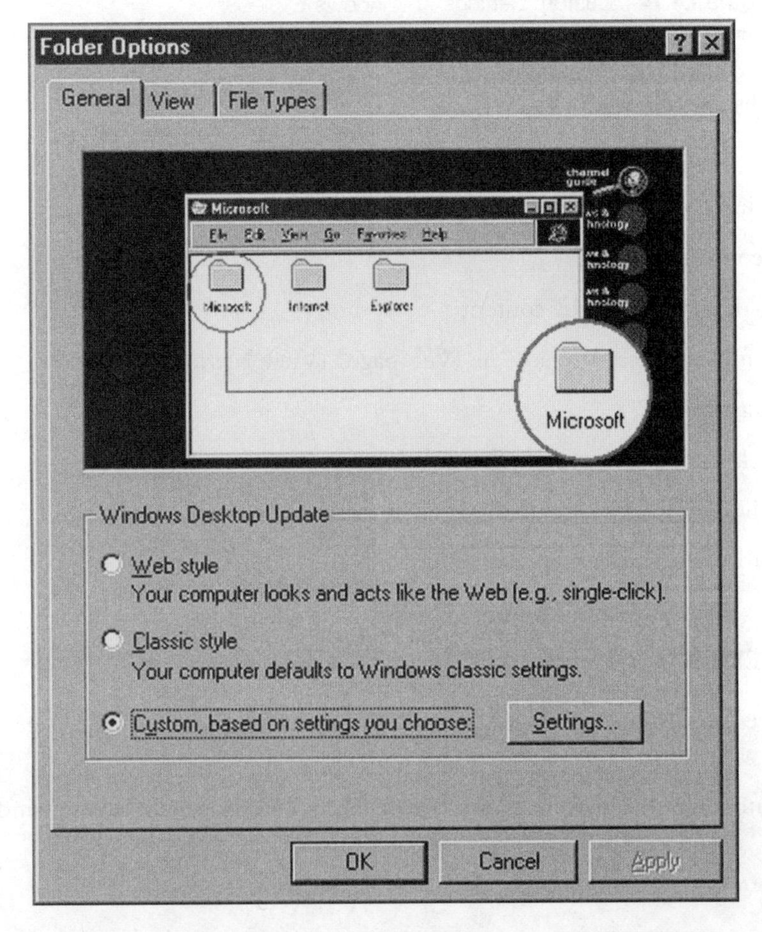

Figure L4.13
Folder Options in Windows Exploder

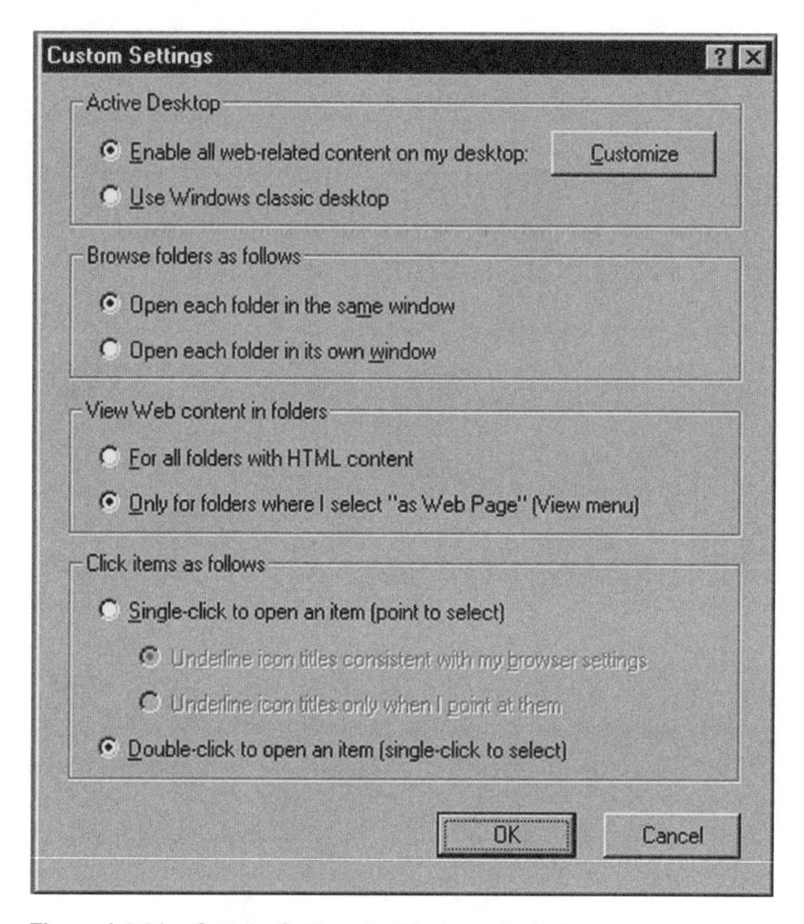

Figure L4.14 Custom Settings in Windows Exploder

- Browse Folders as follows
  - Open each folder in the same window
  - Open each folder in a new window
- View Web content in folders
  - For all folders with HTML content
  - Only for folders where I select "As Web page" (View Menu)
- Click Items as follows
  - Single-click to open an item (point to select)
  - Double-click to open an item (single-click to select)

5. Play around with these options as time permits.

Exercise 2a Review

1. What two pieces of information might you need in order to display a Web page on your desktop?
2. How would you make sure that each item you clicked would open in a new window?

EXERCISE 2B: CONFIGURING DESKTOP EFFECTS

By now, you've already got a desktop that is pretty much unique to you, as long as everyone in class has been picking different settings along the way. Still, in Windows, you can fine-tune the desktop even further. You can configure how windows, menus, and lists behave, and, if you want, you can make sure the contents of a window remain visible even while you're dragging that window across the desktop. Allow me to show you how this is done.

1. Back to Display settings you go for yet another expedition. Click the Effects tab.
2. As you can see, you have six different options.
   a. Hide icons when the desktop is displayed as a Web page: This prevents your icons from cluttering up the Web site you've chosen to appear on your screen. It also ensures that you'll use the Start button a whole lot more.
   b. Use large icons: Umm. That make the icons on the desktop bigger. Bet I didn't have to tell you that.
   c. Show icons using all possible colors: By default, this option is selected. If your display settings are set to True Color, then the colors will blend more smoothly. Deselecting this option reverts all icons back to 256 color images.
   d. Animate windows, menus, and lists: By default this option is selected. When you click the Start menu, it sweeps open in an upward motion. Menus from the top of the screen sweep downward. For most systems this is fine. If resources such as CPU horsepower or available memory are at a minimum you can conserve by deselecting this option. The objects will simply appear when clicked.
   e. Smooth edges of screen fonts: On a low-resolution display, this reduces the stair-step effect seen on the angled edges of larger fonts.
   f. Show Window contents while dragging: When you pull a word processing document across the screen, the words and letters in the document go with the window.
3. As time permits, play around with these options. Note that reconfiguring some of them, such as smoothing screen fonts, requires the restart of the computer.

EXERCISE 2B REVIEW

1. What are the various effects that you can configure in the Windows Display settings?
2. Which of these options requires a restart of Windows before the configuration change will take effect?

LAB REVIEW

1. What happens to icons and font size when you change screen resolution from 640x480 to 1024x768?
2. Which of the Display Properties tabs would you go to in order to increase the size of icons and icon captions?
3. Where would you go to smooth the edges of screen fonts on the Windows display?

4. How could you go about putting a photo that you took on your vacation onto your desktop?
5. Why wouldn't you want to stretch the image of the brick wall to make your wallpaper?

LAB SUMMARY

As you can see, there is a lot of tweaking you can do on the Windows desktop. You could have a dozen computers in a classroom, and no two look alike. This is just one of many ways Microsoft approached the concept of making computing a personal experience.

LAB 5

MANAGING PRINTERS IN WINDOWS

The process of printing in any operating system is one that baffles many. It just seems to happen. As a technician, however, you need to be able to install and configure printers, and then over the course of time, make sure that printer keeps doing what it has to do. To be certain, a lot of this work is hardware related, but the software side is every bit as critical. Updating and reinstalling drivers, mapping networked printers, and managing the print spool are all part of the job. Those are the things I'll go over in this lab.

For this lab, you'll need the lab PC with Win98 installed and, if possible, a printer with driver disks for each PC.

The following CompTIA objectives are covered in this lab:

2.1 Identify the procedures for installing Windows 9x/Me, Windows NT 4.0 Workstation, Windows 2000 Professional, and Windows XP and bringing the operating system to a basic operational level.

2.4 Identify procedures for installing/adding a device, including loading, adding, and configuring device drivers, and required software.

3.3 Recognize common operational and usability problems and determine how to resolve them.

EXERCISE 1: INSTALLING A PRINTER

This is one of those labs where it really doesn't matter what version of Windows you have installed on the system. The procedure doesn't change. Only the pretty pictures do. The biggest difference is that with Win2K or WinXP, the process of installing a local printer is so automated there is rarely much for the technician to do except supply the disk.

I should point out that installing a network printer is part of the process of managing printers. However, since you won't build your network for a couple of more labs, I've decided to include that as part of the networking lab. So for now, I'll concentrate on installing a local printer.

1. The first thing to do is to open the Printers applet from the Control Panel. There are three ways to go about this. The first is to double-click My Computer and then double-click the Printers icon. Another way is Start→Settings→Control Panel and double-clicking the Printers icon. To me, both of these methods are more cumbersome than simply clicking Start→Set-

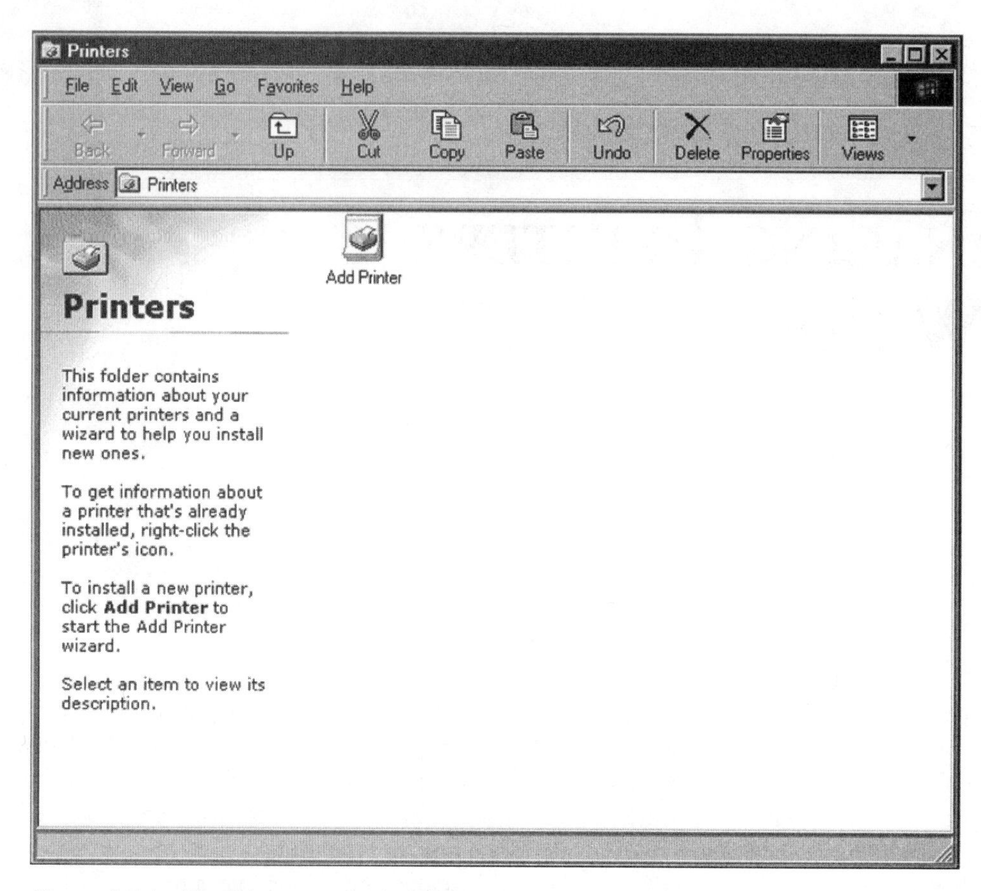

Figure L5.1 The Printers applet in Windows

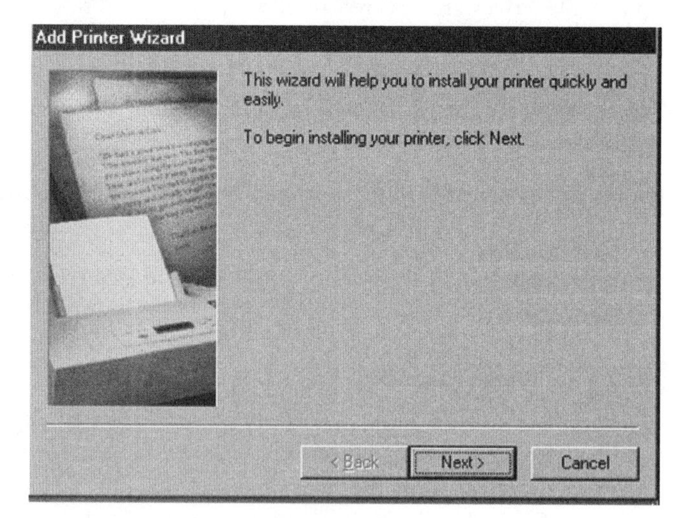

Figure L5.2 Adding a new printer is accomplished by way of a Wizard.

tings→Printers. In WinXP, there is a specific shortcut to Printers and Faxes in the Start Menu, so it's even easier. Whichever method you choose as your own, you'll end up with a screen like the one in **Figure L5.1**.

2. Because these are fresh installations, there is no printer installed, so your only option at this time is to install a new printer. Double-click the Add Printer icon to start the Wizard (**Figure L5.2**).
3. Since the next few screens are merely variations on the same theme I won't waste space or time with screen shots. Click Next and in the screen that follows, click Local printer.

4. In the next screen that appears (**Figure L5.3**) you will be presented with a long list of manufacturers supported by the OS in the left-hand pane. When you click any given manufacturer, a list of printer models appears in the right-hand pane. If you are installing a printer that is not listed, you can click the Have Disk option to install a third party driver. Since it is unlikely that most labs will be blessed with an individual printer for each student PC, you'll simply lie to Windows and tell it you have one.

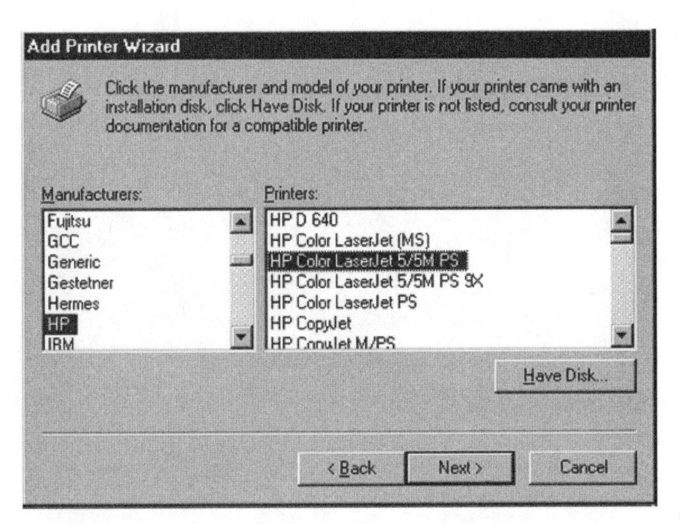

Figure L5.3 While Win98 supported a lot of printer models, it doesn't come close to the number of printers supported by XP!

5. So that everybody stays on the same page, scroll down to the HP entry in the manufacturer's list. You can get there faster by pressing the H key on your keyboard. In the printer model list, select HP Color Laserjet 5/5M PS like I did in Figure L5.3. Those of you with actual printers to install, select the make and model of printer from the list. If it isn't there, select Have Disk. Click Next>.

6. Next, the Add Printer Wizard is going to ask you what port you want your new printer to print to. In Win98 the options are somewhat limited. You have the choice of your serial ports, your parallel ports, or Print to File, as shown in **Figure L5.4**. If you have an actual printer, select LPT1. Printing to file is useful if you have a printer at the office to which you want to output the file. You can save the file the way the printer receives it to a diskette and then just run it off on any printer without having to open it up again in a word processor. Personally, I find it easier to just bring the document itself in on the diskette.

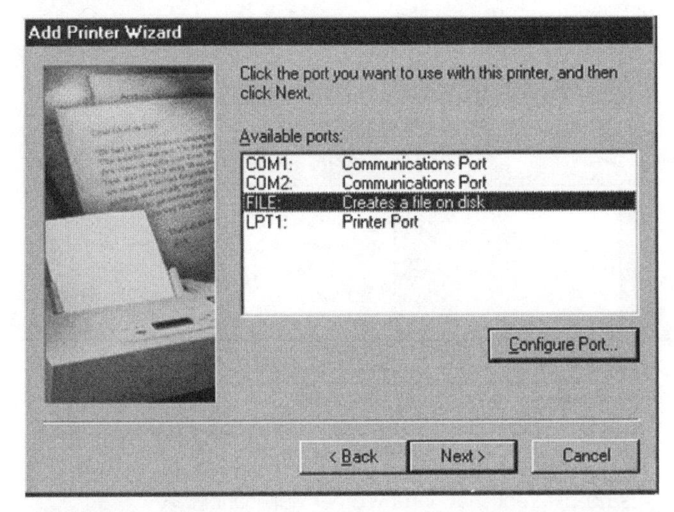

Figure L5.4 Win98 is somewhat limited in the options available for a destination port. Win2K and WinXP both allow you to print to USB and to configure a TCP/IP port from this window.

7. Now you'll be asked to name your printer. A default name will already be filled in. If you like long names, click Next >. As you can see in **Figure L5.5**, I'm going to call my virtual printer Color Laser.

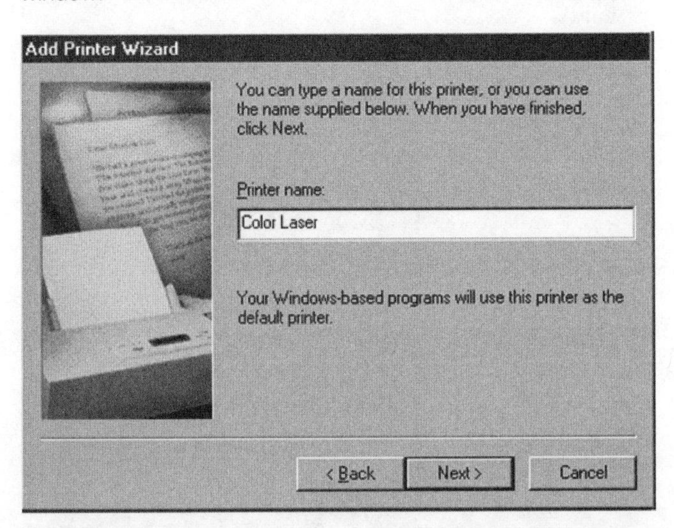

Figure L5.5 You can name your printer whatever you like. Just remember that other people will be seeing it.

8. In the next screen (**Figure L5.6**), you'll be asked whether you want to print a test page. Make sure you have the

Win98 CD in the drive. Under most circumstances, in a new printer installation, you want to click Yes and continue. However, if there is no printer hooked up to your system, click the No button and click Next >. The Wizard will copy a bunch of files from the CD.

9. Should you ever chose to print to file, you'll get the screen shown in **Figure L5.7** asking you to name the file. After the file has been written, you'll get the screen in **Figure L5.8** asking whether the page printed successfully. Whenever you have selected a physical port to print to, Figure L5.8 will be the next screen you see. If you're printing to an actual printer, click Yes. Congratulations! Your printer is installed.

Figure L5.6 Any time you are installing a printer for the first time, it's a good idea to print a test page. That way you know for certain you have connectivity and that you've installed the correct driver.

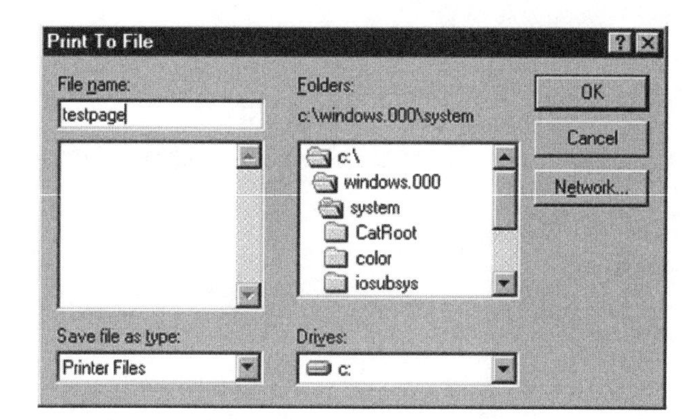

Figure L5.7 Naming a print file when printing to file is no different than in any other application.

EXERCISE 1 REVIEW

1. You're trying to install a brand new printer and realize your make and model isn't on the list of supported printers. What do you do now?

2. What is the extension that allows you to identify a print job that has been printed to file?

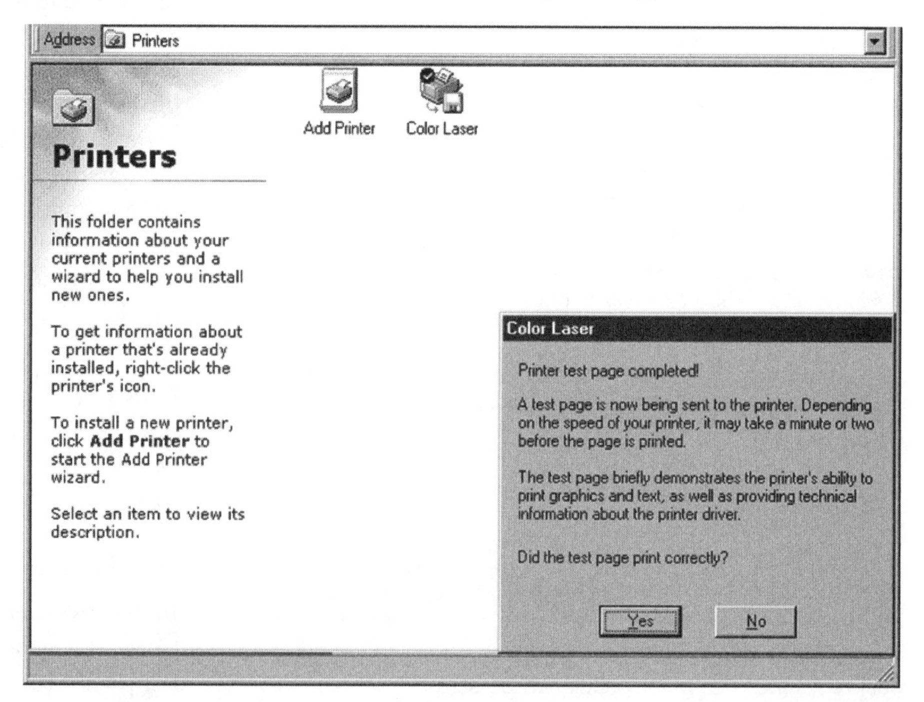

Figure L5.8 When printing to a port, the Wizard will ask you whether the test page printed successfully.

EXERCISE 2: MANAGING THE PRINTER QUEUE

One of the handier things about a graphical interface is having a utility that manages something as complex as the printer queue. What is the printer queue? Simply put, the vast majority of the time when a printer is called upon to perform, a single job gets sent from the PC to the printer, and that's that. However, from time to time things go wrong. Perhaps the printer is shared out over a network, or a user prints a barrage of documents in succession. Then suddenly the printer simply says "Enough's enough" and shuts down. The printer queue provides the user or administrator a way to cancel stalled print jobs, or even bring a critical job to the top of the list when there are numerous jobs waiting in the queue. I'll show you how.

EXERCISE 2A: REMOVING DOCUMENTS FROM THE QUEUE

In the event that a document freezes, or a networked computer locks up while printing a document, the stalled document will prevent all other documents from printing. If you're not familiar with the workings of the printer queue, this can be a perplexing problem. Everything is working properly, except the letter to your mother-in-law won't print. Remove the offending document, and all should be well.

1. The first step is to create an offending print job. With no physical printer hooked up, that ought to be easy to do. Click Start→Programs→Accessories→Wordpad. Open C:\Windows\script.doc by clicking File→Open and browsing to the Windows directory. Most likely that's the only document you will find available. It's a document file that should exist on any fresh Windows installation.
2. Press Alt+P to print the document. As the only printer installed, your Color Laserjet will be selected as the default printer. Press <Enter>. Repeat this step about four times until you have several documents in the queue.
3. Click Start→Settings→Printers to open the Printers applet (or Printers and Faxes in WinXP). Double-click the installed printer's icon to open the window shown in **Figure L5.9**.
4. All of your attempts to print will be visible in this screen. In the Window Title Bar, you will see that the printer is listed as Off Line. The information you can learn from this small applet includes the status of the print job, person who originated any particular print job (useful in a networked environment), how far along the current job is, and what time any given job was initiated.
5. To remove a single document from the queue, highlight that document and on the menu, click Document→Cancel Printing, as shown in Figure L5.9. That job will be deleted.
6. On some rare occasions the printer queue itself may lock up, or you may have to bring a printer offline for an extended period. In either case, you will most likely find it desirable to flush the printer queue completely. In order to do this, open the queue for the targeted printer, and as shown in **Figure L5.10**, click Printer→Purge Print Documents. Most frequently the

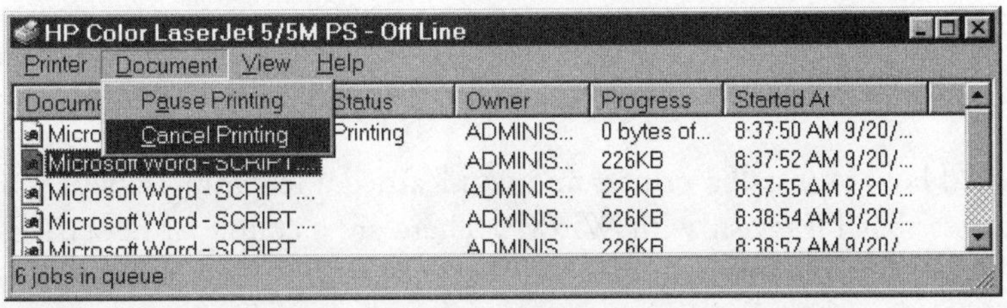

Figure L5.9 Canceling a single document from the queue

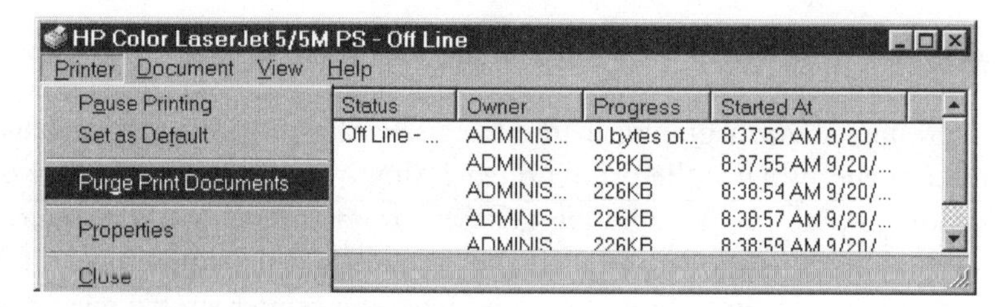

Figure L5.10 Purging the Printer Queue

document that is attempting to print will not clear itself using this method, so you would revert to the method discussed in the previous step for deleting a single print job.

EXERCISE 2A REVIEW

1. Describe the process of deleting a single job from the printer queue.
2. How would you flush all print jobs from the queue?

EXERCISE 2B MOVING A DOCUMENT TO A DIFFERENT POSITION IN THE QUEUE

In a busy office, the only printer can sometimes get quite busy. What if you have an important meeting coming up in 10 minutes and you realize you need a critical document printed. You shoot it off to the printer and realize that there are six jobs ahead of you, and two of them are copies of the boss's 800-page novel. Can you scoot your job ahead of those marathon toner-bleeders? Sure you can. Here's how.

1. Open the printer queue for the selected printer.
2. With the left mouse button, click the print job you want to move up and slide that job up underneath the job that is currently printing. Your job is now next in line. You can also move print jobs down in this same manner if you simply want to move a job to the bottom of the stack.

EXERCISE 2B REVIEW

1. What is the procedure for moving a print job up or down in the queue?
2. What happens if you keep moving the boss's print jobs to the bottom of the order?

LAB REVIEW

1. If you don't see the printer you're installing in the list provided by Windows, what option would you select?
2. Aside from LPT1, what were some of the port options available while installing a printer?

LAB SUMMARY

In this lab you learned how to install a printer and you learned a few things about managing the printer queue. This is one area that I'll revisit with WinXP. There are a couple of new tricks Microsoft taught the printer queue that are worth taking a look at.

LAB 6

WORKING WITH CONTROL PANEL

As I pointed out in the text book, all of the settings that make the Windows OS do what it does, and all of the adjustments that users make, are stored in the registry. However, the registry is an ungainly monster and editing it directly can be dangerous for the uninitiated. Therefore Microsoft provided a tool for making changes to OS settings. This tool is the Control Panel. In this lab you'll take a closer look at each of those pretty little icons you see in Control Panel and learn what they all do.

The only materials you'll need for this lab are the computer onto which you installed Windows 98 and a copy of the Windows 98 CD.

There is only one CompTIA objective covered in this lab:

1.1 Identify the major desktop components and interfaces and their functions. Differentiate the characteristics of Windows 9x/Me, Windows NT 4.0 Workstation, Windows 2000 Professional, and Windows XP

EXERCISE 1: AN OVERVIEW OF THE CONTROL PANEL

Everything that makes Windows do what it does is controlled by the registry. But the registry can be a pretty scary place to be, even for the seasoned veteran. Therefore, Microsoft has provided the Control Panel for adjusting the Registry settings that are most commonly manipulated. There are two ways to get to Control Panel. One is to double-click My Computer and then double-click Control Panel. The other is to click Start→Settings→Control Panel. Either way, you wind up with a screen like the one in **Figure L6.1**.

As you can see, there are a number of icons in this screen. These are shortcuts to the various applets of Control Panel. As other services are installed onto the OS; other icons are added as well. For example, in the figure, there is an icon for HP JetAdmin. You will most likely not have that icon. I purchased a Hewlett Packard Jetdirect as a more efficient method of sharing out the printers on my network than simply hooking up a printer to somebody's computer and sharing it out. When I installed the software, the service was added to Control Panel. Also the icon with the inverted V labeled Modem Settings was added when I installed a USB modem. Other icons you're not likely to see on your screen include Administrative Tools, Adobe Gamma, and Automatic Updates. For the most part, you should see the rest of the icons in Figure L6.1 on your screen. Now I'll go over what each applet controls.

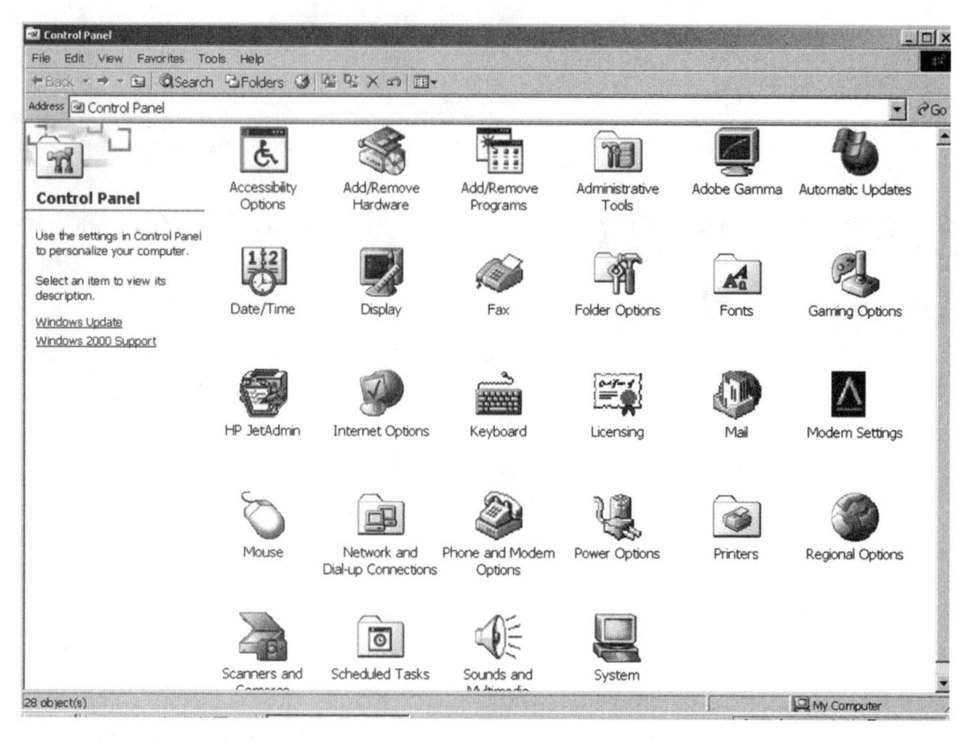

Figure L6.1 The Control Panel

EXERCISE 1A: ACCESSIBILITY OPTIONS

Accessibility Options (**Figure L6.2**) allow you to customize the way your keyboard, display, and mouse function. Although these options are primarily designed to assist the disabled as they use a computer, many of these features are useful to people without disabilities. The various features that can be configured here include the following:

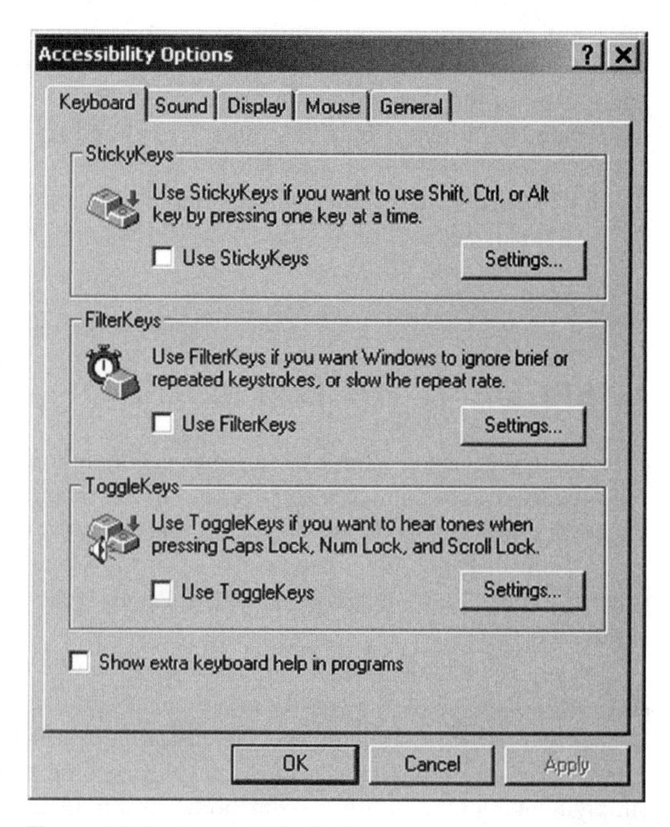

Figure L6.2 Accessibility Options

- StickyKeys: Enables simultaneous keystrokes while pressing one key at a time.
- FilterKeys: Adjusts the response of your keyboard.
- ToggleKeys: Emits sounds when certain locking keys are pressed.
- SoundSentry: Provides visual warnings for system sounds.
- ShowSounds: Instructs programs to display captions for program speech and sounds.
- High Contrast: Improves screen contrast with alternative colors and font sizes.

- MouseKeys: Enables the keyboard to perform mouse functions.
- SerialKeys: Allows the use of alternative input devices instead of a keyboard and mouse.

Set your Accessibility Options so that StickyKeys are enabled and the monitor is adjusted for High Contrast. Can you see how these options might help a person with disabilities?

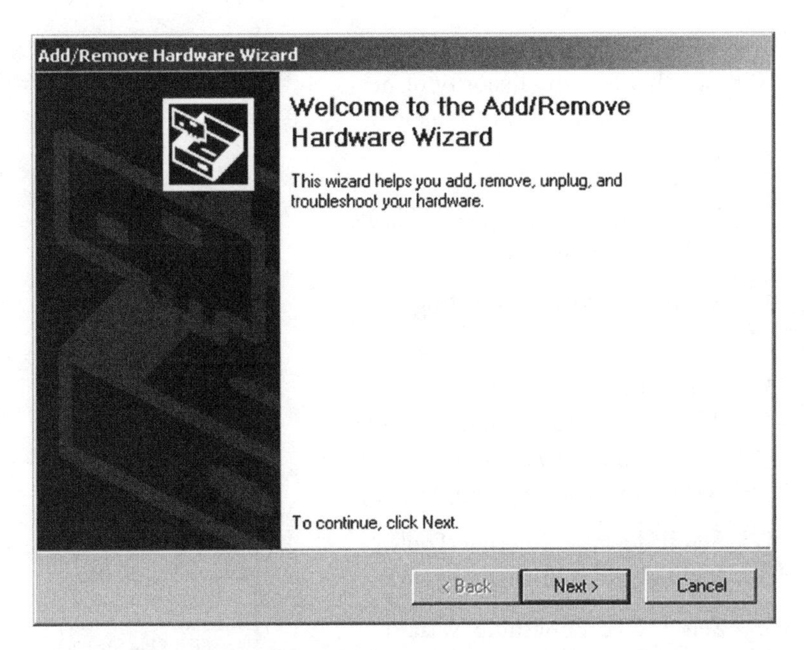

Figure L6.3 Add/Remove Hardware

EXERCISE 1B: ADD/ REMOVE HARDWARE

Double-clicking this icon starts the Add/Remove Hardware Wizard (**Figure L6.3**). For the most part, Windows can automatically detect and configure any new Plug 'n Play hardware you install. Should you decide to install something that is not Plug 'n Play, or should Windows fail to install a device, the Add/ Remove Hardware Wizard comes in handy. It will do a scan of your system and detect any devices that are installed in the system. It can also detect devices that were installed but have not been properly configured to run in Windows. The Add/Remove Hardware Wizard first tries to auto-configure devices. If it fails, it leads the user through a step-by-step process of properly installing that device.

For this exercise, you're going to skip ahead a bit. At the bottom of Control Panel is another applet called System.

1. Open the System Applet.
2. Click the tab that says Device Manager.
3. Click the plus sign next to the entry for Monitor.
4. Delete the Default Monitor. Don't worry. Your screen isn't suddenly going to go away.
5. Now go ahead and run the Add\Remove Hardware Wizard. Just follow the prompts and accept the defaults as they're offered.

EXERCISE 1C: ADD/REMOVE PROGRAMS

Back in the days when Windows 98 was considered state of the art, this applet was a lot more useful than it really is today. Still, even today, it's a very useful application. Or at least it would be if more people actually used it. It isn't the adding of programs that make it useful, but rather the removal of said programs. However, in the days of Windows 98, in order for the applet to properly remove a program, that program needed to be installed by the applet as well. When you use Add/Remove Programs (**Figure L6.4**) to install a program, Windows maintains a log of everything that is change. New folders that are created and new registry entries that are added get recorded in this log. When you decide to uninstall that program later on down the line, Add/Remove Programs uses the uninstall log to back off all changes that were made during installation. Without that log, the majority of new folders and registry entries remain on the system.

1. Make sure you have your Win98 CD available for this exercise.
2. Start the Add/Remove Programs Wizard.
3. Click the Windows Setup tab. There'll be a few moments while the Wizard examines your system for installed components.
4. Scroll down to Internet Tools, highlight it, and click Details.
5. Select Web Publishing Wizard and click OK. The Internet Tools box should now be grayed out, with a checkbox in it. Click OK. You'll be prompted to enter the Win98 CD. You may have to browse for it. It will be in the Win98 directory of the CD.
6. When the Wizard finds the file, it will copy a collection of files to your hard disk. The Publishing Wizard is now installed.

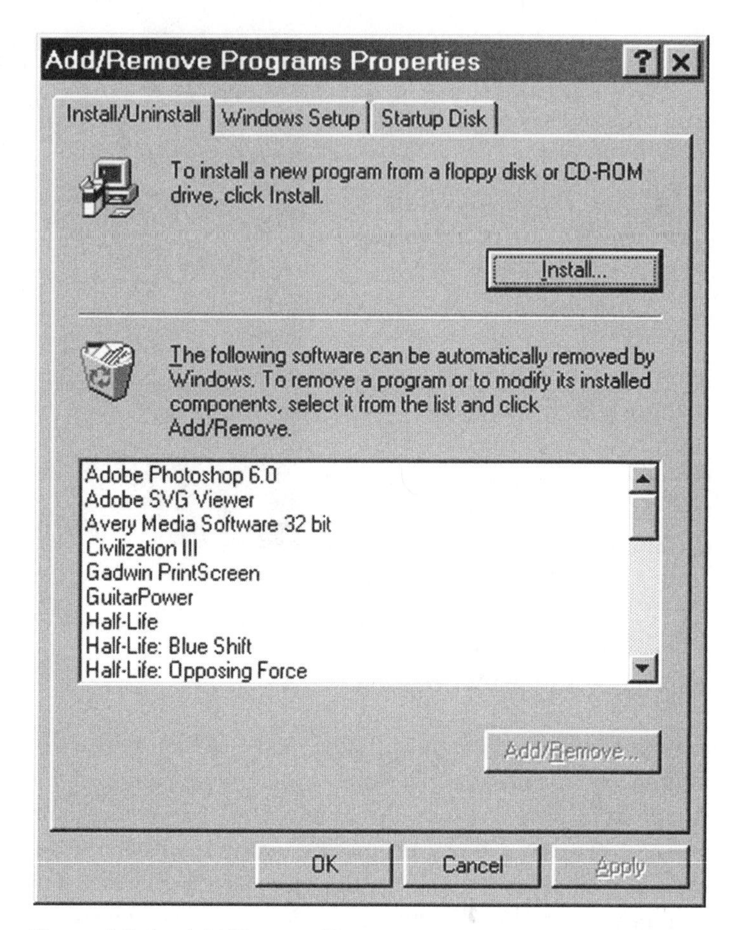

Figure L6.4 Add/Remove Programs

EXERCISE 1D: DATE AND TIME

Hopefully, the applet shown in **Figure L6.5** doesn't require a great deal of explanation. It's, um, where you set your date and time. There is, however, a third function located in this applet that you might find useful if you ever move across the country. That is the ability to change the time zone in which you reside.

1. Double-click the Date/Time icon.
2. Change the year to 1981.
3. Click Apply and then Okay.
4. Did your wardrobe suddenly get tacky and really bad music start pouring from the stereo?

Figure L6.5 Date and Time

EXERCISE 1E: FONTS

This is another often overlooked applet in Control Panel. For most of us, our font collection grows as a result of installing new software. Any new application that provides a collection of fonts assumes you want to use everything they have to offer and installs every single one into your system. The problem with this shotgun approach is that, the more fonts you install, the longer it takes your system to load at startup. Then when you decide to use something other than your normal typeface, you have to scroll through all those hundreds of choices. In the Fonts applet (**Figure L6.6**) you can install and/or uninstall fonts to create the list useful to you. Of course, once again, like most of us, you have no idea what some of these fonts look like.

There are two ways of sorting out the wheat from the chaff. To view a font, double-click on its icon. You'll get a typeface sheet that shows the font in several different sizes. You can print that sheet out, if you so desire. Another useful trick this applet does is to sort fonts by similarity. Click View→List Fonts by Similarity. When you highlight any given font in the list, other fonts are listed as being Very Similar, Fairly Similar, or Not Similar. From what I can tell with these feeble eyes, Very Similar means Identical. If you have two dozen fonts that all show up as being Very Similar, you're better off picking one and uninstalling the rest.

1. Double-click the Fonts icon. You should see a screen that displays an icon for every font installed on your system.
2. Double-click any font and maximize the screen that appears.
3. Now click the Similarity button. The list that appears tells you how similar to the selected font every other font on the system is. Too many similar fonts tie up a lot of disk space. It's safe to eliminate them.

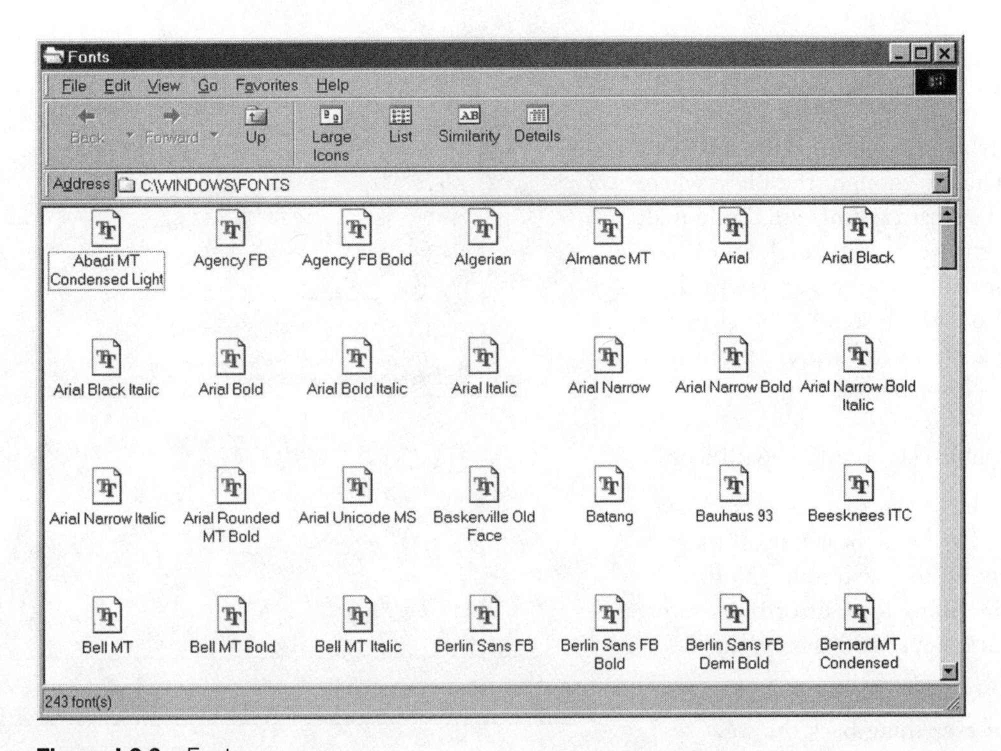

Figure L6.6 Fonts

EXERCISE 1F: INTERNET PROPERTIES

Internet Properties (**Figure L6.7**) is a very busy applet and one in which the average technician spends an inordinate amount of time. This is where you configure all the settings that let your computer successfully communicate with your Internet Service Provider (ISP). But it doesn't stop there. It's also where you can go to make sure your children aren't hopping onto websites like www.crazedmilitants.com and other sites that you'd rather them not be seeing. It is in this applet that you configure how many days worth of history to maintain and to empty the history at your convenience. To go into every setting to be found in this applet is beyond the scope of this lab, but you might want to spend a few extra moments poking around to see what there is to see.

1. Since it is unlikely that most labs will be set up for Internet at this time, simply double-click the Internet Properties icon and follow along as the instructor explains the various options.

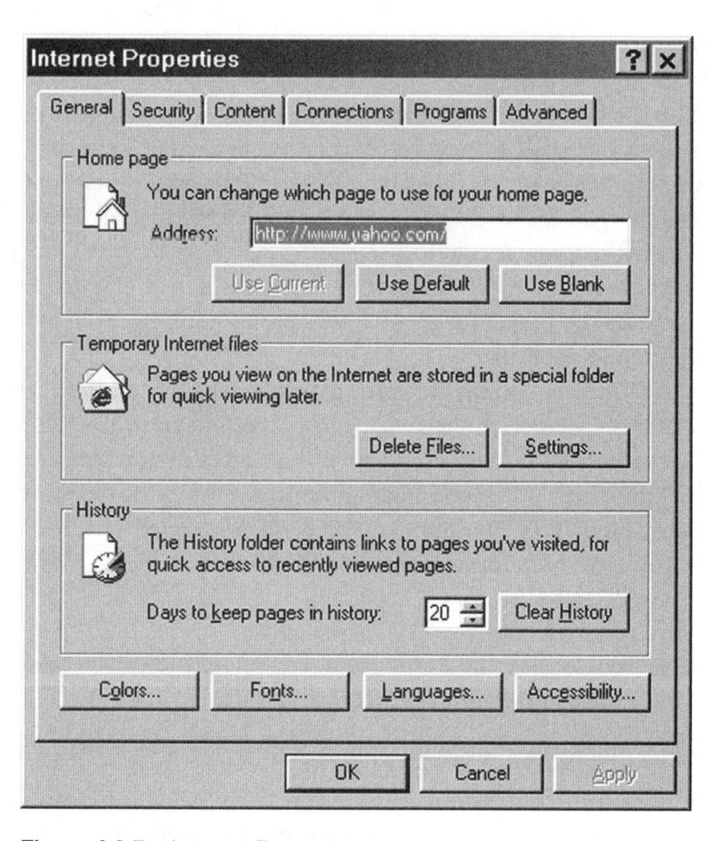

Figure L6.7 Internet Properties

EXERCISE 1G: KEYBOARD

The Keyboard applet (**Figure L6.8**) is, coincidentally enough, the place where certain keyboard settings are configured. These settings include the kind of keyboard installed, the repeat rate for keys that automatically repeat the character as long as the key is depressed and how fast the cursor blinks.

1. Double-click the Keyboard icon.
2. In the screen that appears, slide the bar for Repeat rate all the way up to Maximum. Do the same thing for Cursor blink rate. Click Apply and then Okay.
3. Now, since that's really annoying, put everything back the way it was.

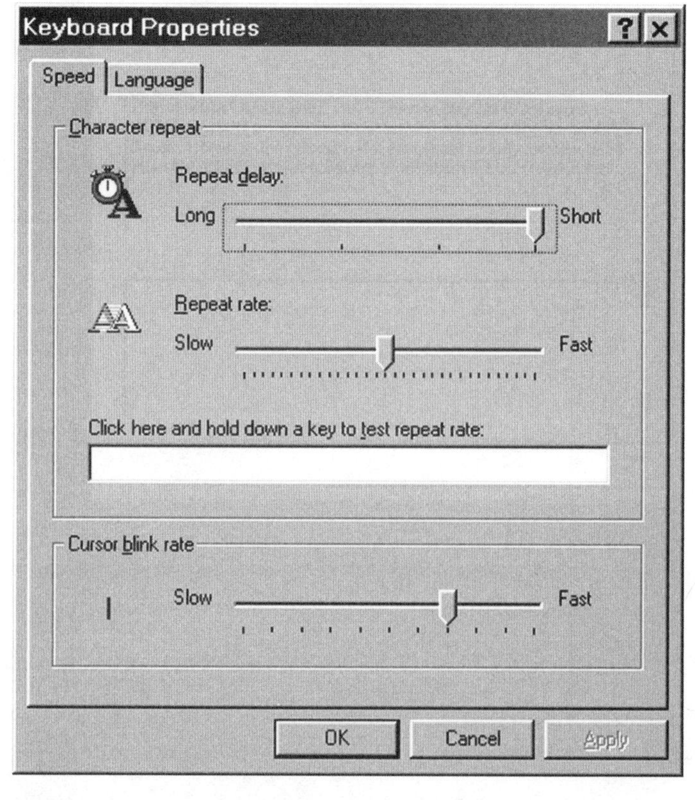

Figure L6.8 The Keyboard applet

EXERCISE 1H: MOUSE

How many times have you sat down at somebody else's computer and found out that they had set their mouse up to be left-handed? Or that the click rate was so slow that you entered the next millennium between clicks? Or so fast that Superman couldn't move his fingers fast enough to get the desired results? The Mouse applet (**Figure L6.9**) is where you change all those settings and more. In this applet you can also change the mouse cursor, enable mouse trails (not on *my* computer, you don't!) and configure how much movement of the mouse is required in order to move the cursor a certain distance. Drive your boss nuts. Make the cursor move as fast as it possibly can, set the click rate to maximum speed and then enable mouse trails. Then delete the Mouse applet from Control Panel.

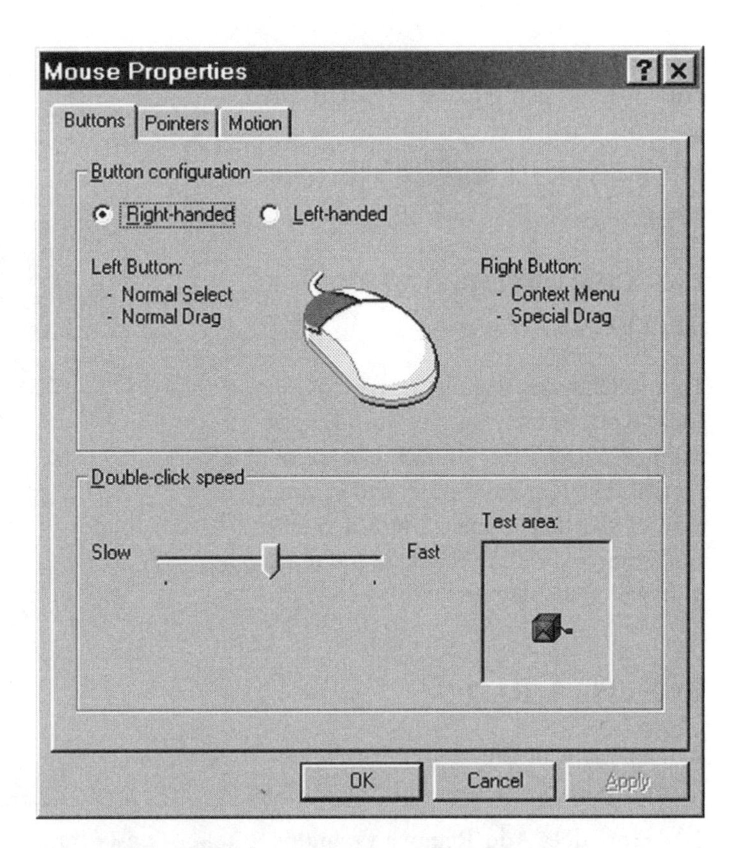

Figure L6.9 The Mouse applet

1. Double-click the Mouse icon.
2. Click the Motion tab.
3. Move the slider for Pointer speed all the way down to slow and click the box for pointer trails.
4. Now since that's even more annoying than fast blinking cursors, put those settings back the way they were.
5. During break, set your partner's mouse to be left-handed, with fast cursors, and slow mouse trails. Expect him or her to do the same to you.

EXERCISE 1I: NETWORK

Another applet that you'll spend a lot of time exploring is the Network and Dial-Up Connections applet (**Figure L6.10**), especially if you pursue a career as a network administrator. This is where all local area connections for the local area network are configured in Windows 98. In Windows 2000 and XP, dial-up con-

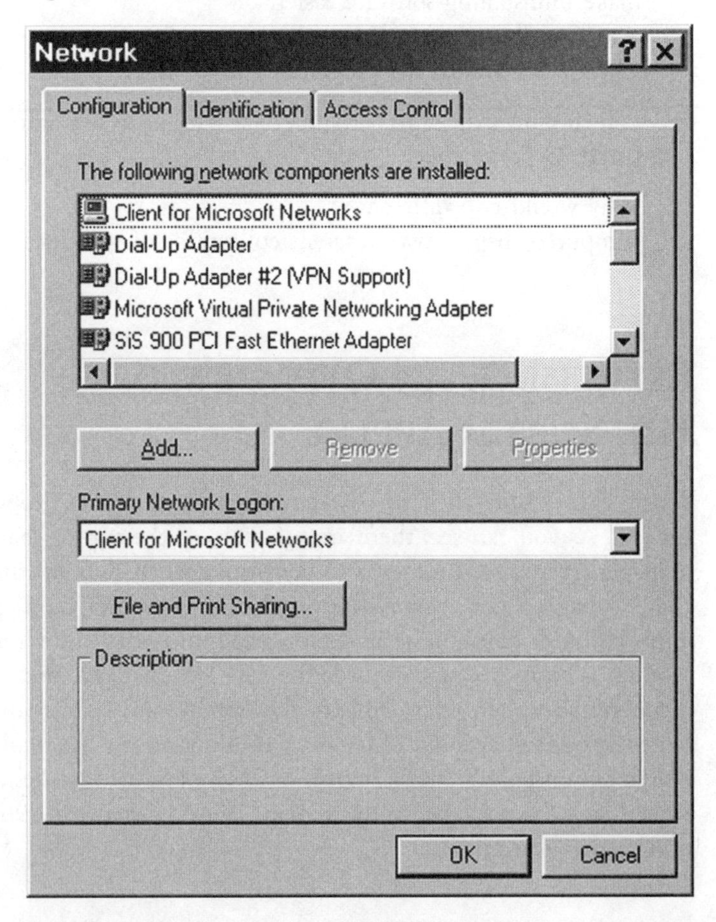

Figure L6.10 Network and Dial-Up Connections

nections were added to this applet. Because there is going to be a separate lab on networking later on, I'll pass on the guided tour at this point in time.

EXERCISE 1J: THE SYSTEM APPLET

To the hardware technician, the System applet is far and away the most useful applet within Control Panel. In fact, it is so important that Exercise 2 is devoted to a review of that applet alone. Which means you're finished with this exercise and ready to move on to the next.

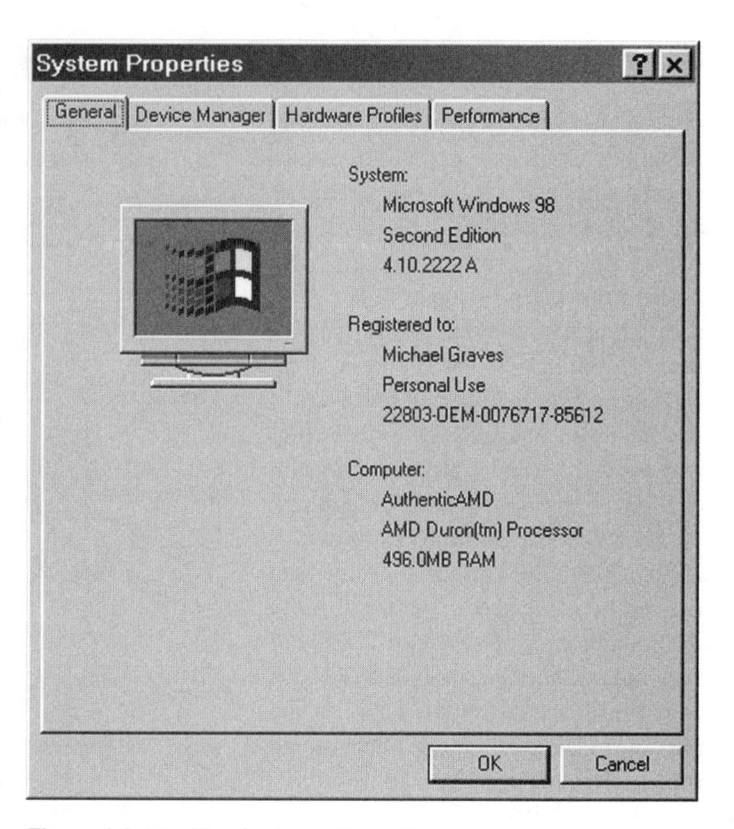

Figure L6.11 The Systems Properties screen

EXERCISE 1 REVIEW

1. In terms of function, what is the purpose of Control Panel?
2. How does Add/Remove Programs make uninstalling software easier, assuming that you used the utility when you installed the program to begin with?
3. Which tab in the Internet applet allows you to configure which URL is your preferred home page?
4. Why would two different computers display two different collections of utilities in Control Panel?

EXERCISE 2: AN OVERVIEW OF THE SYSTEM APPLET

When you double-click the System icon, the System Properties window shown in **Figure L6.11** appears. As you can see, there are four tabs at the top of that screen. These tabs are General, Device Manager, Hardware Profiles, and Performance. By default, the Systems Properties screen opens to the General page. There is nothing on this screen that you can change, but it does show some good information. It tells you what version and build of Windows 98 you're using. It tells you to whom the product is registered and records the CD key that was used to install the software. It tells you how much memory there is available to the system, and it tells you the make and model of CPU running. Note the oddball amount of memory running on this particular system. This is because this particular system has on-board video. There is 512MB of RAM installed, but 16MB have been allocated to video. Since that's not available to the system, Windows reports 496MB as being available. Now take a look at the other screens.

1. Click the Device Manager tab. The screen shown in **Figure L6.12** appears. I deleted the driver files from the NIC and the sound card so that you would have some icons other than the normal ones to view. The yellow exclamation point you see next to PCI Ethernet Controller is the result of that. This indicates that it found a device installed in the system, but couldn't find the driver for that device. A red X across the icon would mean that the registry is telling Windows that a device driver has been installed for a particular device, but Windows doesn't detect the device. Hopefully, your systems won't have any warnings like these.

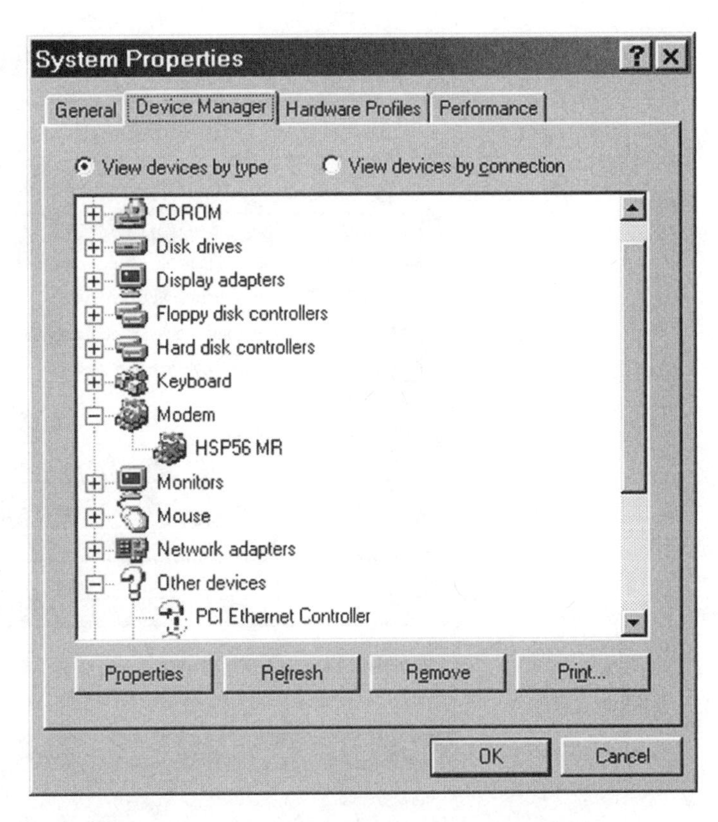

Figure L6.12 Device Manager

2. With Computer highlighted, click the Properties button. This will bring up a screen like the one in **Figure L6.13**. Here, you can view the system properties by IRQ, I/O address, or DMA channel, or view how system memory is being used. By default, Interrupt request (IRQ) appears first. If you scroll down this screen, you'll see how the fifteen available IRQs have been allocated in your system. You will also note that the same IRQ is used more than once. How this works is covered in Chapter Nine, Examining the Expansion Bus of the text.

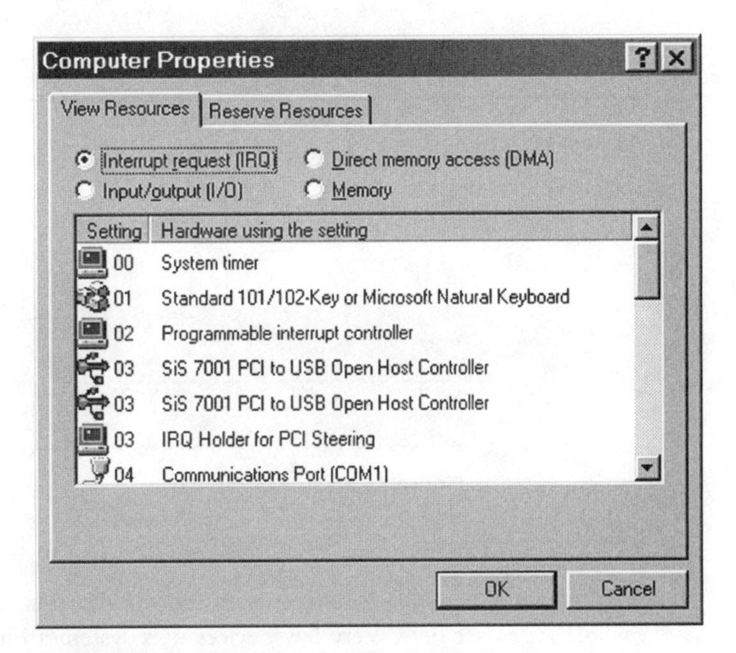

Figure L6.13 The system's IRQ allocations

3. Now click Input/output (I/O). You should get the screen shown in **Figure L6.14**. This shows the base I/O address for every device installed on the system along with areas of buffer memory that have been assigned to that device by Windows. Anytime you get repeated "memory errors" that always occur at the same address, check this list to see whether that address falls within one of the ranges listed here. If so, you know what device is causing the problem.

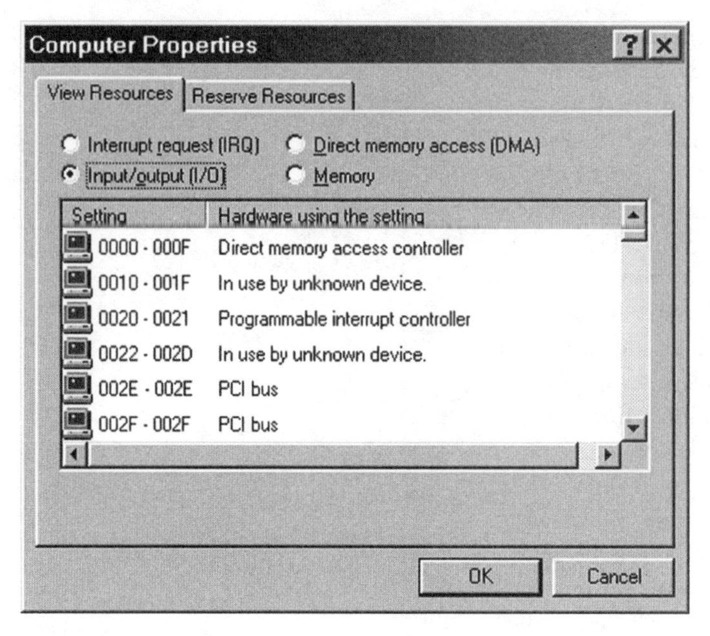

Figure L6.14 I/O properties

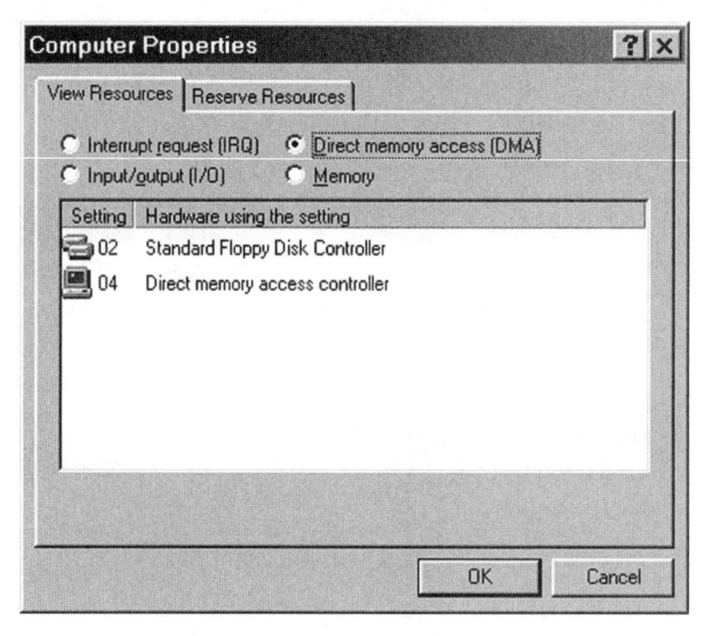

Figure L6.15 DMA properties

4. Next, take a look at Direct Memory Access (DMA). As you can see in **Figure L6.15**, there isn't a whole lot to see here. Very few devices uses system-arbitrated DMA these days. About the only things you would see in this list are the floppy drive, a sound card, and an LPT port if it is configured to ECP.

5. Take a look at the Memory page (**Figure L6.16**). What you see here can vary greatly from machine to machine. If your lab consists of several different makes and models of computer systems, don't expect all of them to have the same information. The numbers you see are the hexadecimal addresses of the device drivers for the devices listed alongside the address. As with I/O addresses, this can be useful in tracing those so-called memory errors Windows is always reporting.

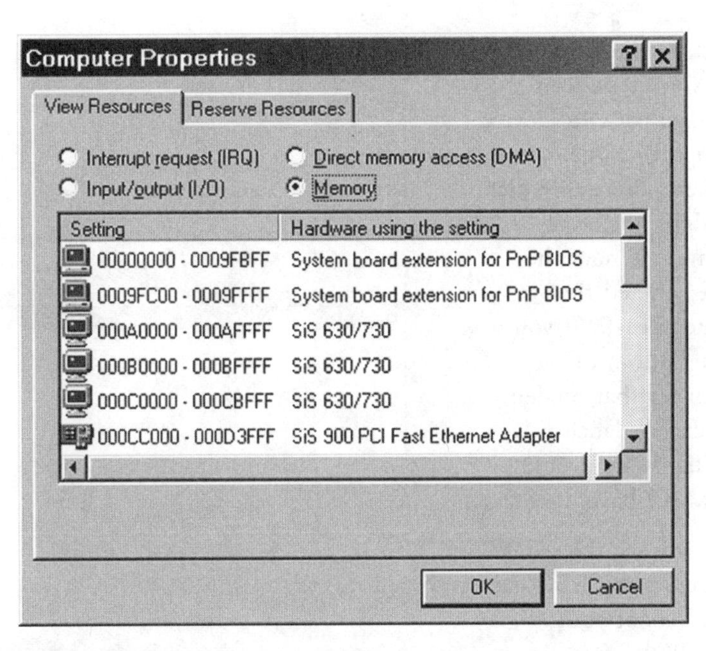

Figure L6.16 Memory properties

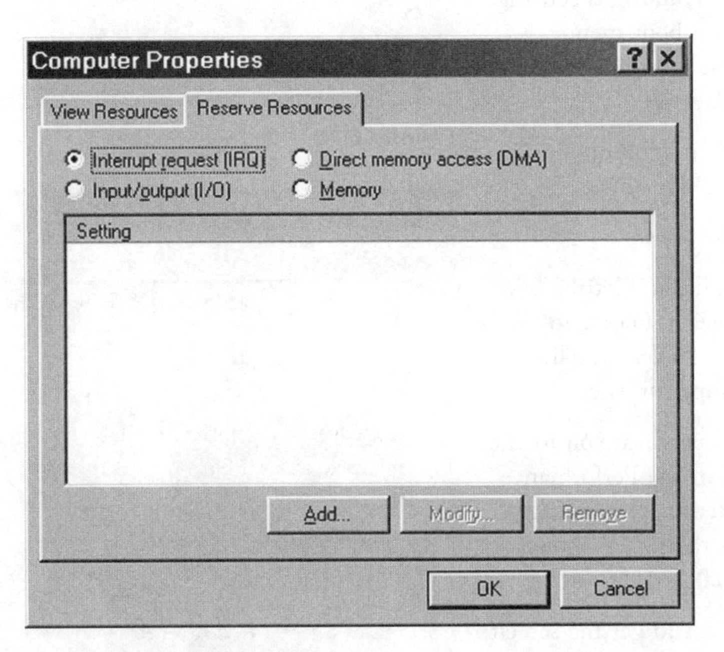

Figure L6.17 Reserving resources

6. Now for that Reserve Resources screen I've been ignoring so far. If you click that tab on any one of the properties screens you just examined, you get a blank screen like the one in **Figure L6.17**. If you click the Add button, you will be prompted to enter a value relative to the type of resource you're trying to reserve. By doing this, you are effectively taking that resource away from Plug 'n Play, and it will not be allocated to any device. This is useful if you have a device that can only be configured manually and Plug 'n Play keeps stealing the resource before your device has a chance to grab it.

7. Click Cancel to get back to the Device Manager screen. Then Click the Hardware Profiles tab. You should get the screen shown in **Figure L6.18**. Notice that, so far anyway, you only have one profile listed. It is named Original Configuration.

8. Click Copy and, in the new screen that pops up, type **`New Profile`**. Now go back to Device Manager and highlight one of the devices listed there. Preferably pick a device that might not be required every time you boot the machine. I have selected the modem in **Figure L6.19**. If you look toward the bottom of the Properties screen for that modem, you'll see a check box labeled Disable in this hardware profile. Check that box, as I have done.
9. Click OK. You will see the red X I described earlier in this lab. Click Close and reboot your machine. When POST has completed, as Windows is starting, you should get a boot menu offering you the option to boot to one of the following:
   - Original Configuration
   - New Profile
   - None of the above
10. Select New Profile and let the boot process continue. If you try to use the device you disabled, you'll be in for an unhappy surprise.
11. Finally, I will introduce you to the options found in the Performance tab of the System applet. Click that tab to get the screen shown in **Figure L6.20**.
12. Click File System to get the screen in **Figure L6.21**. I'm not going to take the time to go through each and every one of the options listed here. That is more the role of a book on operating systems. But if you like, take a look at each of the options listed to see what you could change.

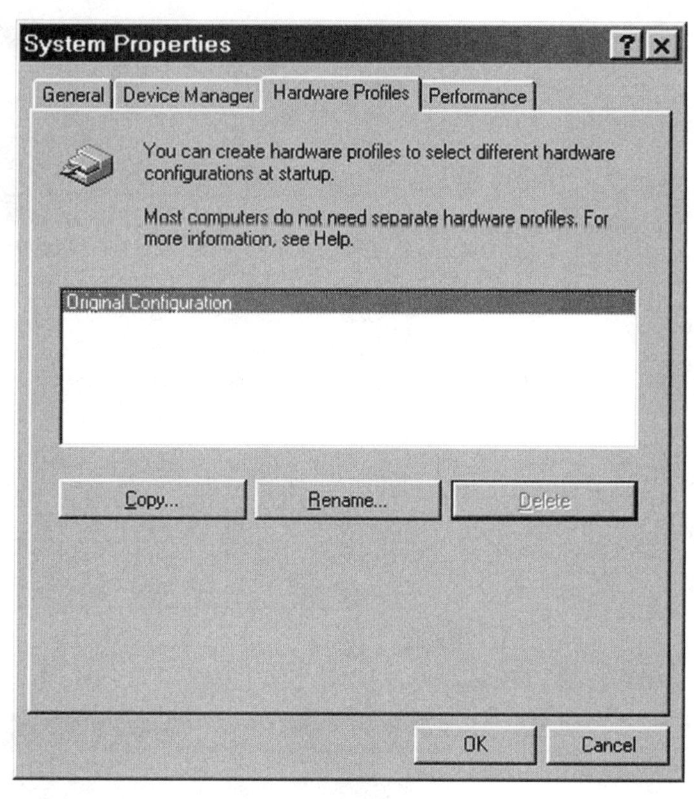

Figure L6.18 Hardware Profiles

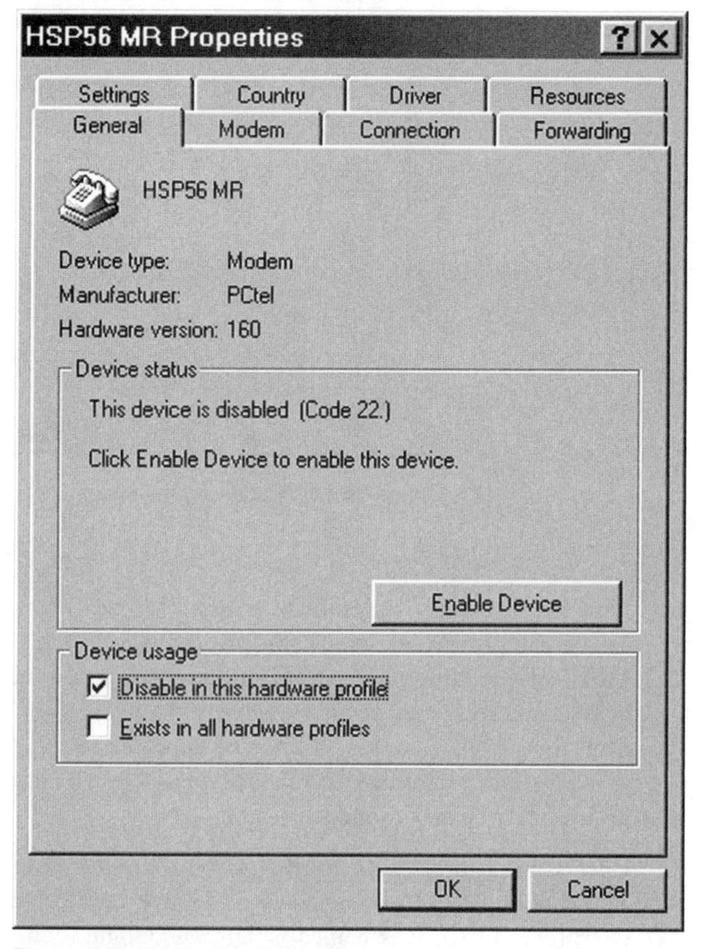

Figure L6.19 Device properties

13. Clicking the Graphics button gives you only one option—how much hardware acceleration you want to apply. Unless your system is giving you fits, the default setting of Maximum should work fine.

14. Clicking the Virtual Memory button brings up the screen shown in **Figure L6.22**. There is rarely any need to change from the default setting of Let Windows manage my virtual memory settings (Recommended). This setting adjusts the size of your swap file in Windows. Your swap file is an area of hard disk space that is treated as if it were installed memory. If your swap file is too small, system performance will drop dramatically. Therefore, if your hard disk is filling up, you might want to configure a fixed swap file so that you'll run out of disk space before your swap file is cut down to unacceptable levels.

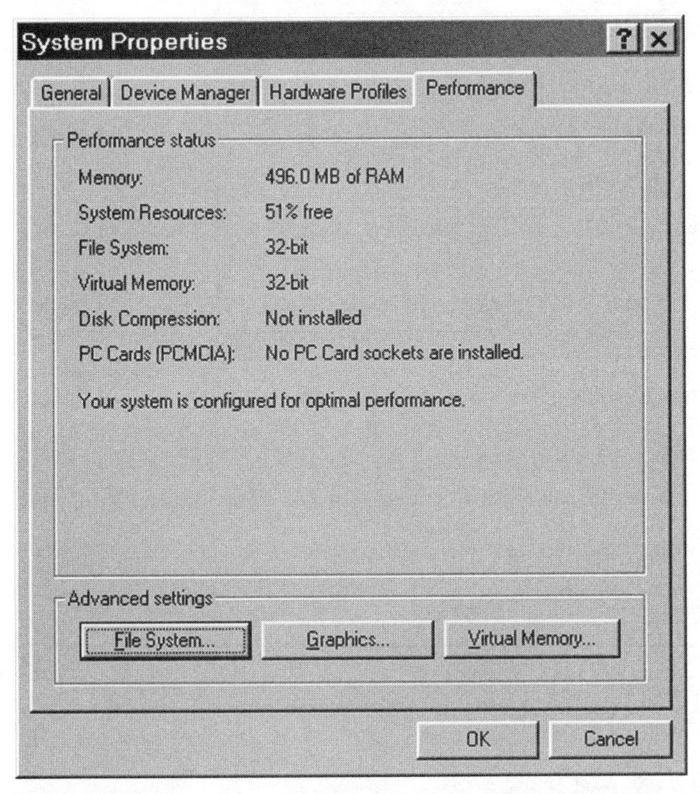

Figure L6.20 Adjusting system performance in the System applet.

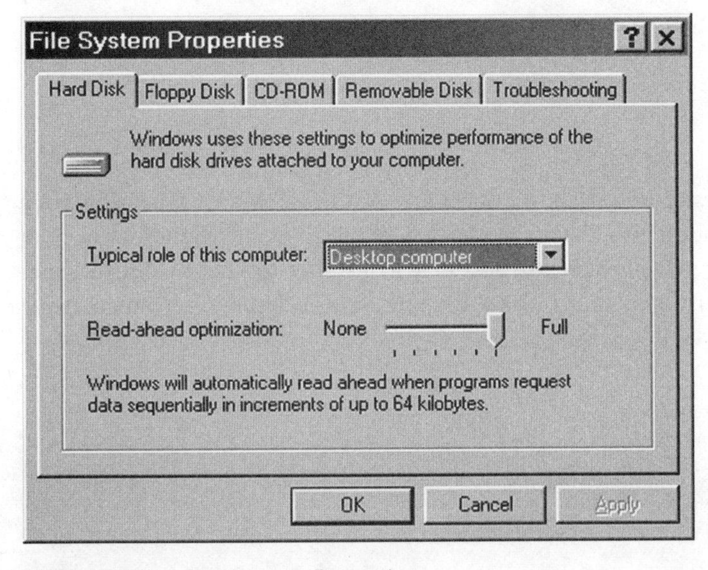

Figure L6.21 File System Properties

15. As you can see, Control Panel is a very handy program. Therefore, the last thing you're going to do is create a shortcut for it on the Desktop. To do so, double-click the My Computer icon on your desktop. Right-click the Control Panel icon and select Create Shortcut. A message will pop up warning you that you can't create a shortcut here and asking whether you want it on the desktop instead. Click OK, and the shortcut will appear on the desktop.

EXERCISE 2 REVIEW

1. What are four different views of the Computer Properties that you can bring up in Device Manager?
2. What would be the purpose of reserving specific resources in Device Manager?
3. What would the effect of reserving those resources be on the system?
4. What are two reasons you can think of for creating two or more different hardware profiles on a system?

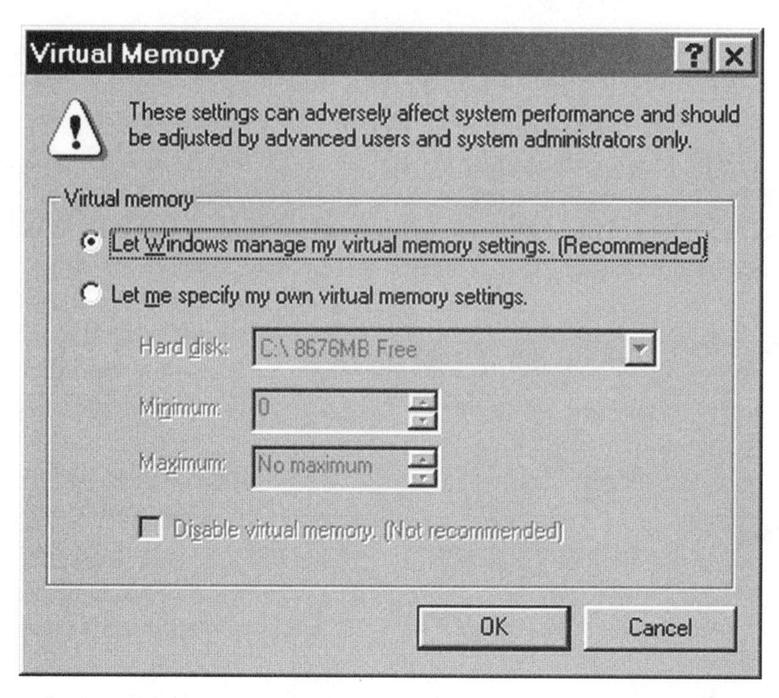

Figure L6.22 Setting Virtual Memory

5. What would be one good reason for manually configuring the size of the swap file in Windows?
6. What are two key functions of the System applet?

LAB REVIEW

1. Just what is the purpose of Control Panel, and what settings are you manipulating when you make changes there?
2. Define two different ways to access the Control Panel.
3. What is one reason why Accessibility Options might not appear in your Control Panel?
4. How would you create a shortcut for Control Panel on your desktop?
5. What are four different sets of resources that can be viewed in the Computer Properties screen?

LAB SUMMARY

Control Panel is a pretty complex space, isn't it? If I didn't cover any of the icons that appear on your screen, or if I covered some that didn't appear, it's all in the way you chose to install Windows to start with. And as I pointed out earlier, adding new services will add new icons. Get to know Control Panel as well as you can, even if you're not personally a Windows user by nature. Ninety percent of your customers will be.

LAB 7

AN OVERVIEW OF THE REGISTRY EDITOR

As I pointed out in Lab 6, the Control Panel is a safe place for making changes to the registry for the most common issues. But once in a while something comes up in Windows that requires that the registry be surgically edited. Should this need arise, *be careful!* With some of the registry settings, simply having a single character missing or out of place can render your system unstable or even unbootable. Fortunately, Windows users have access to a utility that allows them to back off to a previous version of the registry. This utility varies from version to version.

All you'll need for this lab is your lab computer.

There is only one CompTIA objective covered in this lab:

1.5 Identify the major operating system utilities, their purpose, location, and available switches.

EXERCISE 1: AN OVERVIEW OF THE REGISTRY EDITOR

1. The Registry Editor is one of those utilities that Microsoft has deliberately concealed from the average user. There are no pretty little icons to click on. It's a command line utility. It can be run either from a DOS window or from the Start→Run command line. In Windows 98, this utility is launched by typing the command **`regedit`** at either the command prompt or from the Start→Run command line. Windows 2000 and XP users have two different versions of this utility at their disposal. Typing **`regedit`** gets basically the same utility that Windows 98 users have. A safer, but perhaps less potent version comes from typing **`regedt32`** at the prompt. The latter does not have quite as powerful a search function, but it does allow the user to set security settings on individual registry keys within the editor. Since REGEDIT is available to both, this is the one I'll review.
2. Click Start→Run and type **`regedit`** in the command line. You'll get the window shown in **Figure L7.1**. The left-hand window of the screen is known as the navigation area, and the right-hand window is the topic area.
3. The Windows registry has six different keys that are stored collectively in two different files. The files are USER.DAT and SYSTEM.DAT. A third file is created optionally when System Policies are enabled. This file is called CONFIG.POL. The keys are

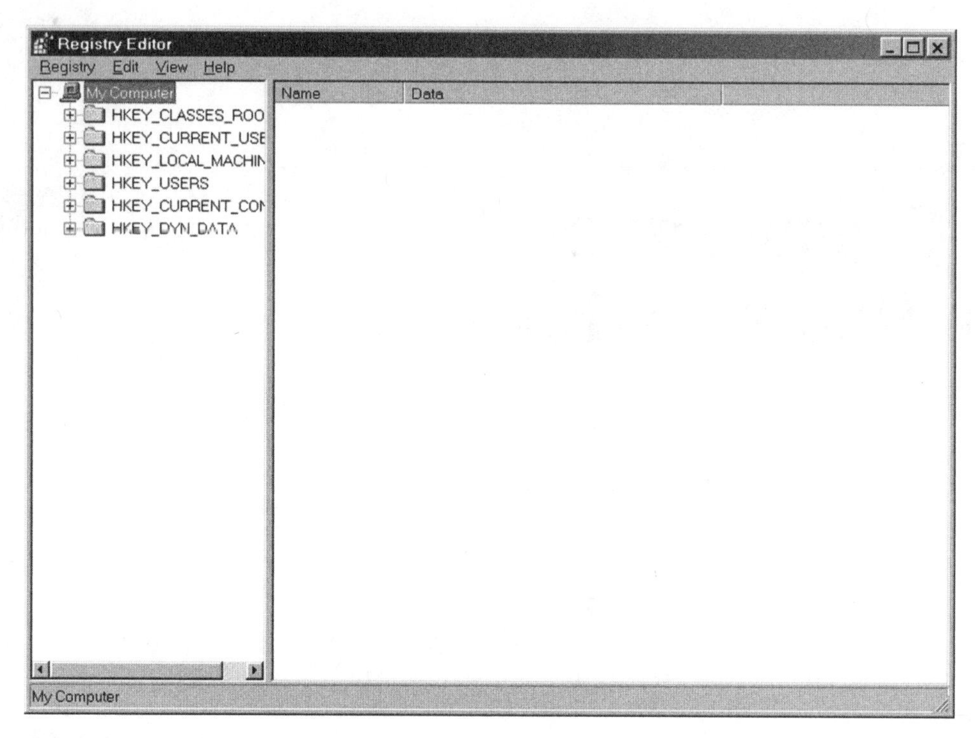

Figure L7.1 The opening screen to the Registry Editor

a. HKEY_CLASSES_ROOT: This key contains the information needed for linking objects between different applications, for determining what file types are opened by what applications, and for mapping specific functions to keystroke patterns or mouse clicks.

b. HKEY_CURRENT_USER: Here is where user-specific information is stored. This would include items such as the programs in the user's Start menu, desktop settings, applications that appear on the desktop, and display preferences.

c. HKEY_LOCAL_MACHINE: This is where information specific to the computer is stored. Device drivers, installed software, and information specific to installed hardware can be found in this key.

d. HKEY_USERS: Windows supports the ability to allow several different users to log on to the same machine, and, if so desired, each user can have individual specific settings and preferences. This hive stores the preferences and settings for all users.

e. HKEY_CURRENT_CONFIG: It is possible to set up multiple hardware profiles on the same computer. Whereas HKEY_LOCAL_MACHINE stores all hardware and software information, HKEY_CURRENT_CONFIG loads the information specific to the profile chosen during boot.

f. HKEY_DYN_DATA: This key stores dynamically configured information concerning the status of Plug 'n Play at the time of boot. Changes to device settings that do not require a reboot are changes that are managed by this key. This key is created on the fly by Windows at each startup and is not stored in any permanent file.

4. Beneath each of these primary keys are collections of hives. Hives are subkeys that contain information specific to a particular aspect of the machine. Click the + next HKEY_LOCAL_MACHINE in the navigation area to open up the hive. You should get a screen similar to **Figure L7.2**.

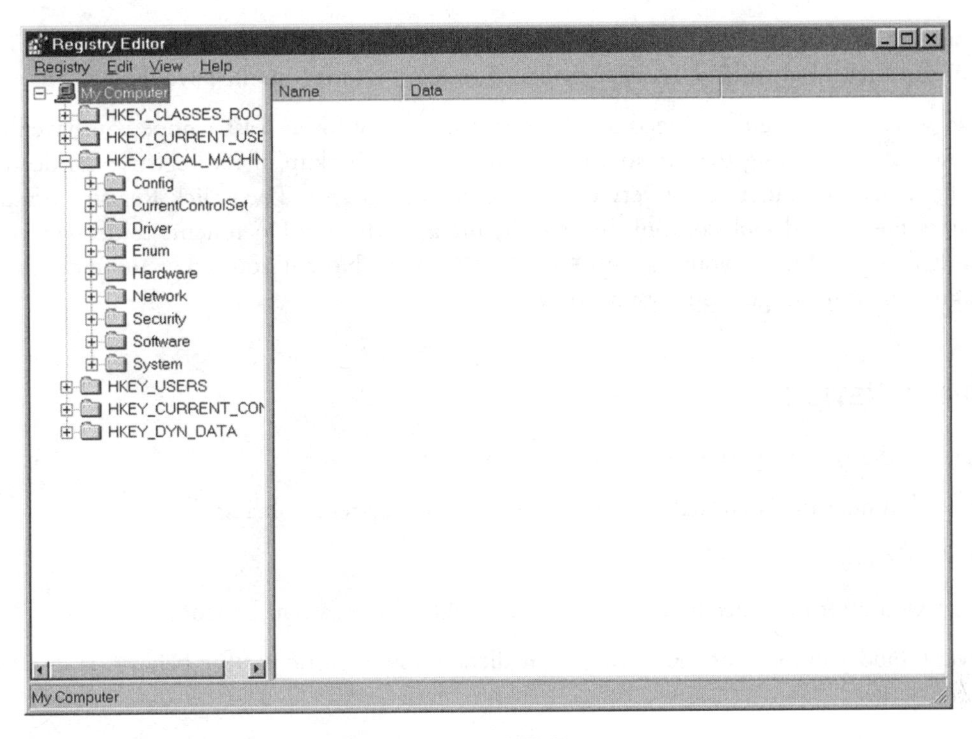

Figure L7.2 The hives of HKEY_LOCAL_MACHINE

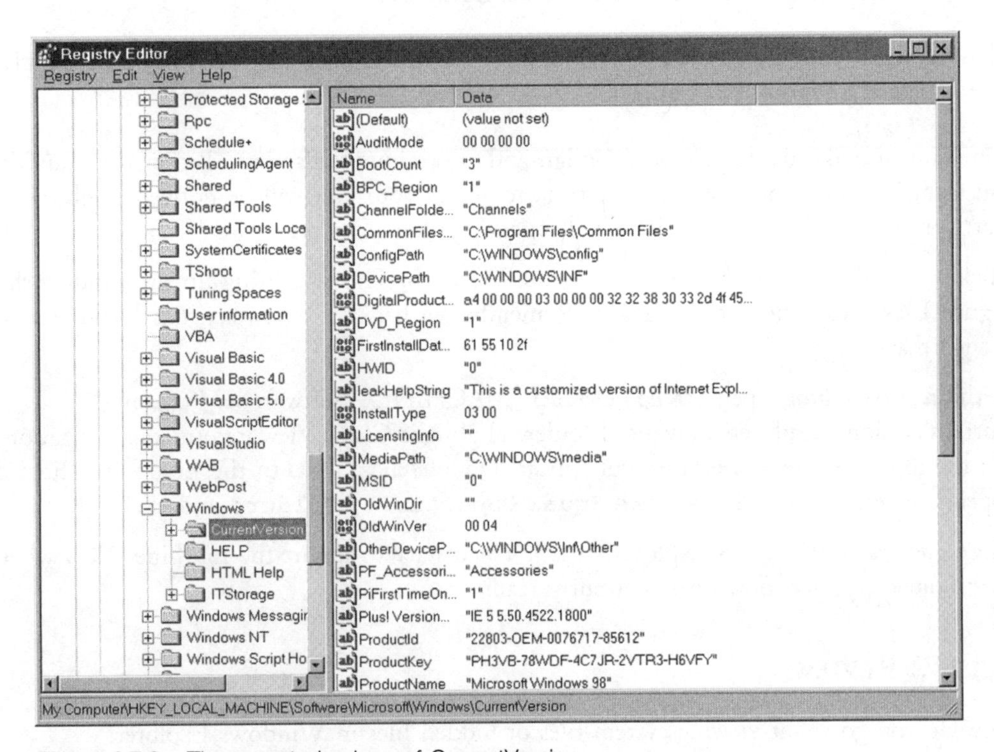

Figure L7.3 The assorted values of CurrentVersion

5. If all you did was click on the + sign, as instructed, as of yet there is still nothing in the topic area. Open the Software hive, then the Microsoft folder, and scroll all the way down to Windows. Open the Windows folder and highlight CurrentVersion. You should get a screen similar to that seen in **Figure L7.3**.

6. To see the type of data that is stored in a particular entry, double-click FirstInstallDateTime. Hmmm. They seem to have encrypted this. Wonder why they might have done that?
7. Now, so far, you haven't changed anything in the registry (or at least I hope you haven't). Before you do anything that drastic, you want to have a backup of the registry. To do that, highlight My Computer at the very top of the navigation area. Then click Registry→Export Registry File. The default location to save the file is in the My Documents folder. Accept the default folder and name your backup **REGBACKUP.REG**. Now if you screw anything up beyond recognition, you can get your system back.

EXERCISE 1 REVIEW

1. What are the two primary files that contain the registry?
2. What additional file is created if you choose to enable system policies?
3. List the six primary keys of the registry.
4. Where would settings specific to hardware installed on the system be stored?
5. Where would you look for the settings that dictate how a particular file behaves if double-clicked?

EXERCISE 2: EDITING THE REGISTRY

If you haven't made your registry backup yet, *do not continue.* Go back to the last step in Exercise 1 and complete it before going on.

1. You want to make a change that is benign and won't hurt the system. But at the same time, you want it to be something for which the results of your edit will be noticed. Right-click the Start button and click Explore. This will open Windows Explorer.
2. Click View→Folder Options. Now click the View tab. This will bring up the window shown in **Figure L7.4**. Note the line that reads "Remember each folder's view settings." You're about to change that.
3. In the registry editor, open HKEY_LOCAL_MACHINE→Software→Microsoft→ CurrentVersion→explorer→advanced folder. Highlight ClassicViewState in the navigation area. On the topic area, several entries will appear. Double-click Text. In the Edit String field that appears, type the words **These are Equal Opportunity Folders** and click OK.
4. Close and restart Windows Explorer. It is not necessary to restart the machine. Now when you view Folder Options, how does that entry read?

EXERCISE 2 REVIEW

1. How do you go about viewing system files or hidden files in Windows Explorer?
2. What was the very first thing you did before editing the registry?

EXERCISE 3: THE SCANREG UTILITY

Of course, now you want to put things back the way they were. Obviously, the easy way is to browse to that registry entry and type in the words the way they used to be. But what if you can't remember

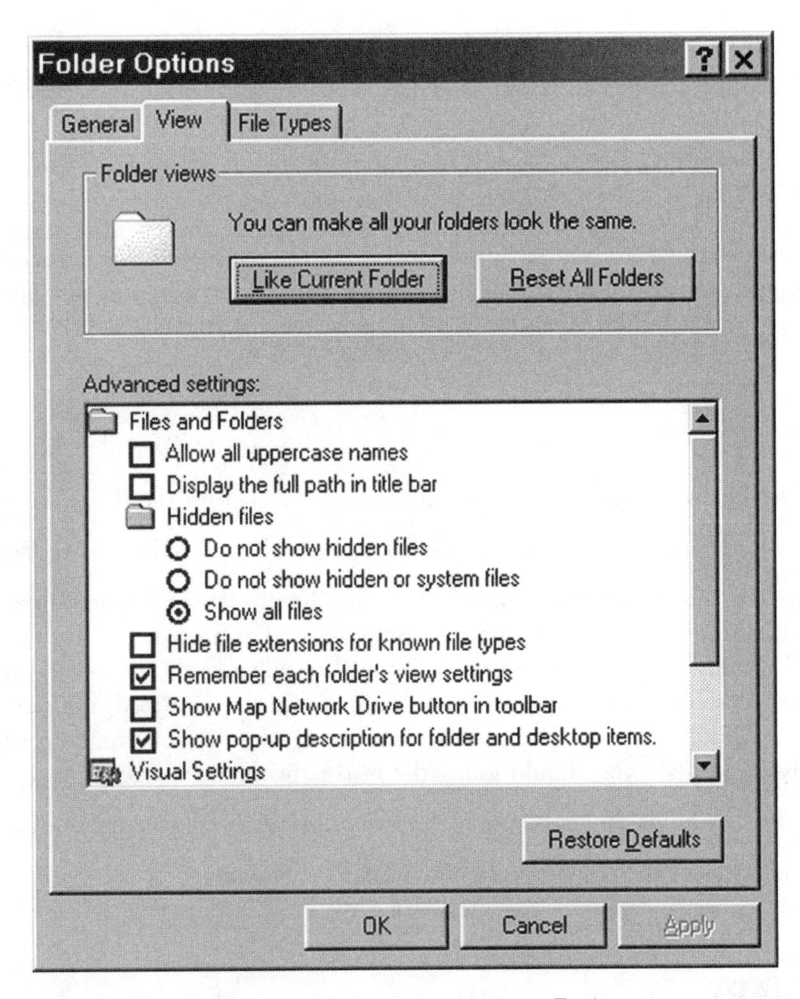

Figure L7.4 Folder viewing options in Windows Explorer

how it used to read? Or if you can't remember just what entry you edited? Or worse yet, Windows blue-screens just as it's entering the graphical mode? There's got to be a way of rolling back the system to a previous setting. And in fact, there are two ways. The first is, of course, to open the Registry Editor and click Registry→Import Registry File and then select the backup of the registry that you made. But that's too easy and doesn't give me the chance to show you the ScanReg utility. Windows 2000 and XP users, unfortunately, don't have this utility at their disposal.

1. Restart your machine, and as POST is completing, just before Windows starts to boot, start pressing the F8 key. This will bring up a boot menu. One of the options is to start Windows to a Command Prompt. Select this option and continue booting. This will bring you to a C:\ prompt.
2. Type **`scanreg`** at the command prompt. The ScanReg utility will start and the first thing it will do is to scan the registry for errors. You can't stop this process despite the fact that, in all the years I've used this utility, no matter how corrupted the registry was, ScanReg always reported no errors.
3. Next you are prompted to either back up your registry or to view existing backups. Obviously, if you're having a problem with the current version of the Windows registry, the last thing you want to do is make a backup of a corrupted registry. Tab over to View Backups. You will see four versions of registry backups listed by the date they were created. Pick the backup previous

to the one with today's date and select Restore. After a few moments, it will prompt you to restart your machine. Windows will boot to the older backup without the changes you made.

EXERCISE 3 REVIEW

1. Since you went out of your way to avoid backing up the registry in this particular exercise, why is backing up the registry an important function of this utility? Why not just do it in Regedit?
2. What does ScanReg do before it allows you to do anything else?

LAB REVIEW

1. Which registry key is not stored in a file, but rather is created on the fly as the system boots?
2. What are two different methods you can use to back up the full Windows registry?
3. You have just installed a new video card and during the driver installation you asked to see a list of all devices. You're so used to another computer that you use every day that you mistakenly selected a completely different make and model of video card. Now every time you boot your machine, as soon as the Windows graphical interface starts to load, the screen goes blank. How might you fix this? (There are actually a couple of ways. If you come up with a way I didn't discuss in this lab, you should lobby the instructor for extra credit.)
4. Which primary key holds the user settings for every user with an account on the system?
5. How many backups of the registry does Windows 98 maintain?

LAB SUMMARY

One of the things I hope you learned from this lab is that every aspect of how Windows performs is a function of some entry in the registry. In Lab 6 you learned how to make safe changes to the registry in Control Panel. Here I showed you the basics of how the Registry Editor can be used to make changes beyond the scope of Control Panel. And, at the risk of sounding like a skipping CD, before you mess around with the registry, *back it up!!!*

LAB 8

INSTALLING WIN2K PROFESSIONAL

There are those who argue that installing an operating system (OS) is not a function of a network administrator. Those are the people who either have the luxury of extremely large and diverse staffs, or simply haven't spent enough time in the real world. There will come a time when you will have to install an OS on a new system or completely rebuild an existing one.

In the following exercises, you will be installing Windows 2000 Professional.

For this lab, you will need your lab computers, a copy of Win2K Professional for each student, and four blank, formatted, high-density 3.5" floppy diskettes.

The following CompTIA objectives are covered in this lab:

1.2 Identify the names, locations, purposes, and contents of major system files.

2.1 Identify the procedures for installing Windows 9x/Me, Windows NT 4.0 Workstation, Windows 2000 Professional, and Windows XP and bringing the operating system to a basic operational level.

2.3 Identify the basic system boot sequences and boot methods, including the steps to create an emergency boot disk with utilities installed for Windows 9x/Me, Windows NT 4.0 Workstation, Windows 2000 Professional, and Windows XP.

EXERCISE 1: THE FLOPPY DISK SIDE OF WIN2K

For the most part, Microsoft has tried to forget the floppy drive ever existed. However, it has made concessions to the fact that many machines still in existence today require the services of the floppy disk drive to boot a system. If you are trying to install Win2K onto a system that is so old that it won't boot to a CD-ROM, you will need the services of a boot disk to access the Win2K CD and a set of four installation disks to install the OS. You also need a new computer.

EXERCISE 1A: PREPARING A BOOT DISKETTE

Most modern machines will easily boot from the CD-ROM drive, and since the Windows 2000 CD is a bootable CD, you would usually simply put the CD in the drive, boot the machine, and follow the yellow brick road. For the purpose of the next two exercises, you're going to attack a worst-case scenario. Your machine refuses to boot from the CD, so you must use the 4-disk set of installation diskettes.

Because this is a lab, you'll carry it a step further. Nobody knows where the setup diskettes are, so you need to make your own.

As of this writing, it is still safe to say that most network environments have a number of systems with Windows 98 installed. If this is not the case, you can download a boot image from www.mwgraves.com. To create a boot disk on a Windows 98 machine, open the Control Panel. This can be done by either right-clicking My Computer and clicking Properties and then double-clicking the Control Panel icon, or by clicking Start→Settings→Control Panel.

In Control Panel, double-click Add/Remove Programs. The right-hand tab at the top says Startup Disk. Click that tab, make sure that there is a blank, formatted, high-density floppy diskette in the drive, and click Create Disk. You now have the necessary tool for starting your computer.

> **NOTE:** If you happen to have a machine that does not have the .cab files installed, you will be prompted for the Windows 98 CD.

EXERCISE 1A REVIEW

1. Where in Win98 is the Startup Disk creation utility located?
2. What size diskette is required to make this disk?

EXERCISE 1B: CREATING THE WINDOWS 2000 BOOT DISK SET

Using the boot diskette you just created (or were supplied), start your machine with the diskette in the drive. Select the option Start computer with CD-ROM support and let the machine boot. If your machine will not boot to the floppy, it is most likely that your CMOS simply needs to be configured accordingly. Consult with your instructor for the appropriate methods for configuring the CMOS on your particular machine

When the machine boots, it will tell you what drive letter it assigned to the CD-ROM drive. With the Win98 Startup Diskette, assuming that there is only one hard drive, this is usually E:. This is because the Startup Diskette creates a virtual drive in memory onto which it copies certain files.

From this point on, I will assume the CD-ROM to be Drive E. If this is not the case on your particular system, simply substitute the appropriate drive letter whenever Drive E is referenced. Now you're ready to begin installation.

1. Log onto the CD-ROM by typing **`E:`** <Enter>. At the E: prompt, type **`CD bootdisk`** <Enter>.

> **NOTE:** Some schools are provided special versions of Windows 2000 for educational purposes. If you are using the 120-day Evaluation (For Educational Use) or the MSDN CD provided by Microsoft, the I386 directory may be a subdirectory buried elsewhere on the CD. If this is the case, your instructor will have the appropriate information

2. At the E:\bootdisk prompt, type **`makeboot`** <Enter>. The screen shown in **Figure L8.1** will appear. Have four blank, formatted, high-density floppy diskettes ready. You will be prompted to enter what drive the diskette is in. Press the A key and make sure that one of the diskettes is in Drive A. This becomes your Installation Boot Diskette. When this diskette is complete, you will be prompted to insert Diskettes 2, 3, and finally 4. To avoid confusion, label the diskettes as you go.

EXERCISE 1B REVIEW

1. How many diskettes are needed for the Win2K installation set?
2. Where is the utility that creates these disks located on the Win2K Installation CD?

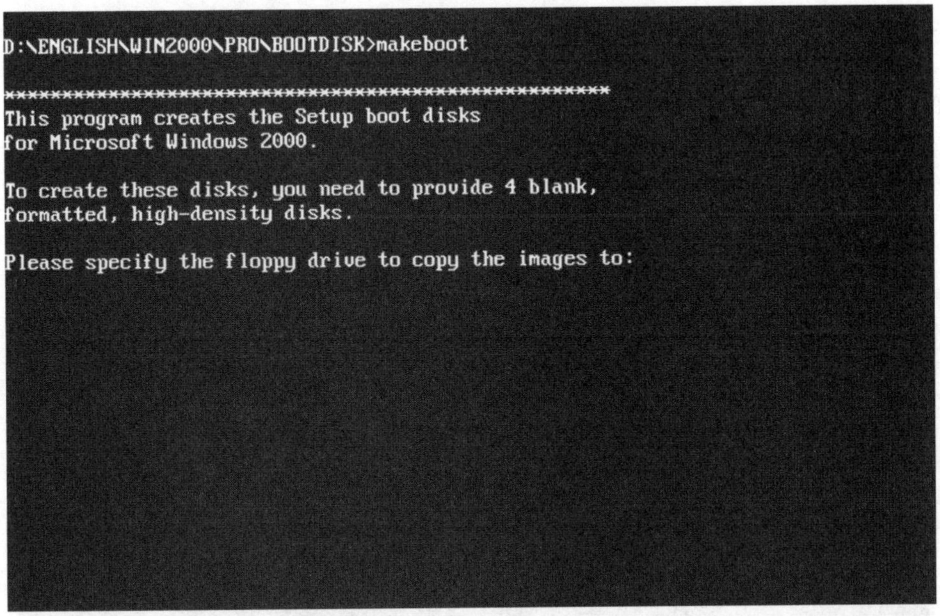

```
D:\ENGLISH\WIN2000\PRO\BOOTDISK>makeboot

*****************************************************
This program creates the Setup boot disks
for Microsoft Windows 2000.

To create these disks, you need to provide 4 blank,
formatted, high-density disks.

Please specify the floppy drive to copy the images to:
```

Figure L8.1 The MAKEBOOT utility is a command line utility.

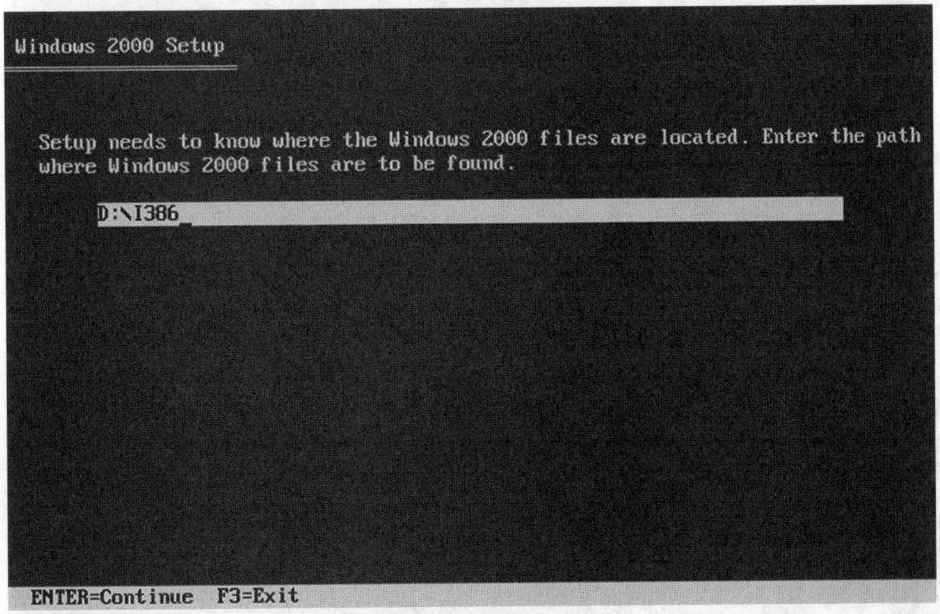

```
Windows 2000 Setup

  Setup needs to know where the Windows 2000 files are located. Enter the path
  where Windows 2000 files are to be found.

      D:\I386_

 ENTER=Continue  F3=Exit
```

Figure L8.2 Out of the gate, the WinNT program asks you to verify the location of the source files.

INSTALLING WINDOWS 2000

Okay, now that you've had the fun of creating those installation diskettes, you're going to love the fact that I'm not going to bother to use them in this lab. Save them for future use in your bag of tricks, but installing from diskettes is far too time consuming to fall within the constraints of a lab session. You'll boot from the CD and go from there.

1. Place the Installation CD into your CD-ROM drive and reboot the machine. The first screen to come up is a screen that asks you to verify the location of the source files (**Figure L8.2**).

Next, a DOS screen (**Figure L8.3**) tells you that Setup is inspecting your hardware configuration. This is NTDETECT at work.

2. Next, Setup must copy some essential files to memory (**Figure L8.4**). (If you are performing this setup from the floppy diskettes set, you will be prompted for each diskette as it is needed.) This is known as the text-based portion of Setup.

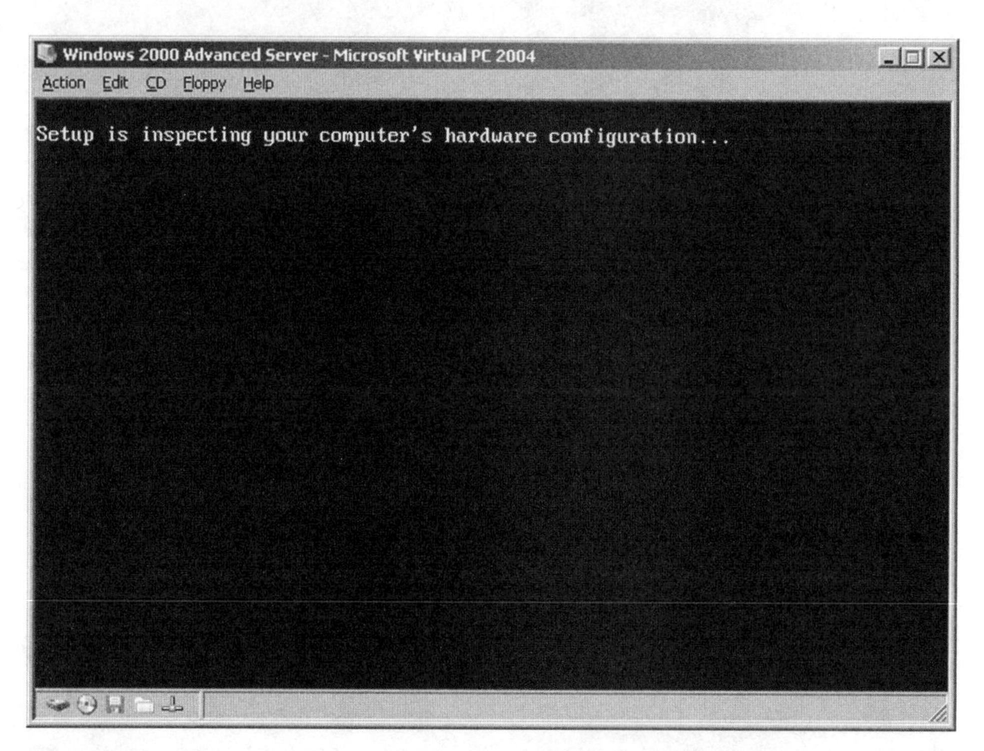

Figure L8.3 Setup's first task is to make sure you have the right hardware configuration to do the job.

Figure L8.4 The first file copy isn't copying files to your hard disk, but rather to RAM. The hard disk hasn't been formatted yet.

3. After these files have been copied a new screen will appear, similar to the one in **Figure L8.5**, giving you three options. Pressing the <Enter> key will begin a new installation of Windows. Pressing <R> allows you to repair an existing installation using the Emergency Repair Diskette (ERD), and <F3> allows you to exit Setup without doing anything.

4. Assuming you're installing your OS to a newly installed disk drive, you'll now see the screen shown in **Figure L8.6**. You will also see this screen if you are installing over an incompatible OS such as Unix or Linux. Press <C> to continue. This will initiate the Win2K disk partitioning utility.

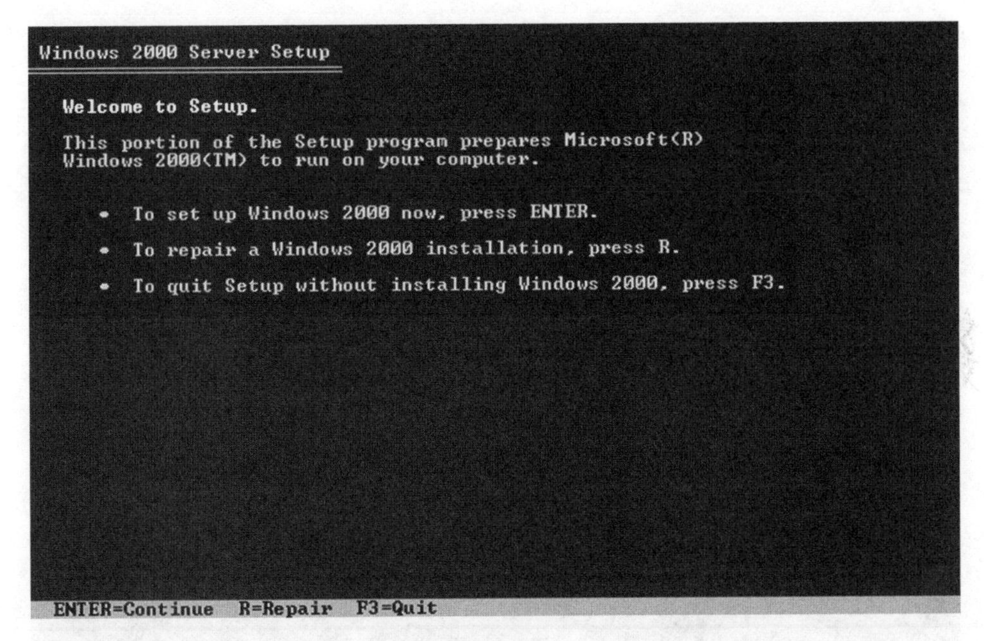

Figure L8.5 Here you have the choice of performing a new installation, repairing an existing installation, or exiting setup. Note that in this illustration, I'm installing Windows 2000 Server. Yours may say Windows 2000 Professional. The installation process is the same.

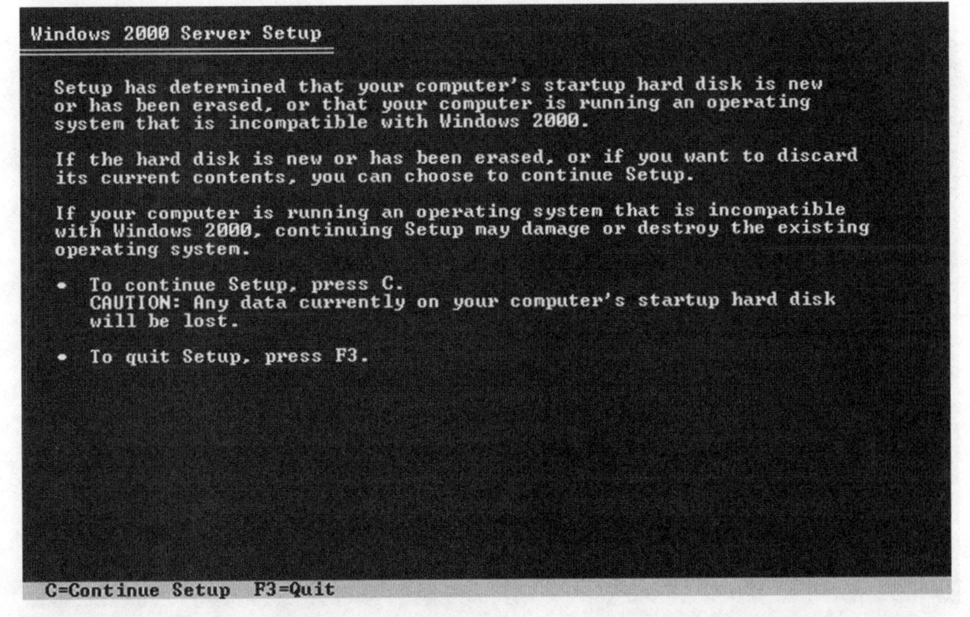

Figure L8.6 On a new or freshly FDISKed hard drive, or if you are replacing an OS such as UNIX or Linux, this window advises you that you are about to wipe your drive.

5. Now read every single word of the licensing agreement that appears in **Figure L8.7**. It's about eight pages long, so give the slower readers time to absorb all of Microsoft's generous terms. Either that, or simply press <F8> to continue. If you don't agree, this is as far as you get, and the rest of the class will have to wait until you get caught up again.

6. Now it's time to create your primary partitions (**Figure L8.8**). Because of the nature of a lab that appears later in this manual, I don't want you to prepare your drive with just one partition. For now, create a partition of 2GB, onto which the OS will be installed. Press <C> to create a new partition.

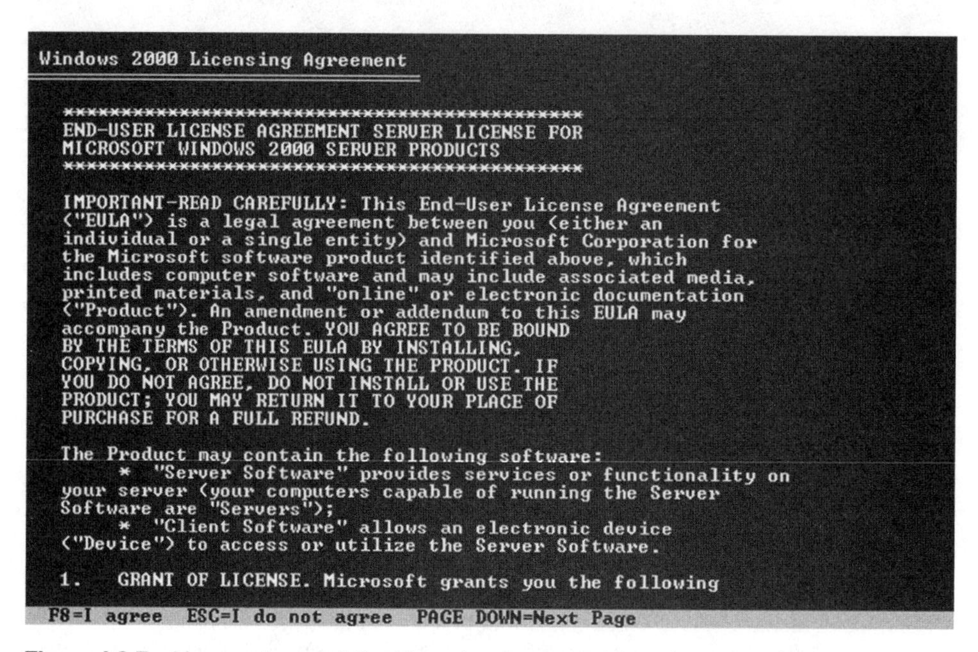

Figure L8.7 You must accept the Licensing Agreement in order to continue.

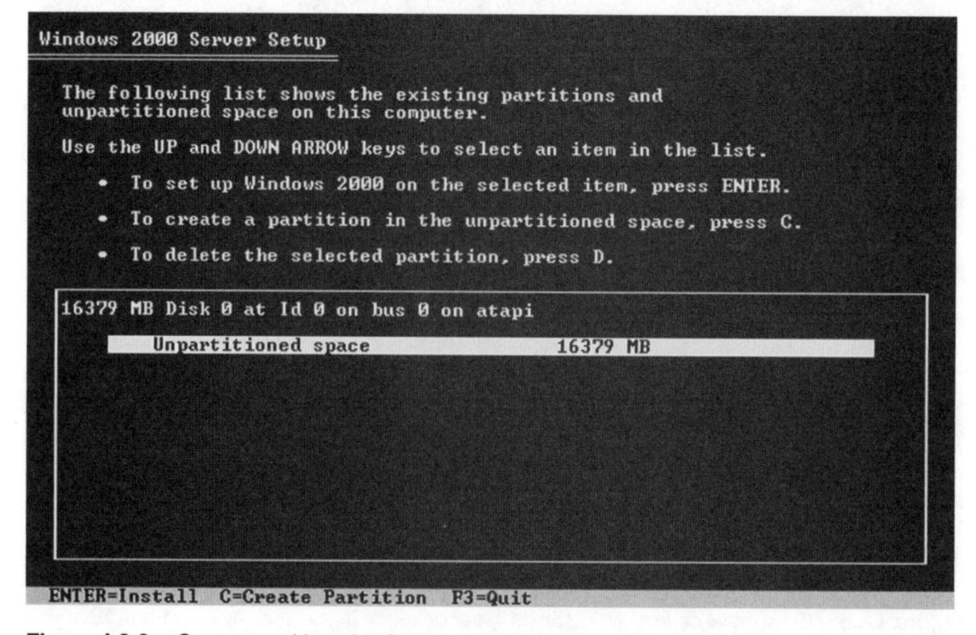

Figure L8.8 On a new drive, the first thing you must do is create the partitions.

7. In the next screen that appears (**Figure L8.9**), you will create your partitions. The default is to use the entire drive. In the bottom field, the number that is filled in represents total drive space. In order to replace that number, you must backspace to the beginning. Fill in the number **`2048`**.

8. When you see the next screen (**Figure L8.10**), which asks you whether you want to install your OS onto the newly created partition or into unformatted space, this may seem like a no-brainer. But in situations where you are installing a second OS onto the system, this is the point where Setup creates the information needed for your system to dual boot.

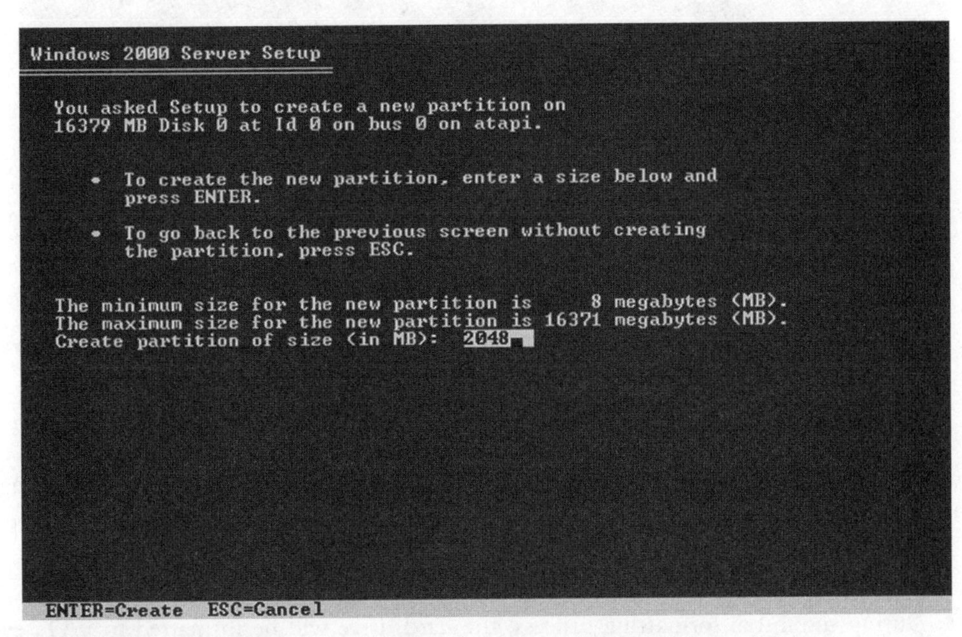

Figure L8.9 It isn't always a good idea to make your hard disk into a single partition. Put your OS and related utilities onto one partition and then install your applications and store user data on separate partitions.

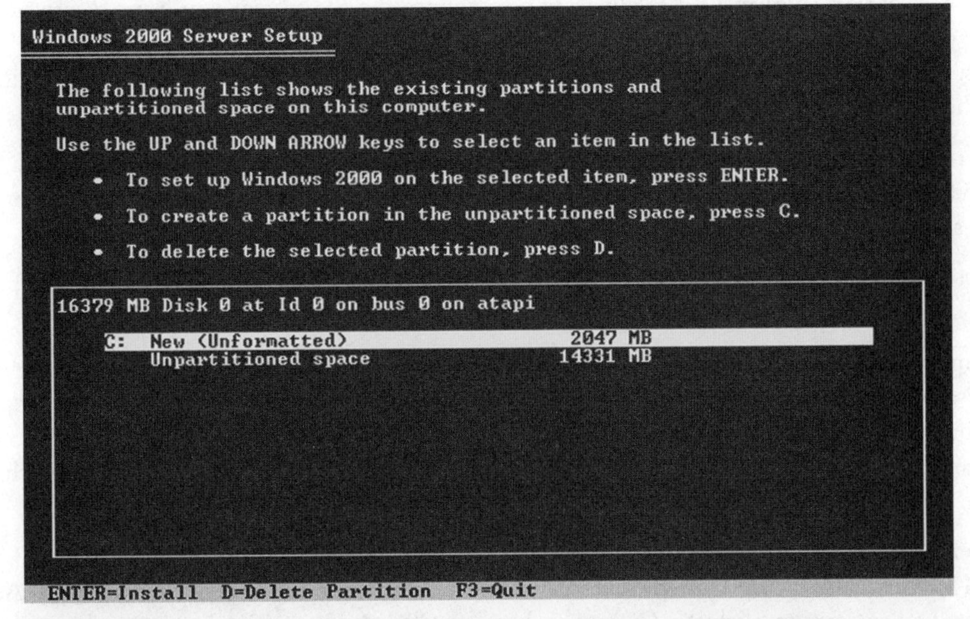

Figure L8.10 If you were installing Win2K onto a previously partitioned disk with another existing OS, this screen would identify the file system installed and how much space was occupied by that file system.

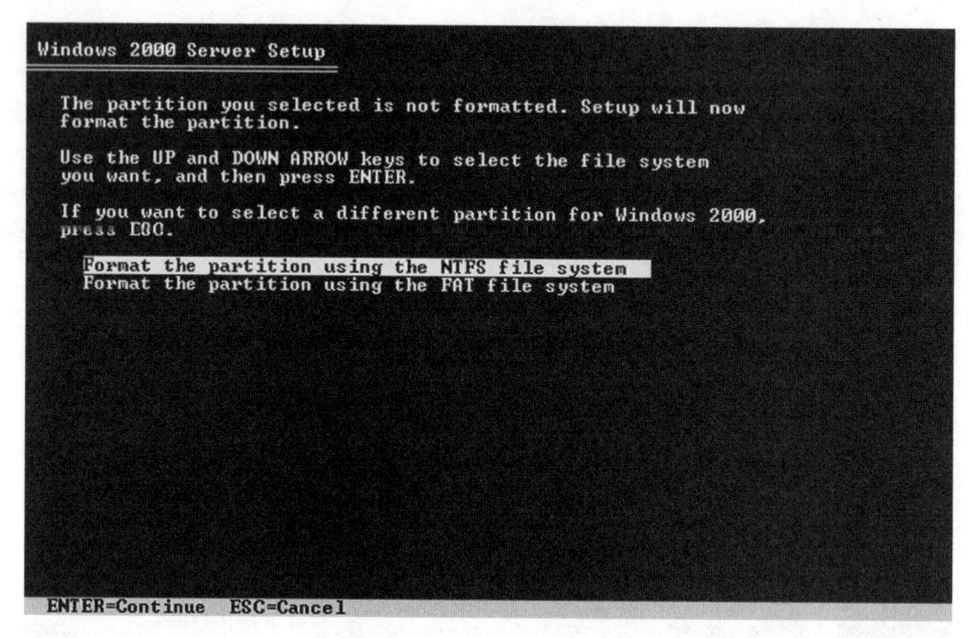

Figure L8.11 One of the bigger advantages of Win2K over previous Windows versions was the NTFS file system. Unless there is a compelling reason not to do so, Win2K computers should always be formatted to NTFS.

9. Now sit back and wait while your partition is formatted. This generally takes long enough for a cup of coffee and a donut while the class mingles in the break room discussing the football playoffs.

NOTE: During the initial formatting process, the hard drive will be formatted to FAT, even if you selected NTFS as your file system of choice. If you are creating a file system of 2GB or larger, it will automatically format the drive to FAT32. Any partition smaller than 2GB will be formatted in FAT16.

10. The next option (**Figure L8.11**) allows you to choose the file system you want to use on your new partition. Your choices are FAT or NTFS. FAT is a poor choice for many reasons. The most important reason to you is that if you ***don't*** choose NTFS, you won't be able to do some of the later labs.
11. On reboot, you enter the graphical portion of the installation process. A lovely screen with the Windows 2000 Professional logo will appear. At the bottom a progress bar labeled Starting up will appear.
12. After that, Setup will convert the drive to NTFS. This takes a minute or two. The computer will automatically reboot once again.
13. Setup will now perform a thorough Plug 'n Play (PnP) scan (**Figure L8.12**), looking for any PnP devices and/or legacy devices previously installed on a prior OS (in the case of an upgrade). If your screen appears to flicker and Setup halts for a few minutes, this is normal. If Setup halts for an abnormally long time, it is probably hung, and you will need to restart your machine once again.
14. When this is finished, you'll have the opportunity to configure your regional settings (**Figure L8.13**). Generally in the United States no changes need to be made here. For overseas users, it might be necessary to click the Customize button. Click Next and in the screen shown in **Figure L8.14**, type your name and organization (organization is optional.)

Windows 2000 Server Setup
Installing Devices
Setup is detecting and installing devices on your computer.
Please wait while Setup detects and installs devices such as your keyboard and mouse. This will take several minutes. During this time, your screen may flicker for a few seconds.
< Back
Next >

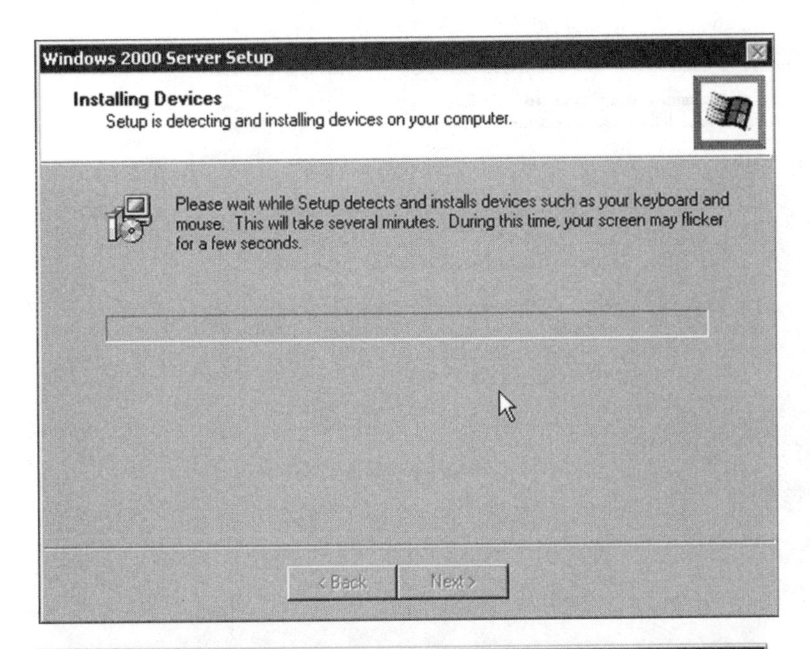

Figure L8.12 The Plug 'n Play scan detects your hardware and creates a list of device drivers to be installed. Contrary to what the screen says, not all devices are being installed at this point. But you do have mouse support now.

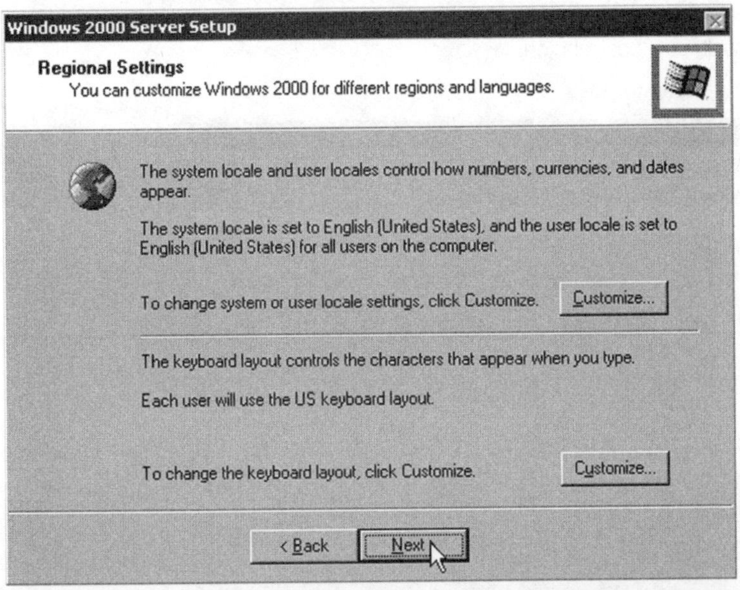

Windows 2000 Server Setup
Regional Settings
You can customize Windows 2000 for different regions and languages.
The system locale and user locales control how numbers, currencies, and dates appear.
The system locale is set to English (United States), and the user locale is set to English (United States) for all users on the computer.
To change system or user locale settings, click Customize.
Customize...
The keyboard layout controls the characters that appear when you type.
Each user will use the US keyboard layout.
To change the keyboard layout, click Customize.
Customize...
< Back
Next >

Figure L8.13 In the United States, it isn't generally necessary to make any changes to the Regional settings, but overseas users can change the currency settings as well as how numbers and dates are displayed.

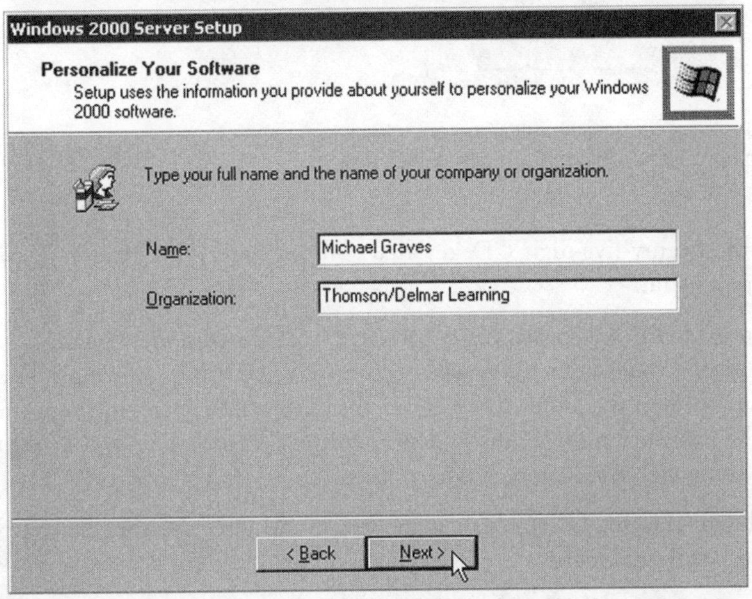

Windows 2000 Server Setup
Personalize Your Software
Setup uses the information you provide about yourself to personalize your Windows 2000 software.
Type your full name and the name of your company or organization.
Name:
Michael Graves
Organization:
Thomson/Delmar Learning
< Back
Next >

Figure L8.14 It isn't necessary to type an organization name, but Setup won't continue until you type a user name.

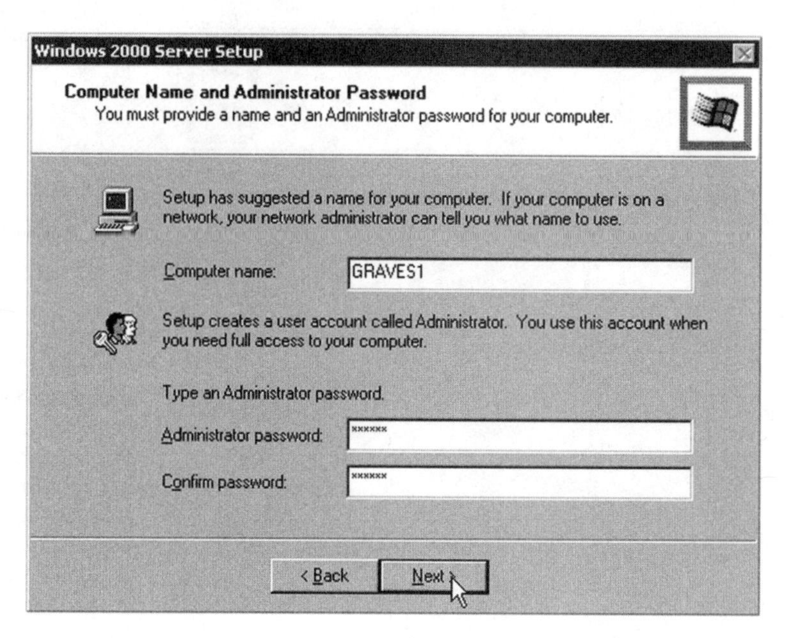

Figure L8.15 The computer name selected at random by the system isn't usually the best choice.

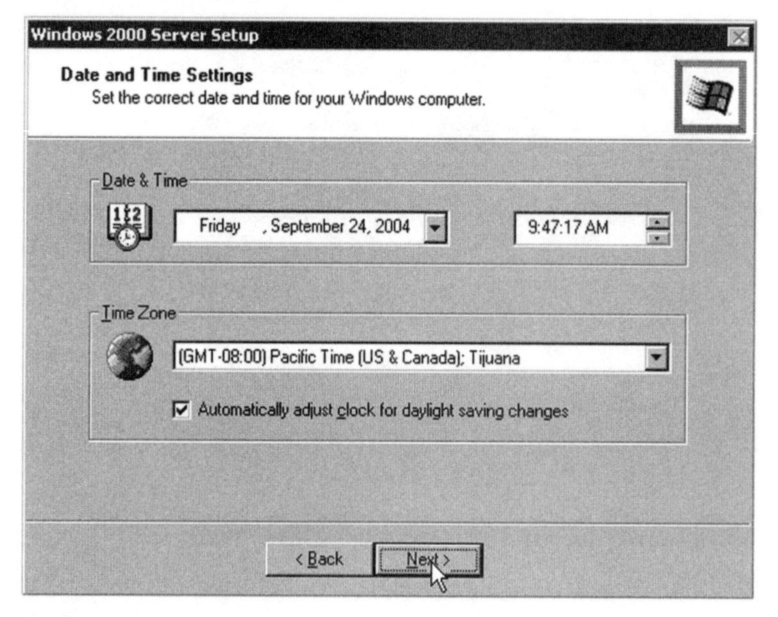

Figure L8.16 Now you know what time and day it was when I wrote this lab. Send me a present on the anniversary.

15. Now it is time to type in the twenty-five-digit CD key that shipped with the software. Type carefully, or you'll be doing it again.
16. The following screen (**Figure L8.15**) will provide a suggested NetBIOS computer name. You won't be using their suggestion. Student machines will be named STUDENT1 through STUDENT12 (or however many student machines there are in the classroom). Here is where the password is selected. For the password *all* students will simply use *password.* This will avoid the inevitable confusion when someone says, "I forgot what I used."
17. Next you set the time and date (**Figure L8.16**), if it is incorrect, and reset the time zone to your own. It will default to Pacific Standard.

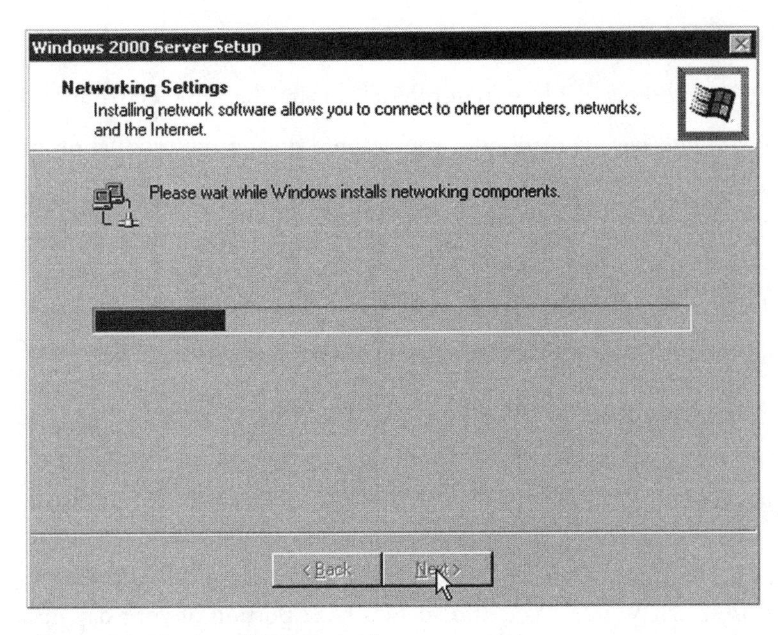

Figure L8.17 Installing networking components

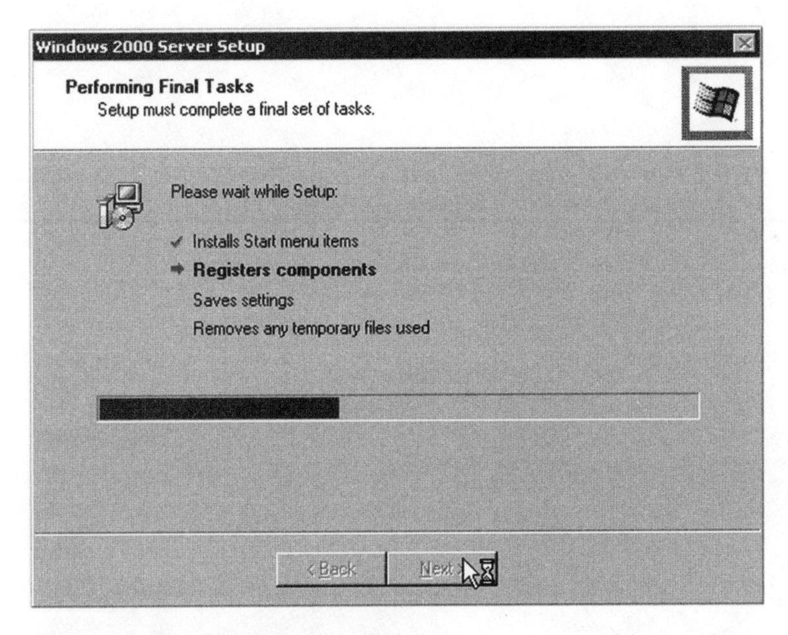

Figure L8.18 Completing the Setup

18. Setup will now begin installing networking components, followed by Windows 2000 components (**Figure L6.17**). Let everything install as per default.
19. In the final step (**Figure L8.18**), Setup installs Start menu items, registers components, saves settings, and finally, removes any temporary files used.
20. When your computer reboots once again, if there are any hardware devices that were detected for which Windows did not have a correct device driver in its database, you will be prompted to search for the appropriate drivers. At this point the drivers can be anywhere, including the network, if networking was configured for DHCP and there is a DHCP server available.

EXERCISE 2 REVIEW

1. What were the two choices of file system offered during the Disk Preparation sequence?
2. At what point did you have control over your mouse during the installation procedure?

LAB REVIEW

1. How many floppies are needed to create the Win2K Installation set?
2. In what directory is the utility for creating boot diskettes located?
3. What happens if you reject the licensing agreement from Microsoft?

LAB SUMMARY

The previous pages led you through a step-by-step procedure for creating all the necessary floppy disks you may ever need to install Win2K. You also spent a large portion of your day installing the product. Now you know why network administrators were so happy Microsoft created methods by which large numbers of machines could be configured at once over a network.

LAB 9

THE WIN2K INTERFACE

I'm going to let you enjoy one brief interlude with Win2K to introduce you to some of the interface changes. Since there are still so many computers out there in the real world running Win2K, it's a good idea if you know where to find things. What I'll be doing in the following exercises is pointing out differences between Win9x (which you just spent a decent amount of time exploring) and Win2K. It's a classic case of, "They're exactly the same, only different."

The only materials you'll need for this lab is your student lab computer, which should now be running Win2K.

The CompTIA objectives covered in this lab include the following:

1.1 Identify the major desktop components and interfaces and their functions. Differentiate the characteristics of Windows 9x/Me, Windows NT 4.0 Workstation, Windows 2000 Professional, and Windows XP.

1.4 Identify basic concepts and procedures for creating, viewing, and managing disks, directories, and files. This includes procedures for changing file attributes and the ramifications of those changes (for example, security issues).

2.4 Identify procedures for installing/adding a device, including loading, adding, and configuring device drivers and required software.

EXERCISE 1: THE START MENU

One of the ways Microsoft made Win2K a bit more user-friendly was to provide a number of different ways in which each user could configure the Start menu to his or her own taste. In the next few pages, I'll show you several different ways to customize the Start menu.

EXERCISE 1A: CONFIGURING THE START MENU

The simple Start menu is the home of some significant changes between Win9x and Win2K. These changes are very subtle, and in fact, cannot be see at first glance. They become available only when configured by the user. In the following pages, you will get acquainted with the Win2K Start menu and learn how to customize it to your taste.

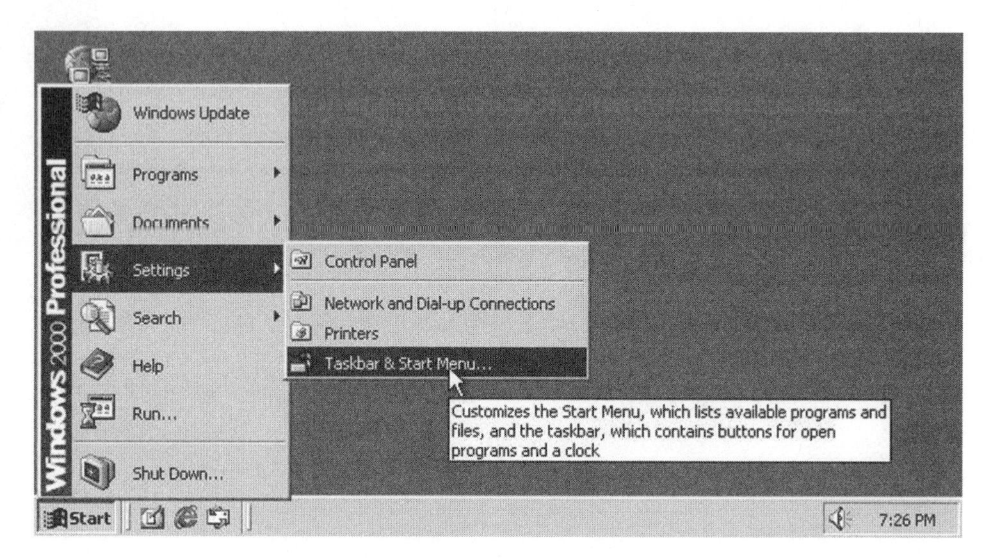

Figure L9.1 Hovering over a menu item in Win2K brings up a description of the item's properties without requiring any further action on the part of the user.

1. Click Start to view the Start menu. Examine the menu closely to see any differences between the Win9x menu and Win2K. There really aren't any are there?
2. Click on Settings→Taskbar and Start menu. (*Note:* You can also get to the Taskbar and Start menu configuration console by right-clicking an unoccupied space on the taskbar and selecting Properties.) If you allow the mouse cursor to hover over the menu selection for a second, you will see a significant change in the user interface. As you can see in **Figure L9.1,** this action brings up a description of the item's properties. Go ahead and click Taskbar and Start menu.
3. This will bring up the Taskbar and Start Menu Properties dialog box. Notice that in this window there are two tabs. The General tab is the one that opens by default. There are five checkboxes available, three of which will be checked by default:
   a. Always on top: Checked by default. Checking this box ensures that even when other programs are running, the taskbar and Start menu are not obscured by any application.
   b. Auto hide: Not checked by default. When checked, the task bar and Start menu disappear from view. When the mouse cursor is pointed to the area where the task bar resides, it will appear.
   c. Show small icons in Start menu: Not checked by default. The pictures used in the Start menu are reduced significantly in size.
   d. Show clock: Checked by default. The time is shown in the lower right-hand corner. Hovering the mouse cursor over the time will also display the date.
   e. Use Personalized Menus: Checked by default. Programs that have not been used recently are not displayed. In order to see the full list of programs, click the down arrows at the bottom of the menu.
4. Click Auto Hide to select it and Show clock to deselect that item. Click Apply and watch what happens. Click Cancel, and the desktop reverts to the way it was.
5. Now click the Advanced tab. This will bring up the screen shown in **Figure L9.2**. There are four buttons on the right-hand side of the window clustered toward the top:
   a. Add: This allows you to add items to the Start menu that do not appear by default. Just for fun, I'll have you do that in Lab 1b.
   b. Remove: I doubt that I need to explain this, but this option allows you to remove items from the Start menu that were added during the OS installation or during the installation of

another application. Since applications frequently add about a gazillion items to your Start menu that you'll never use, this is a handy feature.

c. Advanced: This is actually just another way of adding or removing an item from the Start menu. But instead of using a browse feature, it opens Windows Explorer, and you locate the item you want from there.

d. Re-sort: Here is where you can rearrange the order of items displayed on the Start menu.

6. Beneath these four buttons, discretely distanced by a small space, is a fifth button labeled Clear. Clicking this button wipes out the recent history of opened documents, web pages, or programs.

7. The bottom pane in the Taskbar and Start Menu Properties window is one of the most useful. In a new installation of Win2K the various options offered here are unchecked. By selecting them, you can add the following items to your Start menu:

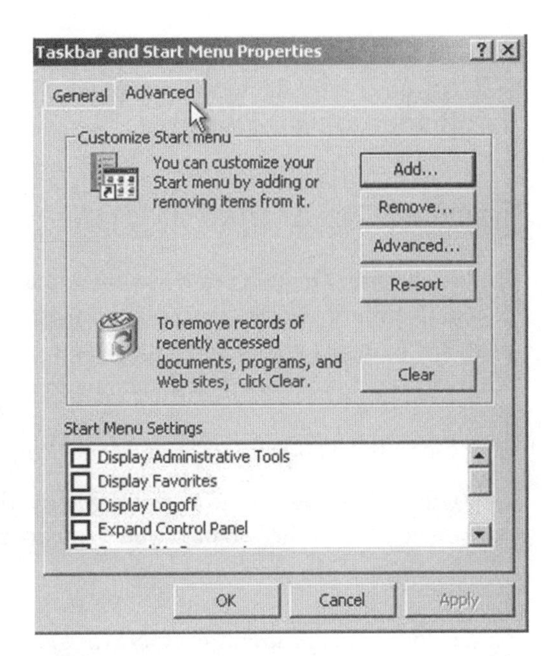

Figure L9.2 The Advanced tab of the Task bar and Start menu configuration screen allows a number of detailed changes.

a. Clicking the Display Administrative Tools box adds a shortcut to the administrative tools to the Start→Programs section of the Start menu.

b. Display Favorites places a shortcut with an itemized submenu of all your Internet Explorer favorite sites.

c. Display Logoff puts an item into the Start menu that allows one user to log off and another to log on without having to restart the computer.

d. I like this one a lot. One of the default items in the Start menu is a shortcut to Control Panel. Clicking that shortcut opens Control Panel. (What a surprise!) The Expand Control Panel option places a submenu in the Control Panel shortcut that allows the user to go directly to one of the individual applets in Control Panel without having to open Control Panel first.

e. Expand My Documents performs that same function for the My Documents entry in the Start menu.

f. Expand Network and Dialup Connections creates a submenu to the Control Panel option that provides shortcuts to each individual DUN or LAN connection configured on the computer.

g. Expand Printers provides shortcuts to each printer installed on the system.

h. Scroll the Programs Menu changes the Start→Programs section of the Start menu from a column to a scroll-down field.

8. Click Expand Control Panel; then click Apply and then OK. Now watch what happens when you Click Start→Settings and then hover the mouse cursor over Control Panel.

REVIEW OF EXERCISE 1A

1. What were the various options located in the General tab of the Taskbar and Start Menu Properties window?

2. What are two different ways to add an item to the Start menu?

3. You've just spent your lunch break searching the Internet for a new job, and you don't want a coworker who shares the computer with you to know what you're doing. How can you hide your tracks from casual eyes?

EXERCISE 1B: ADDING AN ITEM TO THE START MENU

In this exercise, I'm going to have you add a program to the Start menu that does not install by default. A handy little program for the administrator is the Microsoft Management Console (MMC). This program is useful for creating your own customized administrative tools, but by default it is only a command-line function. You'll create a Start menu shortcut for it.

1. Open the Taskbar and Start Menu Properties window and click Advanced.
2. Clicking the Add button will bring up the window shown in **Figure L9.3**. If you know the exact path to the program you want to add, simply type it into the field labeled Type the location of the item. Because everyone knows where MMC.EXE is located, type it and click Next. What? You *don't* know where MMC.EXE is? Neither do I, so go ahead and click Browse....
3. In the window that opens (**Figure L9.4**) you will see a screen that displays My Documents, My Computer, My Network Places, and Connect to the Internet. Each one of these represents a shortcut that you can add to the Start menu to make your computing life easier. Adding a document creates a shortcut to the document that automatically launches the default program to edit that type of document. Adding an Internet location creates a shortcut that will launch Internet Explorer and automatically browse to that URL. You're going to add an executable, so, as shown in Figure L9.4, click the + symbol next to Local Disk C to open it. Click the + symbol next to the System32 subdirectory and scroll down to MMC.EXE. Life will be much easier and this lab will go faster if you click the first file you see under System32 and press the M key. That will highlight the first file with a name beginning with M. and scrolling will be much faster. Double-click MMC. and the file will appear in the location field. Click Next.

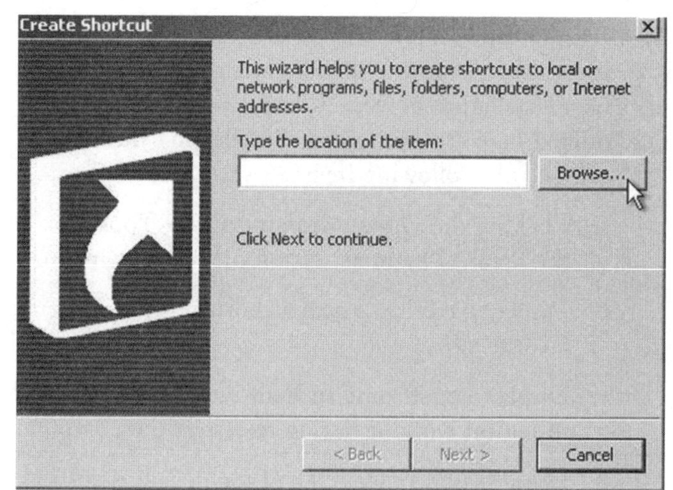

Figure L9.3 The Browse function of the Add button allows you to search your hard drive for the program you want to add.

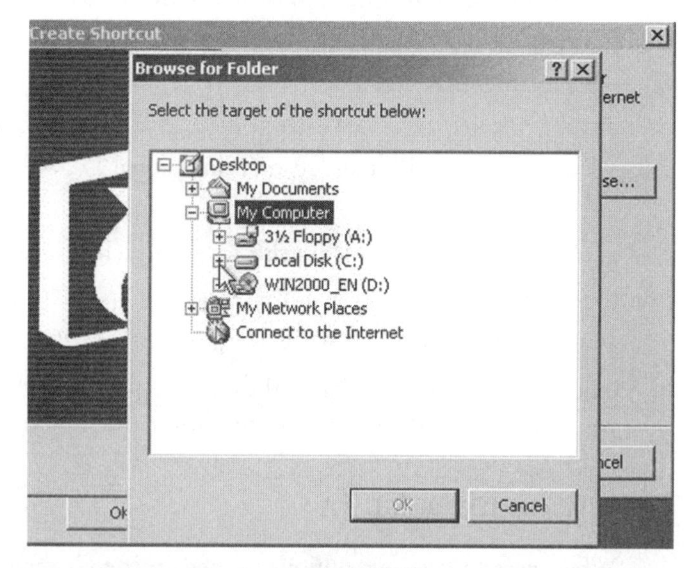

Figure L9.4 The Browse function allows the user to locate shortcut targets without having to know the exact location.

4. In the next screen (**Figure L9.5**) you will be prompted to select which folder should house the new shortcut. The default is Program Files, but there is also an option for a New Folder. Click that button to automatically create a new folder with the same name as the shortcut.

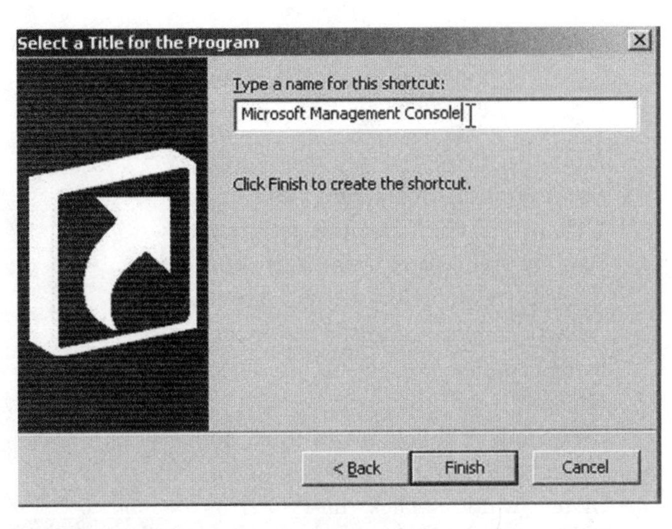

Figure L9.5 One of the options in creating shortcuts is to put each shortcut in its own folder.

5. Now a screen like the one in **Figure L9.6** pops up, prompting you to give your new shortcut a name. The default is the name of the executable. This might be occasionally useful, but if you happen to be creating a shortcut to a program whose executable is WXKV785.EXE, that might not be so useful to other people using your computer. Or you, for that matter, three days after you create the shortcut. Call your new shortcut Microsoft Management Console.
6. Click Finish and then click OK in the Taskbar and Start Menu Properties screen. Your new item now shows up in the Start Menu.

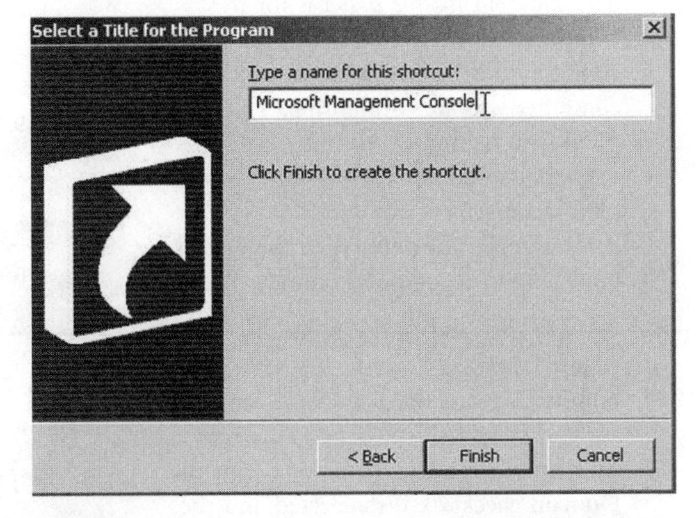

Figure L9.6 Make sure you give your shortcut a name you can recognize later.

EXERCISE 1B REVIEW

1. What is the purpose of adding new items to the Start menu? Aren't all installed applications automatically added?
2. Why is it not a good idea to accept the default name for a new shortcut?

EXERCISE 2: NAMING A COMPUTER IN WIN2K

In Win9x, naming a computer was done in the Network applet at the time networking was set up. If a network card is detected during installation, naming is done during installation. Microsoft made it slightly different in Win2K.

1. The first thing you have to do is open the System applet in Control Panel. There are three ways to do that. One is to click Start→Settings→Control Panel and then double-click System. A second way is to double-click the My Computer icon on the desktop, double-click Control Panel, and then double-click System. Far and away the easiest method is to simply right-click My Computer and select Properties. Any of these methods will bring up the screen shown in **Figure L9.7**.

2. Click the Network Identification tab at the top. That brings up the window shown in **Figure L9.8**.

3. Note that there are only two configuration buttons on this panel. One is Network ID and the other is Properties. You are going to examine both of them. Click Network ID. This will start the Network Identification Wizard. Since I intend to have you set up a network in a later lab, I am not going to have you run the wizard at this point in time. So Cancel the Wizard and, back in the System window, click the Properties button. That will bring up the screen shown in **Figure L9.9**.

4. The top field in this panel is for the computer name. Here is where you configure the NetBIOS name for the computer you are configuring. There can be no two computers on the network with the same NetBIOS name. A complete discussion of computer naming conventions can be found in the text book. Fill in a computer name.

5. Beneath that and to the right is a button labeled More... I'll get to that one in a minute. Toward the bottom of the panel are two more fields in a box labeled Member of. By default the one with the Domain checkbox is deselected and the field is grayed out. The one labeled Workgroup is checked and the word WORKGROUP is already filled in. In a workgroup setup, all computers that are going to talk to one another must be a member of the same workgroup. Were you to set up a network in which half the computers in the classroom were part of the CLASSONE workgroup and the other half were part of the CLASSTWO workgroup, even though they were part of the same physical network, CLASSONE computers would not be able to communicate with CLASSTWO computers and vice versa.

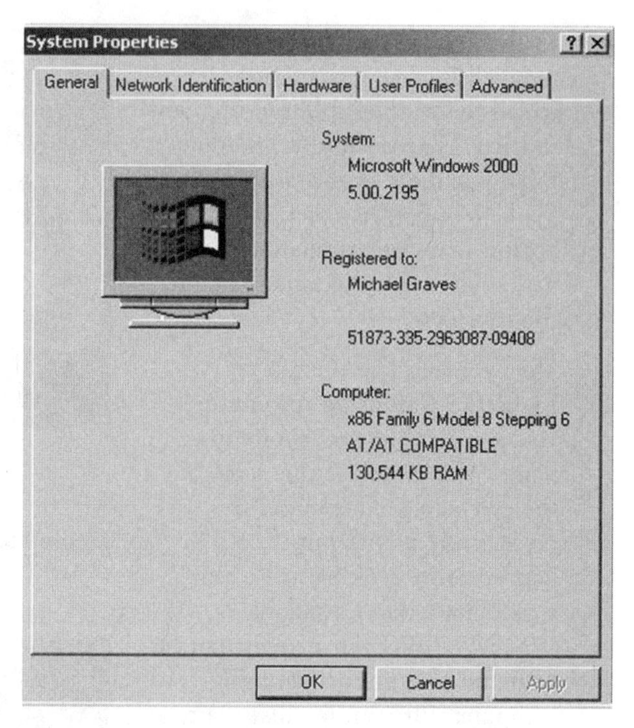

Figure L9.7 The System applet in the Win2K Control Panel

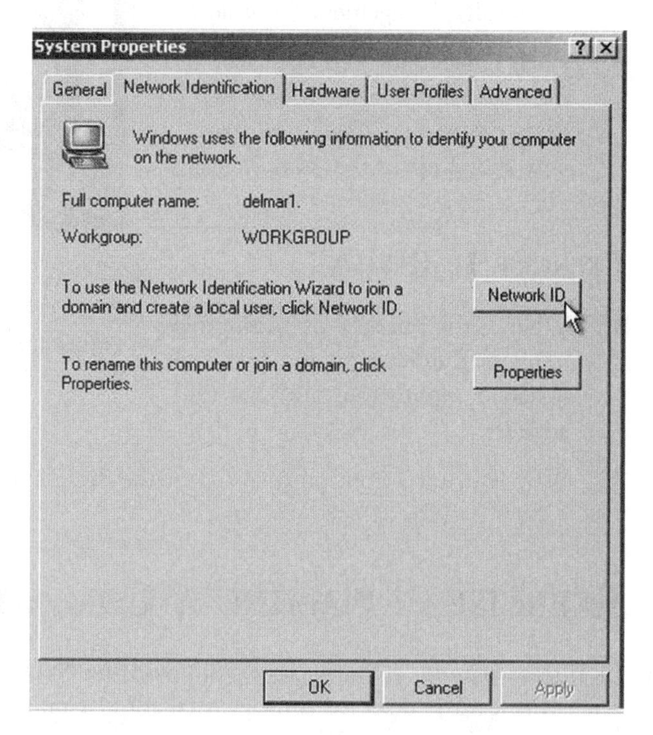

Figure L9.8 The Network Identification tab

6. Now take a look at that More... button (**Figure L9.10**). This button has one function: to change the primary DNS suffix for your computer. So what the heck is a primary DNS suffix and why would you want to change it? I'll answer the last question first. Unless an administrator tells you otherwise, you wouldn't want to change it. DNS is the Domain Name Services and is how different servers are named on the Internet or in a Win2K domain. The primary DNS suffix is a key part of your computer name. This feature only comes into play when the computer is a member of a domain. My only reason for showing you this screen is to point out that little check box labeled Change primary DNS suffix when domain membership changes. By default that box is checked. Now if I move this computer from the GRAVES.ORG domain to the DELMAR.COM domain, as soon as the administrator adds my computer to the DELMAR.COM domain, the computer automatically assumes the new suffix. 99.99% of the time, you don't want to fool with this setting. But if, for any reason, this box is deselected and you change domains, it can cause issues later on.

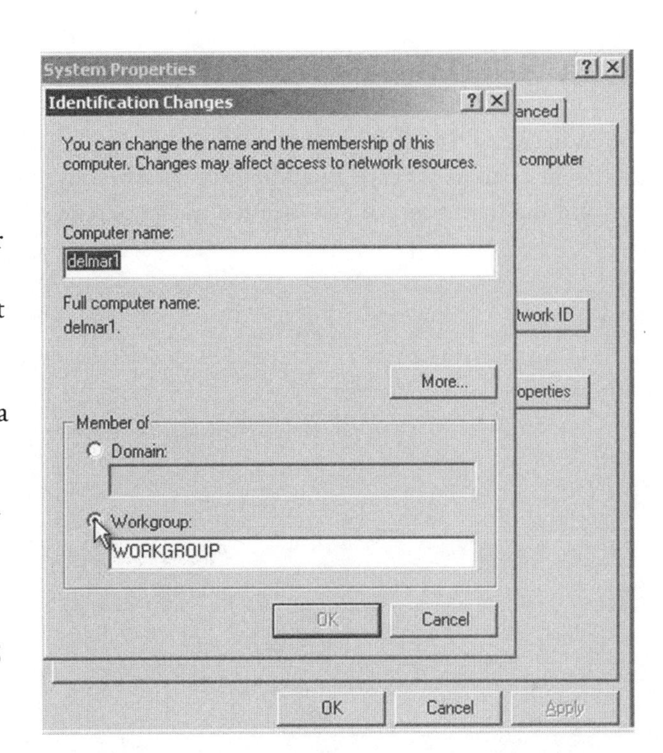

Figure L9.9
The Properties configuration screen

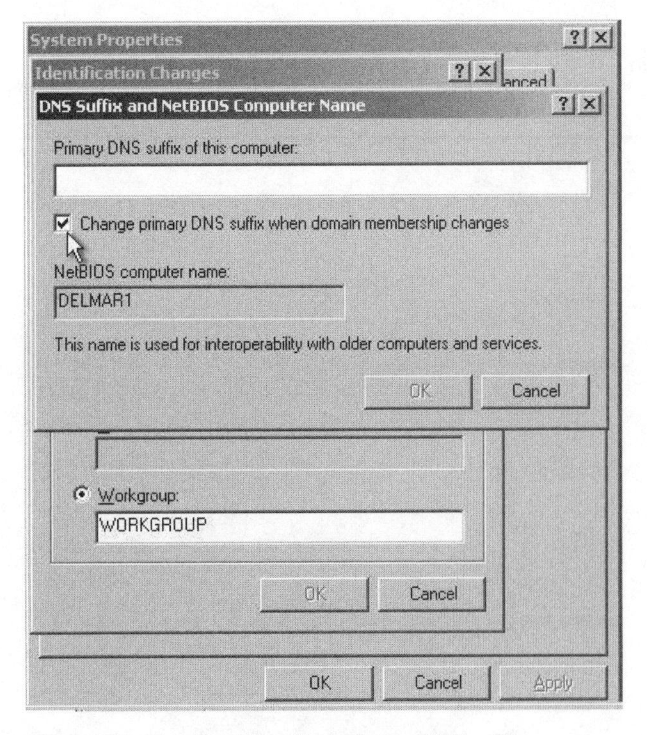

Figure L9.10 Changing the primary DNS suffix

EXERCISE 2 REVIEW

1. What are three ways to get to Control Panel in Win2K?
2. Where does one change the computer's NETBIOS name in Win2K?

LAB REVIEW

1. What is the MMC, and what does it allow you to do?
2. Where would you go to change the NetBIOS name of a computer?
3. You want to clear your history of recently opened documents. Where do you go to do that?

LAB SUMMARY

So Win2K isn't as different from Win9x as you initially thought, is it? Internally, the two OSs are as different as dogs and cats. But Microsoft wisely chose to keep the interface as similar as possible in order to ease the transition. As you will see in the next few labs, they weren't quite as friendly with WinXP.

LAB 10

INSTALLING WINXP

In this lab you will install Windows XP onto the lab machines. The only real difference between installing XP and Win2K is that there is no option for setting up a computer from floppy disks. If you have computers that do not boot to a CD-ROM, you must download a file called WinXP_EN_PRO_BF.EXE from Microsoft's website. As of this writing, that file was located at www.microsoft.com/downloads/details.aspx?displaylang=en&FamilyID=55820EDB-5039-4955-BCB7-4FED408EA73F. Since this is a copyrighted file, it is not possible for me to make it available to you from my website or delmar.com.

Since the procedure is identical to that of installing Win2K, I am not going to waste precious natural resources on ten pages of identical text. The procedure is very automatic, but if you do require the assistance of instructions and screenshots, make use of Lab 8.

The materials you'll need for this lab include your student lab computer and a copy of Windows XP for each student.

The CompTIA objectives covered in this lab include the following:

1.2 Identify the names, locations, purposes, and contents of major system files.

2.1 Identify the procedures for installing Windows 9x/Me, Windows NT 4.0 Workstation, Windows 2000 Professional, and Windows XP, and bringing the operating system to a basic operational level.

2.3 Identify the basic system boot sequences and boot methods, including the steps to create an emergency boot disk with utilities installed for Windows 9x/Me, Windows NT 4.0 Workstation, Windows 2000 Professional, and Windows XP.

LAB 11

Working with Accounts

In the following exercises, you will be creating several different user and group accounts. These accounts will be used in later labs as you learn how to associate permissions and apply security to individual users and groups. You will also learn to copy an account, so that its permissions and settings are automatically applied to a new account that you've created. In the final exercise, you will rename and finally disable the account. In the exercises on groups, I have taken the liberty of using a Windows 2003 Server to show some advanced options. These are optional exercises. If you don't have access to either a Win2K Server or a Windows 2003 Server, simply follow along.

Sadly, this is an area that CompTIA does not deem sufficiently important to cover on the exam. It is, however, information critical to anyone working with computers on a professional level.

Exercise 1: Creating a New Account

Any time a new user is added to the network, that person will require a unique user account. This account, complete with user ID and password, is the ticket to the network. In order to create the account you will perform the following procedures.

1. Click Start→Programs→Administrative Tools→Active Directory Users and Computers (as shown in **Figure L11.1**).
2. You should get a screen similar to that in **Figure L11.2**. Highlight Users in the left pane then, in the right pane, right-click in any blank area. From the pop-up menu that appears, select New→User.
3. You should now have the screen shown in **Figure L11.3**. Type the user information as requested. In the User logon name field, type the User ID for that user. This must be a unique value. There can be no duplicate User IDs anywhere on the network. Click Next.
4. In the next screen (illustrated in **Figure L11.4**), you will be prompted to enter the user's password. You must enter it a second time in order to confirm the

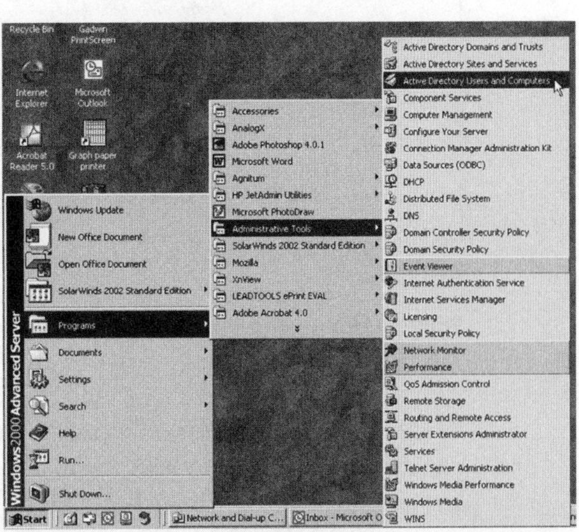

Figure L11.1 A roadmap to Active Directory Users and Computers

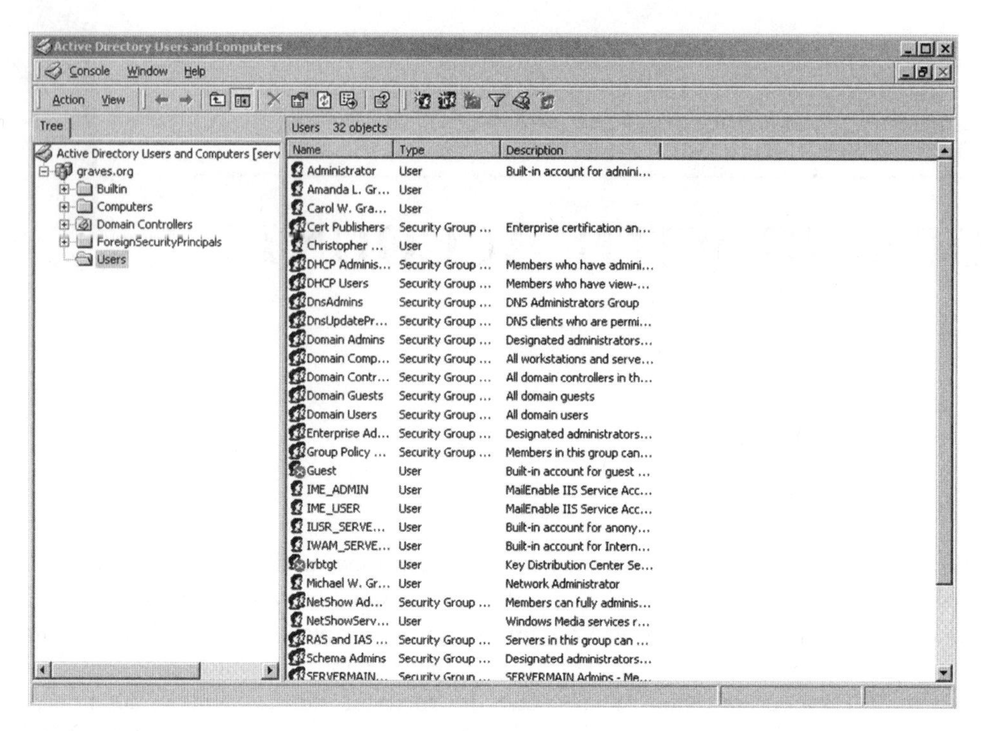

Figure L11.2 The Active Directory Users and Computers console

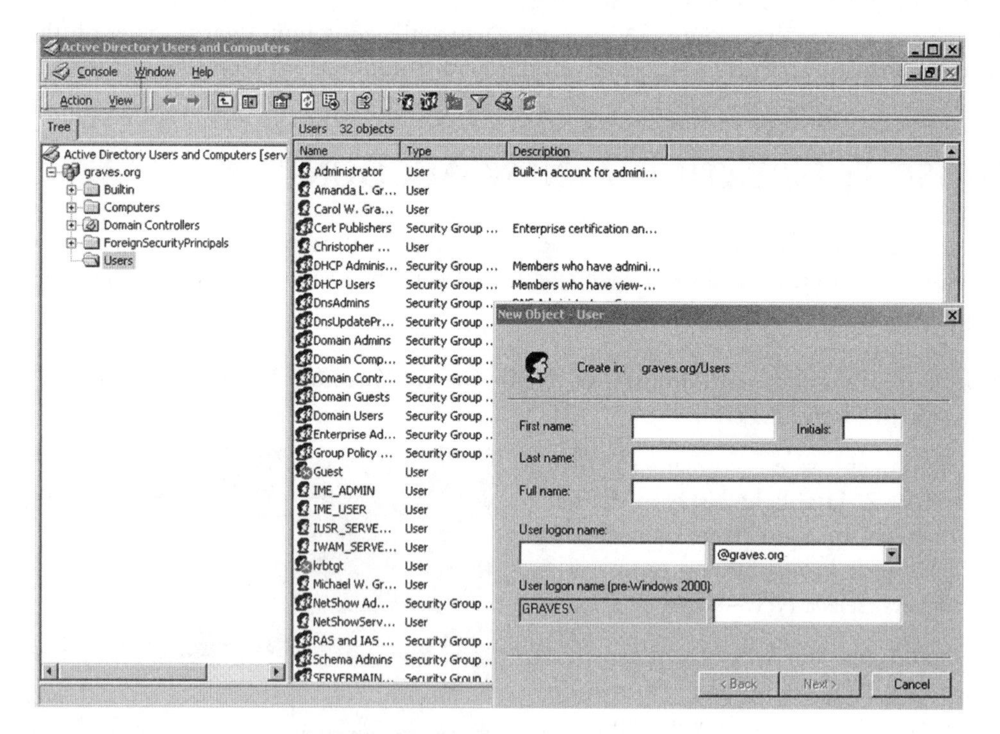

Figure L11.3 Fill in the user information and provide a unique User ID.

password. Should you inadvertently enter it differently the second time, the password will be rejected, and you will have to start again. There are four checkboxes beneath the password fields for password options:

a. User must change password at next logon: If this choice is selected, the first time users log onto their new accounts, they will be told that their password has expired and will be prompted to enter a new one (twice, for confirmation). This is the option to select if you want your users selecting their own passwords.

b. User cannot change password: As the phrase implies, after you have assigned a password, it is etched in stone. Only an account administrator or one with administrative privileges can change the password.

c. Password never expires: If this field is selected, the password will remain valid until changed by an account administrator or someone with administrative privileges. This is the case even if the password policy has been set to force users to change their password periodically.

d. Account is disabled: This option prevents anyone from logging onto the network using that particular account. It does not, however, delete any security settings or permissions.

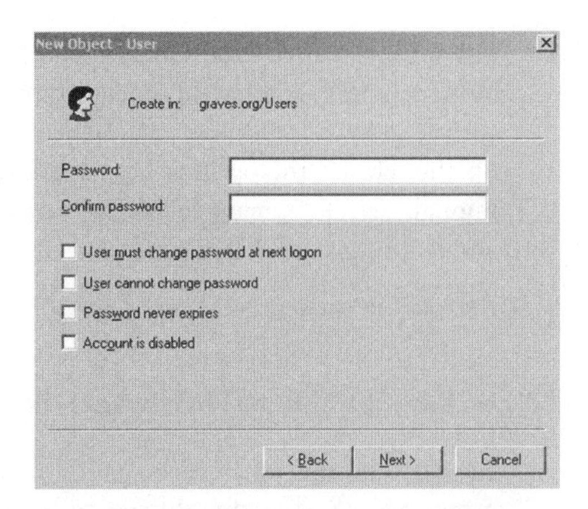

Figure L11.4 Next, enter a password, confirm it, and select the password options.

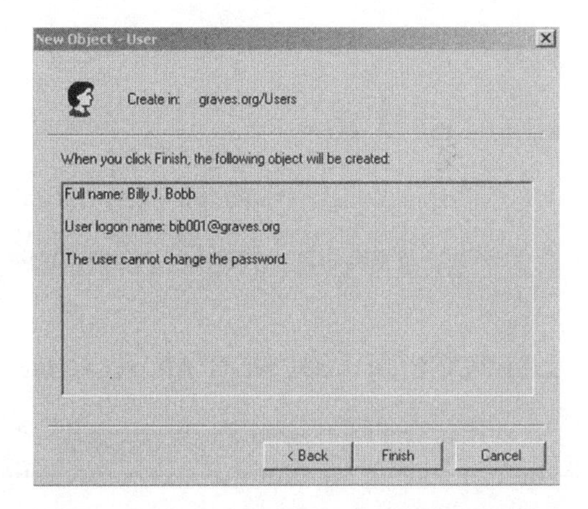

Figure L11.5 The User summary screen

5. For all accounts in your lab exercises, you will be using *password* as your standard password. This will prevent forgotten passwords from becoming an issue. Obviously, in a real-world scenario, this would be a very bad idea. Select User cannot change password and click Next.
6. You will get a summary screen like the one in **Figure L11.5.** All the information you typed will be displayed except for the password. Click Finish. Your new account has been established.
7. Repeat the previous steps until you have created a total of twelve new accounts. Don't forget to use *password* as the password for all user accounts.

EXERCISE 1 REVIEW

1. Where do you go to create a new user account in WinXP?
2. What happens if you don't configure a password for XP?

EXERCISE 2: CREATING GROUP ACCOUNTS

Every network administrator quickly learns that managing groups of accounts all at once is much simpler than trying to manages the users one at a time. In this section, you will create two forms of group accounts. You will create local groups to manage resources, and you will create global groups to manage users. Later on you will use these global groups to manage permissions.

EXERCISE 2A: CREATING A LOCAL GROUP

1. Start Active Directory Users and Computers, just as you did in Exercise 1. Right-click a blank portion of the right pane and select New→Group from the pop-up menu. You'll get the screen shown in **Figure L11.6.**

2. For Group Name, type Documents. Notice that Windows fills in the field labeled Group Name (pre-Windows 2000) for you. Beneath those fields, on the left are the options Domain local and Global. Select Domain local. For now, don't worry about group type. Click OK.
3. Repeat the process, creating a group called DATA.

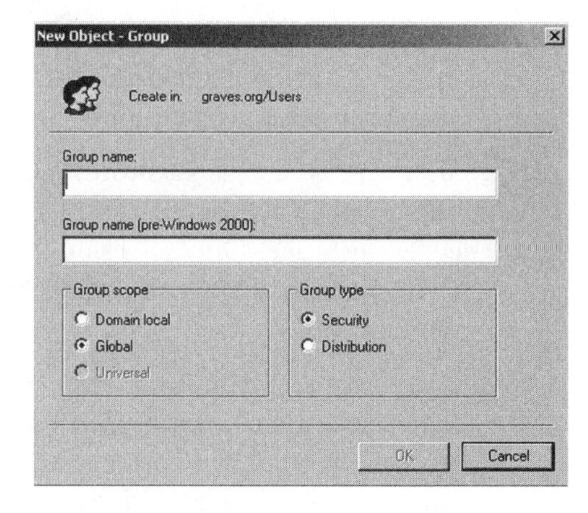

Figure L11.6 Creating a new group in Active Directory Users and Computers

EXERCISE 2B: CREATING A GLOBAL GROUP

1. Repeat the steps outlined in Exercise 2a. Name the group SALES. The one difference is that, instead of selecting Domain local in the second screen, select Global.
2. Repeat this process twice, creating global groups called MANAGEMENT and ADMINISTRATION.

EXERCISE 2 REVIEW

1. What is the difference between a local group and a global group?
2. What is the advantage to using groups?

EXERCISE 3: COPYING AN ACCOUNT

Now that you've created all those nearly identical groups and accounts the hard way, you'll learn how you can take an account that has been configured the way you want and make a new one using the first one as a template.

MANAGING GROUPS

When you're first getting started with this networking business, it sometimes gets confusing as to when to use groups and when not to. And when it comes to managing groups, what's with this *global group* versus *local group*?

It isn't really all that complicated. Local groups are used to manage local resources. You might have a database containing your customer information. In order to allow access to that database, you create a local group called DATA. Permissions are assigned at this level.

Global groups are used to give users with similar sets of responsibilities and resource needs the permissions they need to do their work. For example, you might have a global group called SALES. Every salesperson needs access to the same resources and generally needs the same permission sets. Therefore, when you hire a new salesperson, rather than go through the rigmarole of assigning those permissions independently (and remembering what they are), you simply create a new account and add it to the SALES group. In order to give all sales reps access to the database, you add the global group SALES to the local group DATA. In one step, all sales reps are given exactly the same permissions to use the database.

A simple little mnemonic will help you remember what's going on. AGLP. *A*ccounts go into *G*lobal groups, which are added to *L*ocal groups, which are given *P*ermissions.

1. The first thing you want to do is customize an account so that you know it is different than the others you created. Select one of the accounts that you created in Exercise 1 and double-click it in the right pane of Active Directory Users and Computers. You'll get the screen shown in **Figure L11.7.**

2. Click the tab labeled Member Of. Then click Add. This will give you the screen shown in **Figure L11.8.** As shown in the illustration, add this account to several different built-in groups. Also, add it to your newly created SALES group. Click OK.

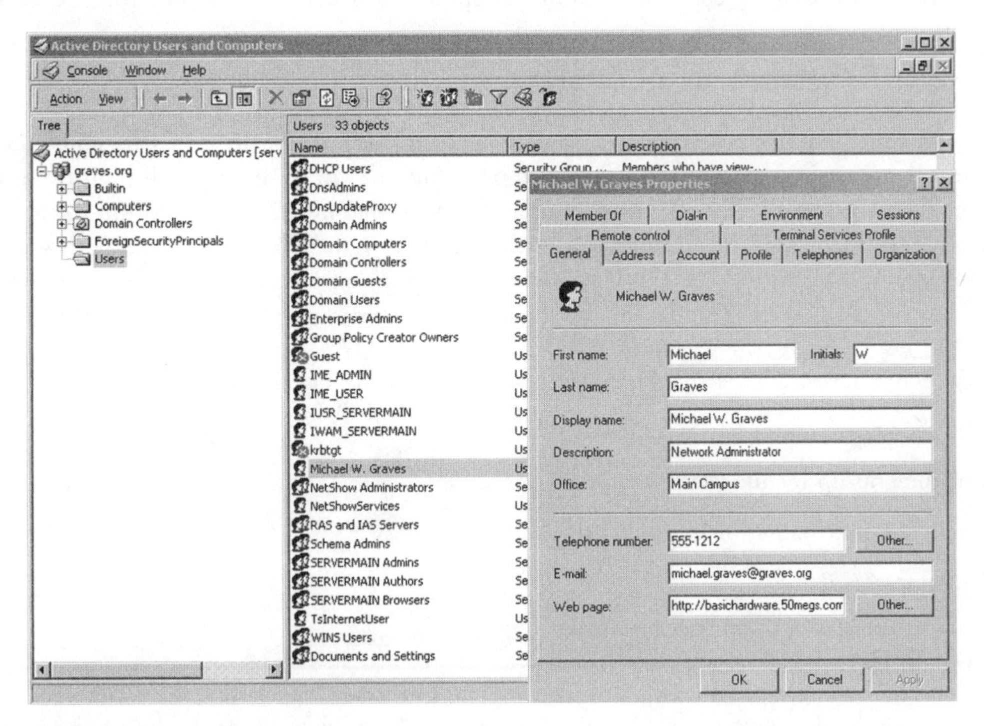

Figure L11.7 Customizing an account

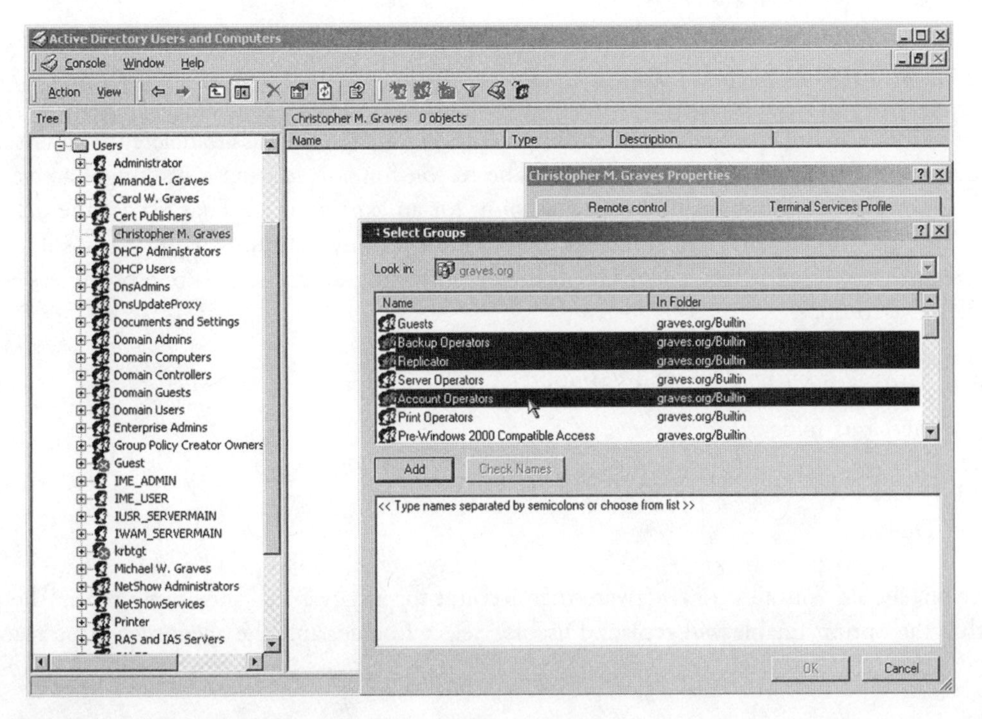

Figure L11.8 Making an account a member of a group

3. Open the Users Folder in the left pane of Active Directory Users and Computers and right-click the account you just modified. Select Copy. The screens that follow are the same ones you saw when creating a new account. That is because that's exactly what you're doing. Except this new account brings with it all the accoutrements of the account you copied.

EXERCISE 3 REVIEW

1. Why would you want to copy an account as opposed to simply creating one from scratch?

EXERCISE 4: RENAMING AN ACCOUNT

Once in a while it becomes necessary to rename an account. It's all too tempting to simply delete the old one and create a new one. However, there is a problem inherent in that procedure. It is not the user name, user ID, or password—or any combination of those—that identifies the account to the OS. The account is identified by a 32-bit number that was generated by the OS when the account was created. This is the account's security ID (SID). If you want to keep the entire history of the account intact, you need to keep the SID intact. You do this by renaming the existing account. Here's how to do it:

1. Open Active Directory Users and Computers and open the Users folder.
2. Right-click the account you want changed.
3. From the pop-up menu, select Rename.
4. Type in the new name for the account.

   It's as simple as that.

EXERCISE 4 REVIEW

1. What is the disadvantage of deleting the account of a user when he or she leaves the company?
2. What is the purpose of the SID?

EXERCISE 5: DISABLING AN ACCOUNT

When a user leaves an organization, the first thing many administrators do is to delete that user's account. This can be (and frequently is) a critical error. The reason for not deleting a no-longer active account is the same one I gave for not creating a new account for an existing user. That SID is the ticket to the account's history. Should you need to access that account for any reason, it won't be possible if it was deleted. Simply recreating it won't work. Fortunately, disabling an account is one of the easiest things you'll ever have to do.

1. Open Active Directory Users and Computers.
2. Open the Users folder.
3. Right-click the account you want disabled.
4. Select Disable.

Later on, should you need to reactivate that account for any reason, you simply repeat the process, except that the option Enable will replace Disable. Select Enable, and the account will be reactivated.

LAB REVIEW

1. You have just created a new account for a user on the network, but you want him to select his own password. How do you make sure he has no choice but to create a new password?
2. What is the advantage of copying an account over creating a new one?

LAB SUMMARY

WinXP was designed from the ground up to be an OS that supports multiple users. Therefore, from an administrative standpoint, being able to manage those users is a critical ability. Although this lab only touches on managing accounts, without those accounts in place, the system is not much more secure than a Win9x box.

LAB 12

THE EVENT VIEWER

One of the better troubleshooting tools provided by Win2KS is one called Event Viewer, which collects information on different activities that are generated by either hardware or software action. These events range from benign to critical, and Event Viewer frequently can provide information that helps the administrator diagnose what led up to the event.

Event Viewer reports three degrees of severity in its logs.

Table 12.1 Event Viewer Severity Classifications

Symbol	Severity	Description
	Information	Information describes the successful operation of an application, driver, or service.
	Error	A significant problem, such as loss of data or loss of functionality.
	Warning	An event that is not necessarily significant but may indicate a possible future problem.

With this information in mind, take a look at Event Viewer and see what you can find.

The only materials you'll need for this lab are your lab computers. The CompTIA objectives covered in this lab include the following:

1.5 Identify the major operating system utilities, their purpose, location, and available switches.

3.1 Recognize and interpret the meaning of common error codes and startup messages from the boot sequence and identify steps to correct the problems.

3.2 Recognize when to use common diagnostic utilities and tools. Given a diagnostic scenario involving one of these utilities or tools, select the appropriate steps needed to resolve the problem.

EXERCISE 1: AN OVERVIEW OF EVENT VIEWER

1. Click Start→Programs→Administrative Tools→Event Viewer. The screen in **Figure L12.1** will appear. Here, I added a computer that had not been on my network since rebuilding the domain. That gave me some very interesting errors to examine.
2. Notice in the left-hand pane that there are six different aspects of system performance that are logged.
   a. Application Log: Here is where events logged by applications or programs are recorded.
   b. Security Log: Events such as invalid logon attempts are recorded here. If you have auditing enabled, this is where auditing events will be stored.
   c. System Log: Any event generated by a system component, whether it be hardware (such as a memory error) or OS related, will be stored here.
   d. Directory Service Log: Events directly related to Active Directory are recorded here.
   e. DNS Server: Events generated by DNS services are stored here.
   f. File Replication Service: As its name implies, events generated by the File Replication service are stored here. An example of this event would be the failure of two domain controllers to successfully replicate the SID or SYSVOL.
3. Highlight the Application Log in the left-hand pane. Click Action. Click Properties. This will bring up the screen in **Figure L12.2**. The two tabs in this screen are General and Filter. Under General, you can configure several different things.

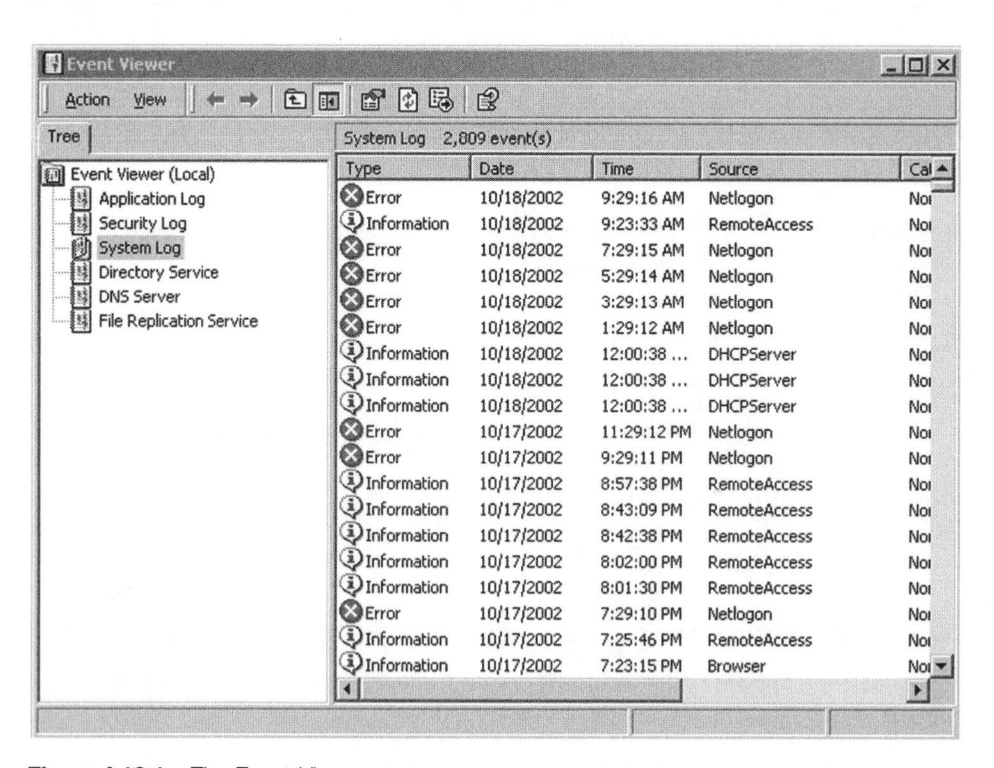

Figure L12.1 The Event Viewer screen

4. Under Display Name, change Application Log to Server Applications. Click Apply and then OK. Notice the change on your Event Viewer Screen.

5. Go back to the Properties screen for the Application Log and change it back to its original name. Notice that the default Maximum log size is 512KB. Also, by default, when the log size exceeds 512KB, it is set to Overwrite events older than seven days. If hard drive space is not an issue, I suggest that you increase your log size to 2048KB (2MB) and that the selection Overwrite events as needed be selected. Make these changes

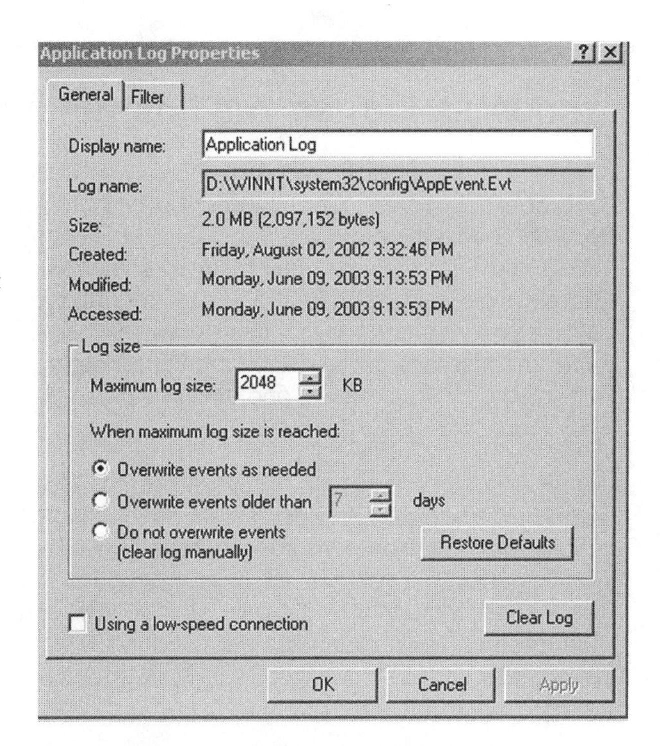

Figure L12.2 The Application Log Properties window

6. Another option on this screen is to Clear log. Clicking this button will completely delete all events recorded in this log. You will be asked whether you want to save the log files before you continue (**Figure L12.3**). You don't really want to clear your log, so click Cancel and move on.

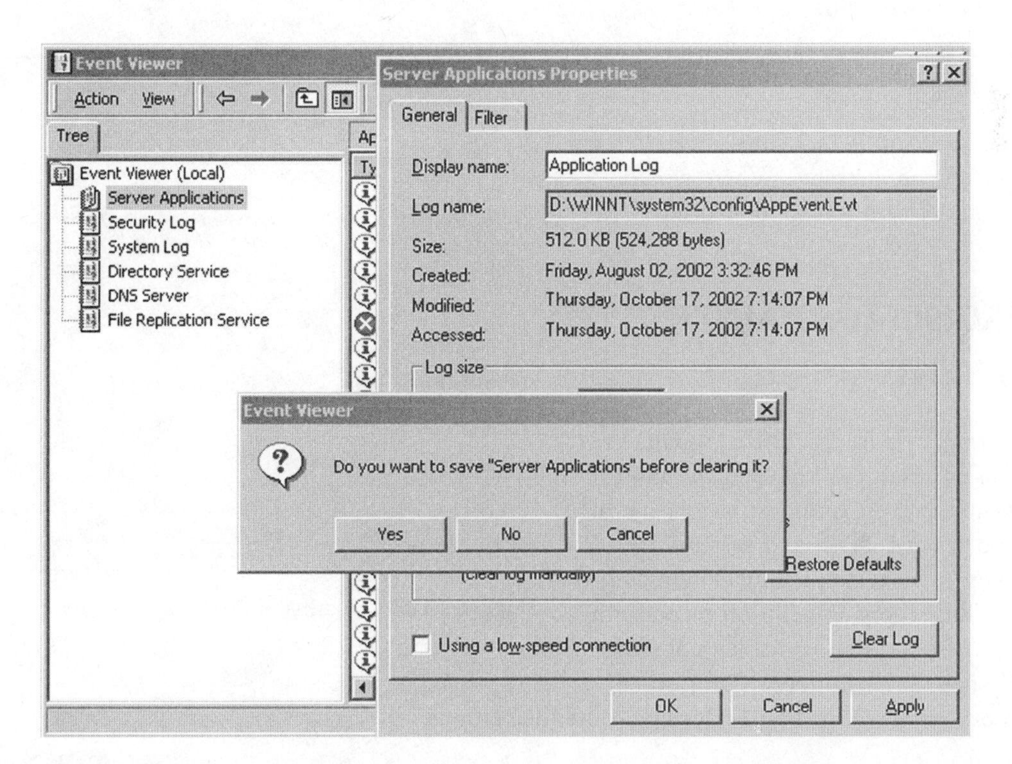

Figure L12.3

TROUBLESHOOTING THE NOS THROUGH EVENTS

When you're first getting starting with this network administration thing, it can appear to be overwhelming at first. You'll soon get over that. You'll find that all providers of network operating systems provide a substantial amount of support for their products. In Windows 2000 and XP, the Event Viewer provides information on what caused a failure. If this doesn't help, you can take it a step farther and make use of their TechNet services on Microsoft's web page (currently at www.microsoft.com/technet). A search of key words from the message is very likely to bring up several articles related to your problem. Novell offers very similar services, and Linux help can be obtained from Red Hat, Mandrake, and numerous other Linux vendors.

Another good resource for Microsoft users is the Windows 2000 or Windows XP Resource Guide. Again, Novell provides similar references for its NOS. In this kit you will find reams of information. Nearly every error message generated by the NOS is explained, and most causes of service or driver failure can be found in this guide. These are not inexpensive books, but compared to the cost of your NOS and/or the cost of the administrator's time, the resource guide is an essential tool for any administrator.

SUMMARY OF EXERCISE 1

1. Where would you find the Event Viewer in Windows 2000?
2. If a service fails to start, what kind of icon will it display?
3. You have configured your server to audit failed logon attempts. Where would reports of these events be logged?

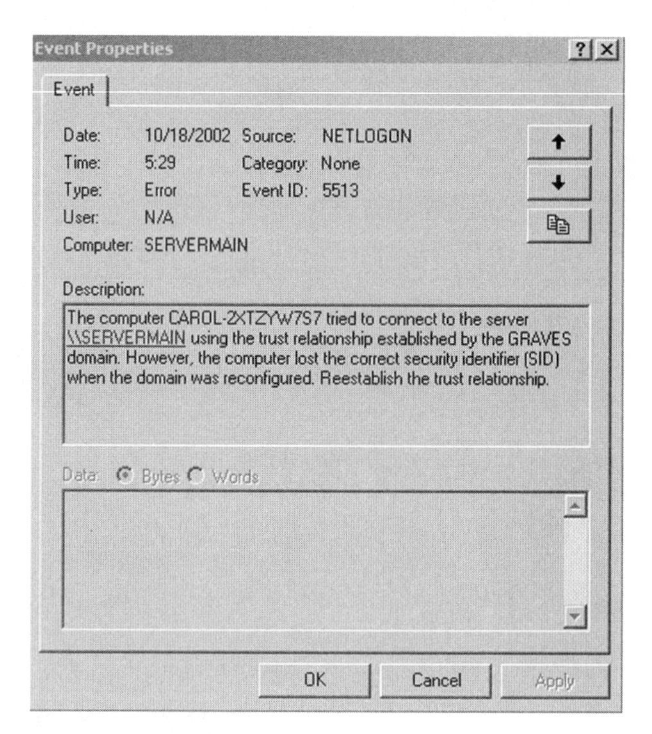

Figure L12.4 The Event Properties window

EXERCISE 2: ANALYZING AN EVENT

1. For this exercise, go to the System Log. This is where you will find the most events. Since it is impossible for me to predict what all of your systems are going to look like, follow closely with the illustrations in addition to performing these steps on your own computer. My descriptions of events and other information will be based entirely on the illustrations.
2. Double-click any error your System Log may be reporting. If there are no errors, find an Information event. Lacking that, double-click any event but follow the text carefully. Double-clicking any event will bring up the Event Properties screen (**Figure L12.4**).

3. If you are looking at an error message, such as the one in the illustration, the description screen will tell you precisely what failed. In the case of the error in the illustration, you are even told how to fix the problem. All I need to do is rejoin this computer to the domain.
4. Close Event Viewer.

SUMMARY OF EXERCISE 2

1. What kinds of information can you learn from an event if you double-click it?
2. If a service fails to start, what can you learn by examining the event?

LAB REVIEW

1. What are the different logs kept by Event Viewer?
2. Describe the three little icons used by Event Viewer to identify the severity of an event and explain what each one means.

LAB SUMMARY

The Event Viewer is one of the first places a systems administrator goes for information when something goes wrong. This lab provided a glimpse into the reasoning for that. The Event Viewer is actually a very powerful tool when you get the hang of using it, you'll make it one of your first stops as well.

LAB 13

SETTING UP A PEER TO PEER NETWORK

In the following exercises, you'll get your first taste of actually networking multiple devices. You will interconnect the lab computers onto a small peer to peer (P2P) network. But before you do that, you're going to need NICs installed.

The materials needed for this lab are the student machines, a NIC for each machine with drivers (if necessary), technician's toolkits, a patch cable long enough to connect the computer to the wall panel, and a hub.

The CompTIA objectives covered in this lab include the following:

2.4 Identify procedures for installing/adding a device, including loading, adding, and configuring device drivers and required software.

4.1 Identify the networking capabilities of Windows. Given configuration parameters, configure the operating system to connect to a network.

4.2 Identify the basic Internet protocols and terminologies. Identify procedures for establishing Internet connectivity. In a given scenario, configure the operating system to connect to and use Internet resources.

EXERCISE 1: INSTALLING A NIC

1. Place the computer on the desk in front on you. Depending on the model, you will either need to remove the case or the access panel in order to add components. Since the methods for doing this vary greatly from one model of computer to another, it isn't practical to provide instructions on how to open the computer in this text. If you are unclear on how to open your computer, consult with your instructor.
2. Now it's time to read any instructions that come with your NIC. Some brands, such as 3-Com, require that you run a small setup program before installing the NIC, while others have you install the driver after the card is in place.
3. Find a free PCI slot and remove the backplane cover for that slot (see **Figure L13.1**). Firmly seat the NIC into the slot and replace the backplane screw.
4. Start the computer and let Plug 'n Play do its thing. With Windows 2000, the NIC should automatically be detected. Depending on your card and the installation process used, PnP will

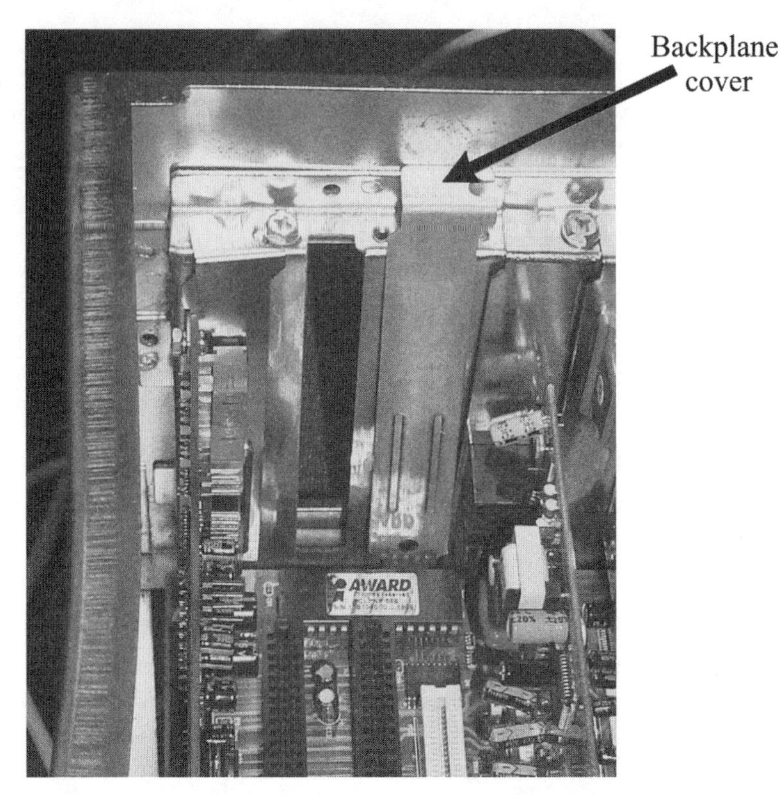

Figure L13.1 The backplane cover (raised in this illustration) is actually an essential part of your computer's thermal regulation system. Any time you remove any card, fill the open slot with a cover.

either identify the card and find the appropriate driver in its database, or it won't. If you ran a setup program such as 3-Com's prior to installing the card, that added the necessary drivers to the database. If no driver is found, during the installation process you will get a screen like the one in **Figure L13.2**, followed by the one in **Figure L13.3**. Specify the appropriate location of the disk containing your drivers and click Next.

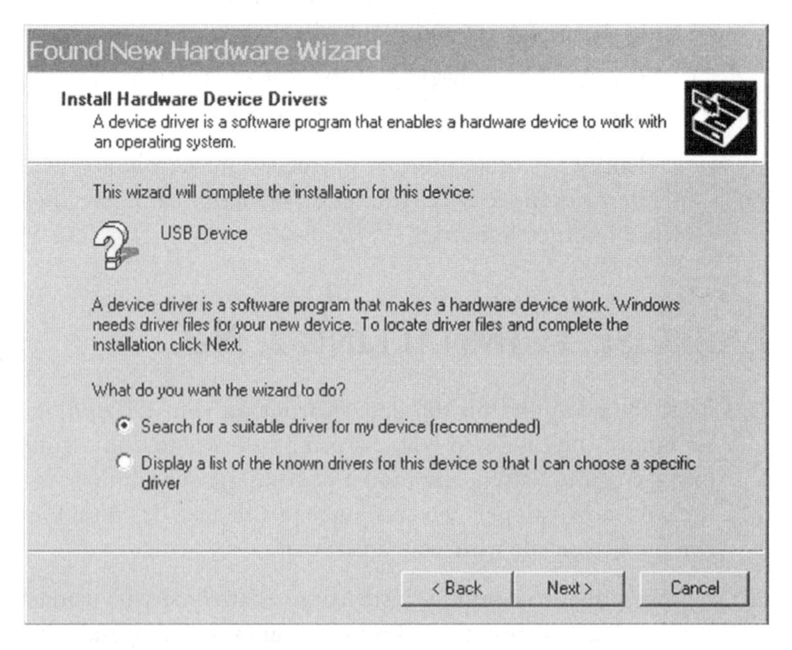

Figure L13.2 In most circumstances, it is best to let Windows search for a device driver. Select that option for this lab.

5. If you get a screen warning you that the driver does not contain a Microsoft signature, don't worry about that. Continue the installation and let the driver install. Depending on the brand of NIC and its drivers, you may or may not have to restart your computer once again.

6. Your NIC installation is complete.

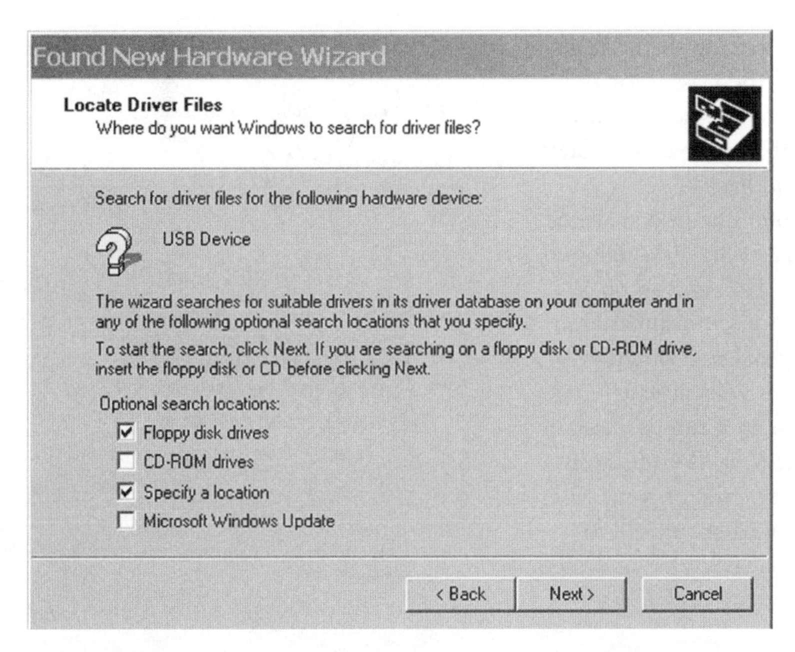

Figure L13.3 Click the appropriate box that specifies where your driver is located. To save a little time, deselect everything else.

EXERCISE 2: CONFIGURING THE PROTOCOLS

After installing a NIC driver, there are certain networking functions that Windows automatically installs. By default, you have installed a networking client in Client for Microsoft Networks. It also installs File and Printer Sharing for Microsoft Networks and Internet Protocol (TCP/IP). TCP/IP is configured to automatically obtain an IP address from a DHCP server. Therefore, your machine is configured as a DHCP client as well. You're going to change some of that.

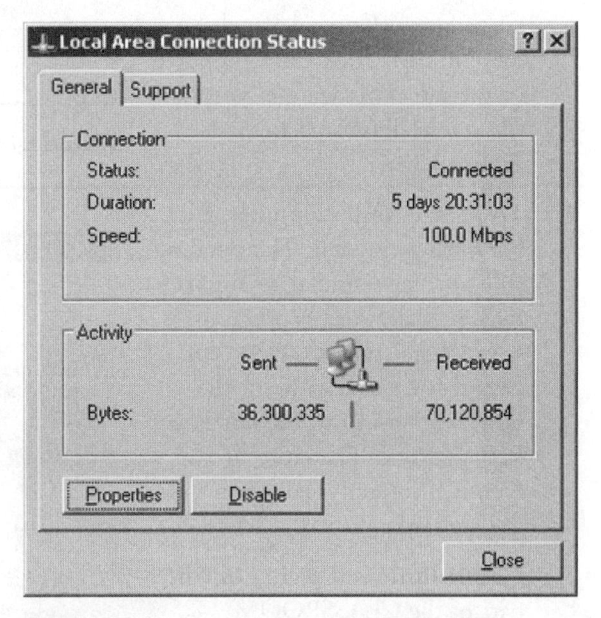

Figure L13.4 Local Area Connection applet

STEP 1: RECONFIGURING TCP/IP

The first thing you'll do is statically assign IP addresses to each machine on the network.

1. Right-click My Network Places on the desktop and select Properties, or click Start→Control Panel→Network Connections→Local Area Connections.
2. The screen shown in **Figure L13.4** will appear. Click Properties.
3. Now you will have the screen shown in **Figure L13.5**. Scroll down to Internet Protocol (TCP/IP) and click Properties.
4. The screen in **Figure L13.6** will be the next thing you see.
5. You will statically configure each of the machines in the classroom. To do this, click Use the following IP address and type the address assigned to your machine. You will derive the

addresses by starting in the front left corner of the classroom and moving left to right and then to the back, one row at a time. Start with the IP address of 192.168.1.100. The next machine would be 192.168.1.101, followed by 192.168.1.102, and so on. Make sure no two machines are inadvertently assigned duplicate addresses. This will cause a conflict. Type in a subnet mask of **255.255.255.0**. If you simply press Tab after entering your IP address, this field should fill in automatically. Click OK, and then on the next screen click Close.

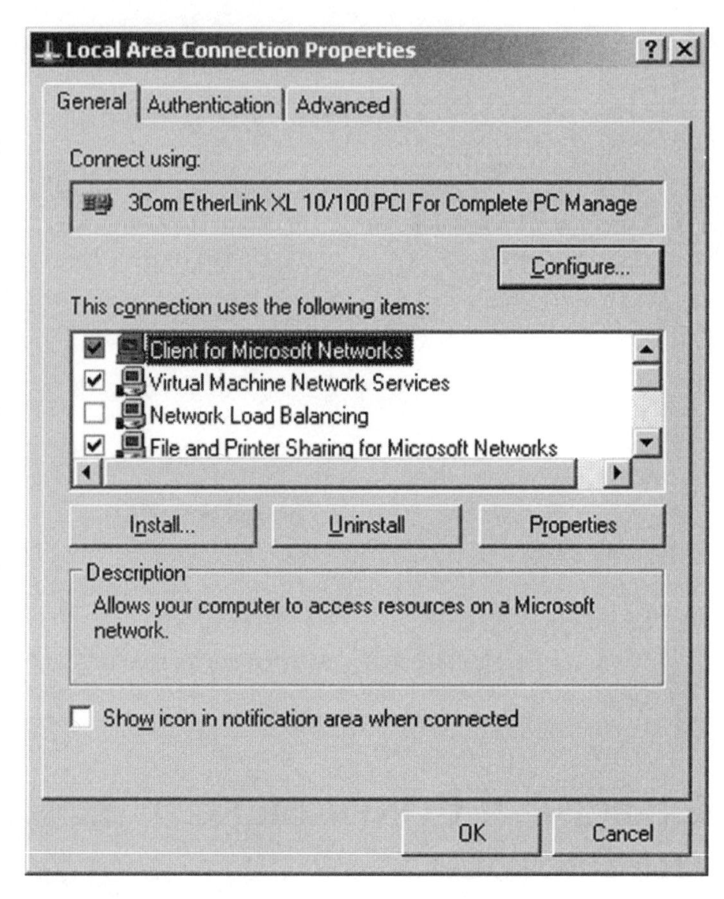

Figure L13.5 Local Area Connection Properties

STEP 2: CREATING A WORKGROUP

1. Click Start→Control Panel→System, then click the Computer Name tab. This will get you to the screen illustrated in **Figure L13.7**.
2. To rename your computer, click the Change button. The window will now look similar to **Figure L13.8**. Make sure Workgroup is selected and type **CLASSROOM**. Everybody needs to be in the same workgroup to be part of a P2P network. Therefore, if you type it incorrectly, you won't join the network.
3. Congratulations. You're now all part of the CLASSROOM workgroup. You should be able to see the CLASSROOM workgroup in My Network Places. If you double-click this icon, you should be able to see each other's machines. Note, however, that you won't be able to see any of the contents of these machines as of yet.

Figure L13.6 TCP/IP Properties

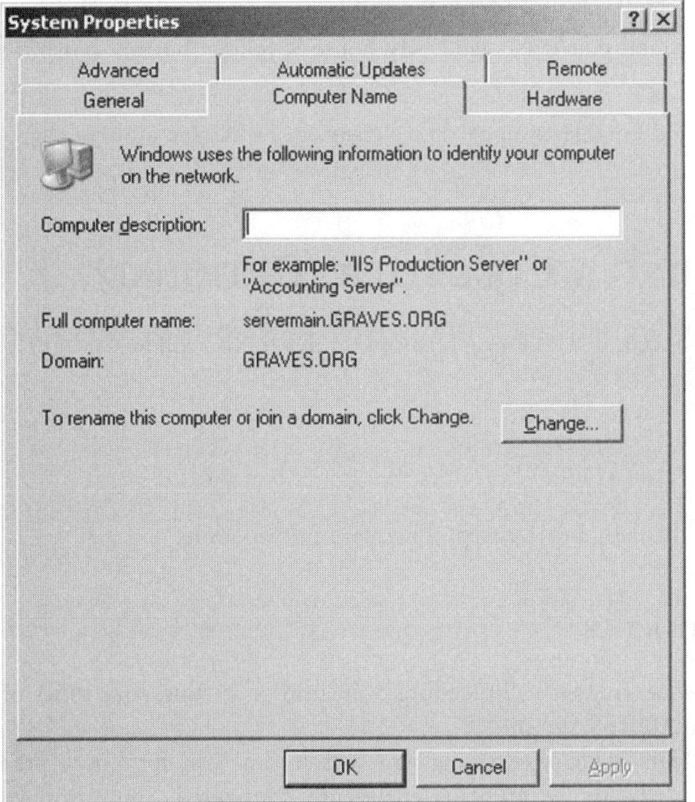

Figure L13.7 Naming your computer in WinXP is done in the System Properties applet.

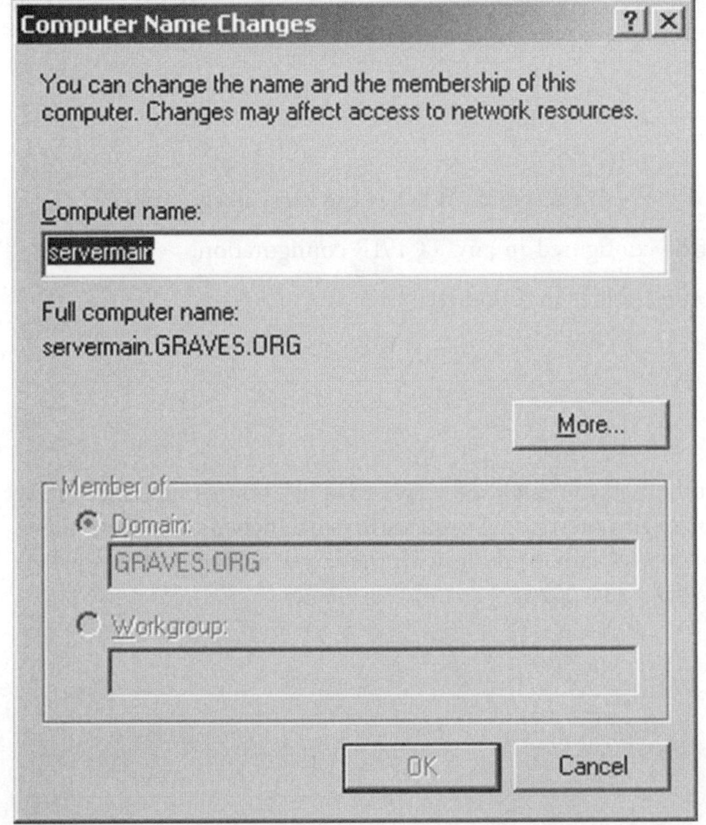

Figure L13.8 The Computer Name Changes window

STEP 3: SHARING RESOURCES

1. Right-click the Start button and select Explore. This will open Windows Explorer. You're going to create a new folder in which you can store your shared files.
2. Highlight Drive C: in the left-hand pane. Select File→ New and then Folder. Give the folder your first name.
3. When the new folder appears in the left-hand pane, right-click that folder and, in the pull-down menu that appears, one of the options will be Sharing. Click that option.
4. Select Share this folder and leave the default share name in place. Don't worry if more than one of you have the same first name. Just don't try to put two shared folders with the same share name on the same computer. You won't worry about permissions in this lab, so simply click Apply and then OK.
5. Now, in the left pane of Windows Explorer, double-click your shared folder. The right-hand pane should be empty. Right-click anywhere in that pane, and you'll get a pop-up menu. Select New, and then in the next menu that appears, select Text Document.
6. Type the following text. "My house is brown, but my horse is yellow." Don't worry about how stupid that sounds. One of your classmates is going to fix that for you. Close the document and when it prompts you to save the file, save it as house.doc.
7. Now everybody pick a teammate. Pick somebody you don't know so that you can learn to work together and maybe make a new

friend at the same time. In Windows Explorer, double-click My Network Places and browse to your partner's machine. Open the file and edit it to read, "My house is yellow, but my horse is brown." Save the file and close it.

8. When you're both finished, you should be able to open your version of house.doc and see the revisions your partner made.

EXERCISE 3: DUAL-HOMING A COMPUTER (OPTIONAL)

In order to perform this lab, you will need a second NIC for each computer. Each NIC will be configured to work on a separate network.

STEP 1: INSTALLING THE NIC

This is easy. Simply repeat Exercise 1 of this lab, step by step. There are no variations.

STEP 2: CONFIGURING THE PROTOCOLS

Repeat Exercise 2 of this lab. However, when you get to Procedure 5, instead of starting your series of IP addresses at 192.168.1.100, start with 192.168.10.100.

Now when you open Network and Dial-up Connections, you will see an icon for Local Area Connection 1 and Local Area Connection 2. Each one can be independently configured. You now have two networks running simultaneously in the classroom.

Have half the classroom reconfigure their Network Identification in the System Properties screen so that they are members of a workgroup called WORKGROUP. You will have to restart these machines for the change to take effect. Now, in My Network Places, you should be able to browse to both workgroups.

LAB REVIEW

1. You've just installed a new NIC, and it doesn't respond. What is the most likely problem?
2. What are the two settings that must be configured in any TCP/IP configuration?
3. What are the basic steps in sharing out a folder in Windows?

LAB SUMMARY

If this is the first time you've set up a network, then you might be surprised at just how simple configuring a peer-to-peer network really is. Many people with no training at all set up small networks in their homes with no difficulty. Where it gets fun is when you start working with the larger networks. That's where a book like *The Complete Guide to Networking and Network+* comes in handy.

LAB 14

BACKUP AND RECOVERY

In the following exercises, you're going to get a brief overview of the Windows Backup utility. Then you'll go through the process of performing a backup and subsequently deleting and restoring the data you backed up. Optimally, in order to do this lab, each computer should be equipped with a tape backup unit. However, it is assumed that is not the case in the majority of classrooms, and the backup will be done to file in these exercises.

For this lab, you'll need your student computers, tape drive (if possible), and backup tapes.

There's only one CompTIA objective covered in this lab:

1.2 Identify basic concepts and procedures for creating, viewing, and managing files, directories, and disks. This includes procedures for changing file attributes and the ramifications of those changes (for example, security issues).

EXERCISE 1: AN OVERVIEW OF THE BACKUP UTILITY

1. To start Win2K backup, click Start→Programs→Accessories→System Tools→Backup. This will bring up the screen shown in **Figure L14.1**.
2. The three options shown in this window are Backup Wizard, Restore Wizard, and Emergency Repair Disk. You won't be working with any of the Wizards in this lab. You'll be learning to perform manual backups and recoveries.
3. Click the Backup tab. You should now have a window like that in **Figure L14.2**. Note that you can back up any or all of your local drives, from your CD-ROM drive, the System State, and from Network Places. If you click your C: (or any other) drive, you will see the various folders on that drive. You can choose which files and folders to back up.
4. At the bottom of the screen you have two other options. Backup destination allows you to select where that file is going to be stored. If you have no tape drive installed on your machine,

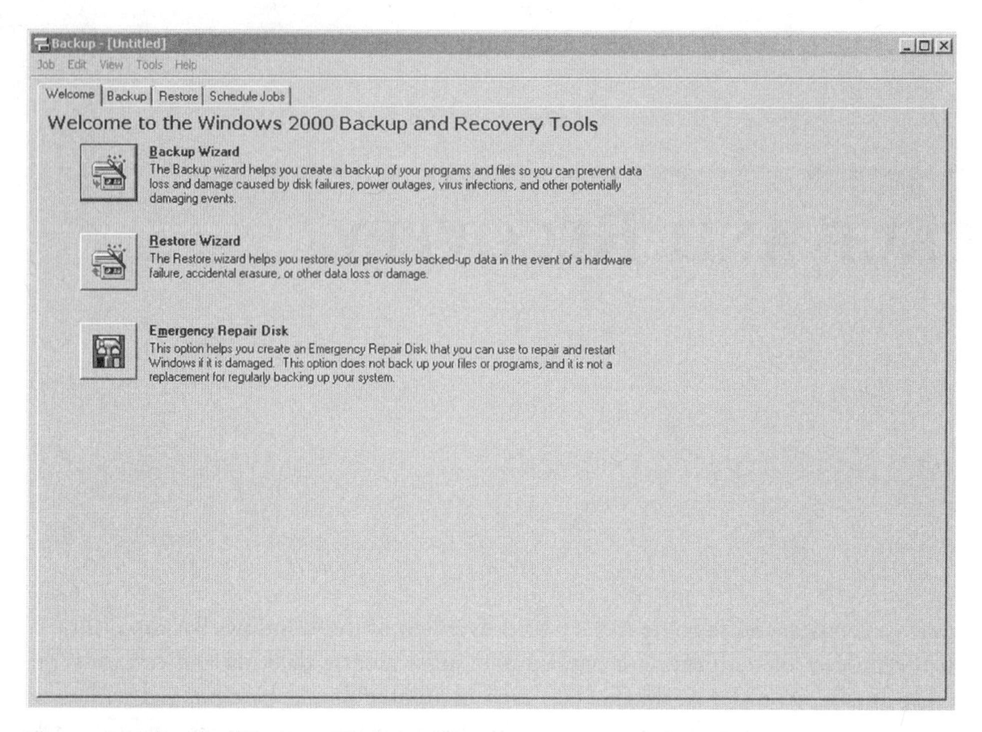

Figure L14.1 The Windows Backup utility

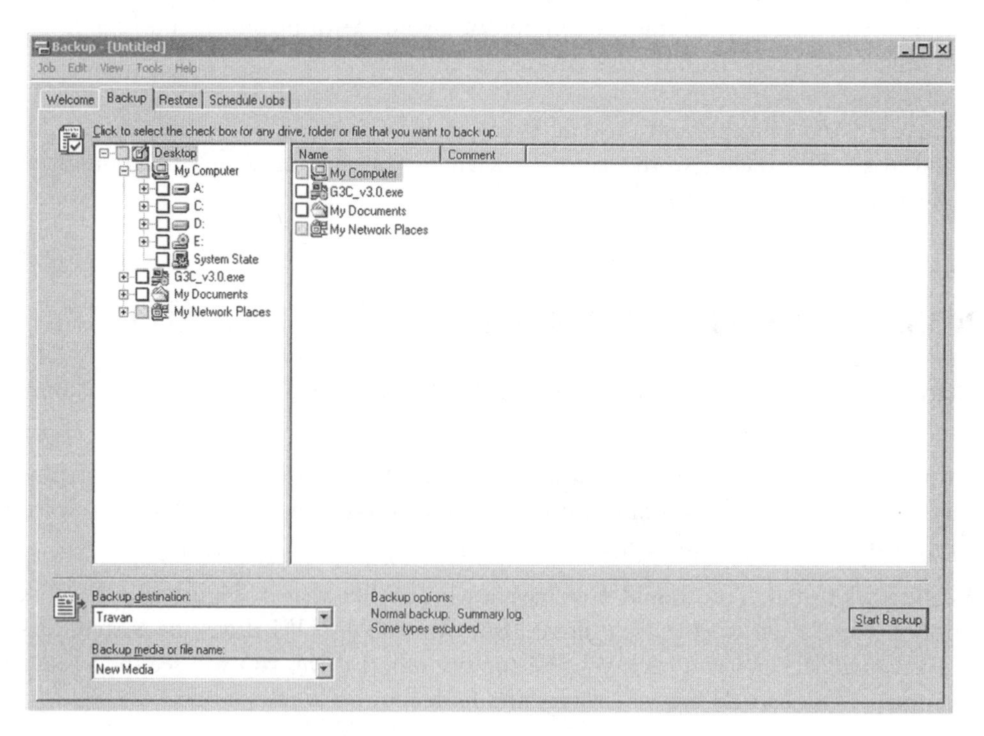

Figure L14.2 Backup options

the only option will be File. Note in **Figure L14.3** that I have the option of backing up to a miniQIC, Travan, or File. Backup media or file name allows you to indicate the form of medium you're going to use or select a file name (with full directory path) for your backup.

5. Now click the Tools option in the menu and select Options (**Figure L14.4**). Under Backup Type you can select Normal, Copy, Differential, Incremental, or Daily. You'll be looking at this section in closer detail in Exercise 2, so for now, move on to the next section.

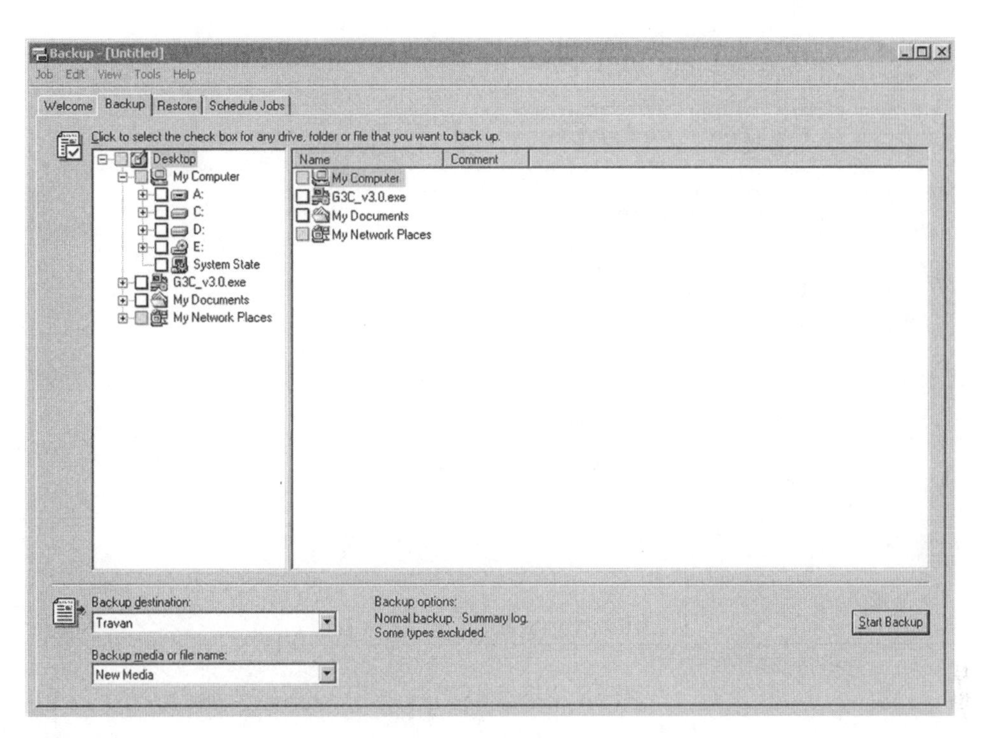

Figure L14.3 Selecting the destination for your backup

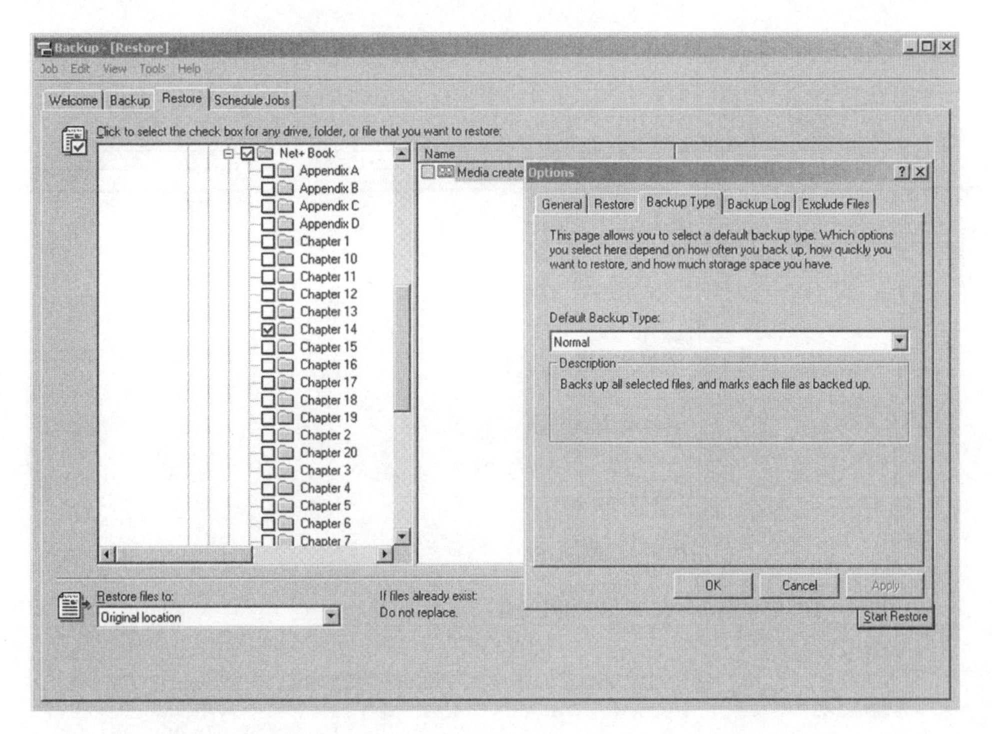

Figure L14.4 Selecting the backup type

6. Click the Restore tab. In this screen (**Figure L14.5**), you are presented with all possible locations on your computer where a backup could exist. If you have no tape drive installed on your machine, the only option available to you will be File.
7. In Figure L14.5, I've opened the Travan option to show that my last backup included my C: drive and my D: drive. In **Figure L14.6**, I've opened the contents of the D: drive. When you do this, your tape drive will go into action as it tries to load the contents of that folder. When

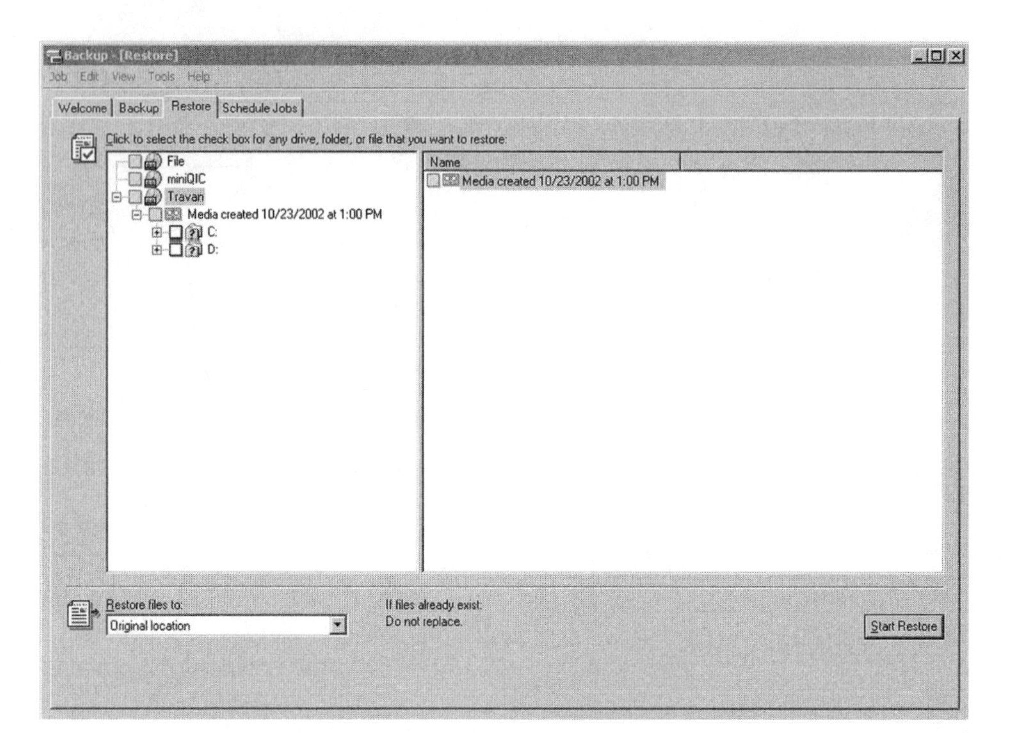

Figure L14.5 Restore options in the Windows Backup utility

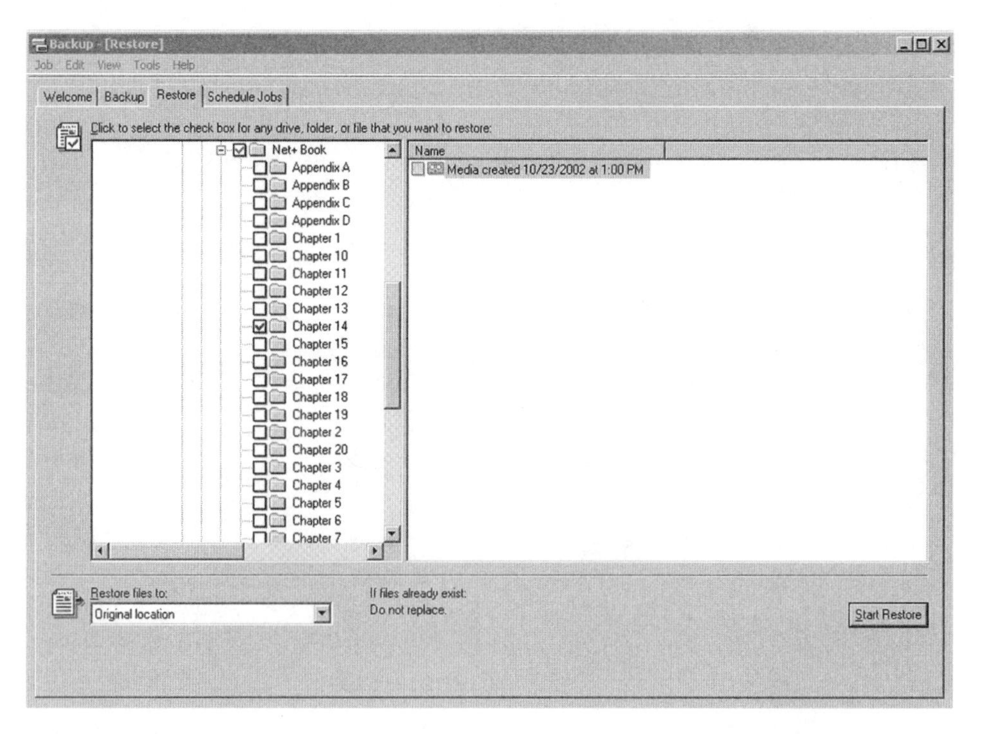

Figure L14.6 The Windows Backup utility allows you to selectively restore files.

it has done that, it will rewind the tape. This can take several minutes on Travan drives. DAT or DLT drives are usually somewhat quicker.

8. Notice that by clicking just a single subdirectory or file (as I've done in Figure L14.6), I can restore just that file or directory. By clicking an entire drive, I will restore the contents of that entire drive.

SUMMARY OF EXERCISE 1

1. Where do you find the backup utility in Windows XP?
2. What is the difference between a differential backup and an incremental backup?
3. What is the difference between copying your files and backing them up?

EXERCISE 2: PERFORMING A BACKUP

In this exercise, you will back up a single directory on your hard drive to a file. In order to expedite the procedure, you will select a small directory. You will use the one you created using your own first name.

1. On the Backup screen, click the Backup tab. Highlight the hard disk drive that contains your folder, and then click the checkbox next to that folder (**Figure L14.7**).
2. Under Backup destination, select File, and under Backup media or file name, change A:\backup.bkf to C:\backup.bkf. (Note that in the real world, backing up files from your hard drive to your hard drive is not a very sane practice. If your hard drive fails, it all fails, not just selected directories!)

NOTE: Most backup software still offers the option of backing up your files to floppy. This is a viable option for backing up just a few files, but it can also be used when you have a file that is too large to fit onto a floppy disk. The Backup utility will split large files onto several floppy diskettes. If you want, you can back up your entire hard drive to a collection of floppy diskettes. However, I would like to go on record as saying that the idea of backing up my 40GB hard disk to 27,778 diskettes is not a project that is close to my heart.

3. Click Start Backup. Since you've selected an extremely small backup set, this should take only a second or two. When it is finished you will get a screen like the one in **Figure L14.8**.

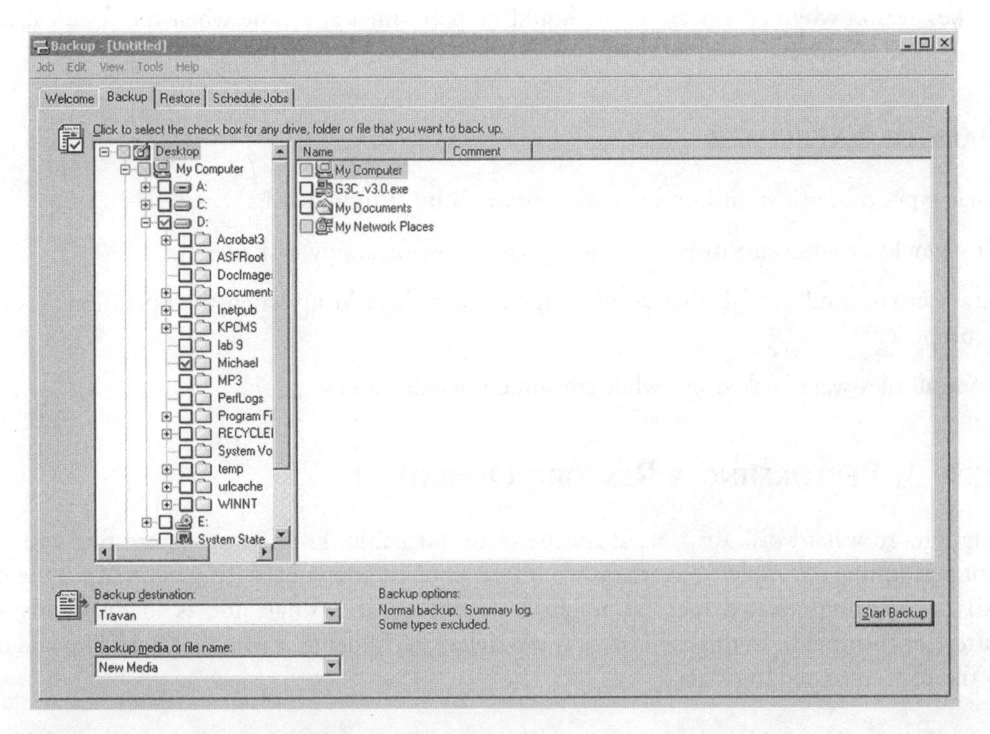

Figure L14.7 Selecting the files to be backed up

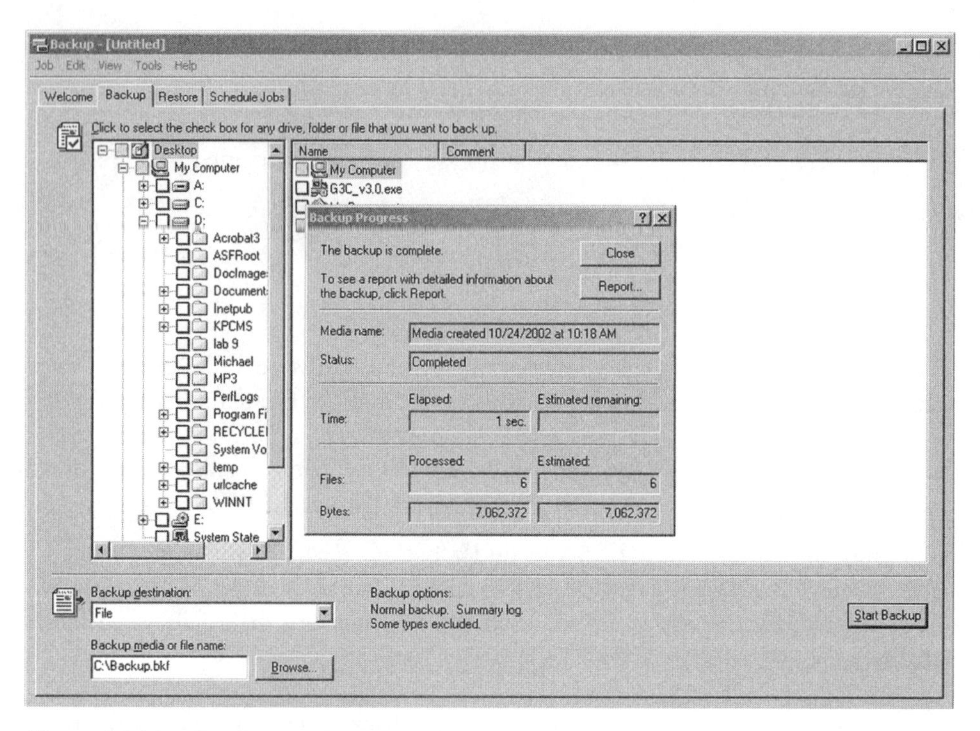

Figure L14.8 The Backup Progress screen

4. Here you are informed of the time and date of the backup along with whether it was successful or not. In addition, you can see how long the backup took, how many files were processed, and the total number of bytes that were backed up. Now click the Report button.

5. For **Figure L14.9**, I performed a backup to my tape drive of the My Documents folder on my hard drive. In order to generate some failure messages, I left Microsoft Word, along with several documents, open. Notice the number of files that were skipped because they were in use. This is a key reason why network backups should be performed at a time when the fewest users (none at all, if possible) will be active on the network.

SUMMARY OF EXERCISE 2

1. What types of destination locations are supported by Windows XP?
2. Why wouldn't you want to back up your hard drive to floppy diskettes?
3. How can you find out whether all of your files were backed up when the operation is completed?
4. If not all files were backed up, what are some possible causes?

EXERCISE 3: PERFORMING A RESTORE OPERATION

Restoring data to a hard disk drive need not be cause for panic. From your restore file, you have the option of performing a complete restore (as would be required after a hard disk failure once the disk was replaced) or restoring selected files (as might be necessary if a single file is inadvertently deleted, overwritten, or corrupted). In this exercise, you will delete the folder that you just backed up and use your backup file to recover the lost data.

1. First of all, go into Windows Explorer and delete your folder. Since you shared this folder out in an earlier lab, you will be warned that others might be using the folder. Click OK.

```
Backup Status
Operation: Backup
Active backup destination: Travan
Media name: "Media created 10/23/2002 at 1:00 PM"

Backup of "C: "
Backup set #1 on media #1
Backup description: "Set created 10/23/2002 at 1:00 PM"
Backup Type: Normal

Backup started on 10/23/2002 at 1:04 PM.
Backup completed on 10/23/2002 at 1:32 PM.
Directories: 4
Files: 180
Bytes: 826,099,901
Time:  28 minutes and  3 seconds
Media name: "Media created 10/23/2002 at 1:00 PM"

Backup of "D: "
Backup set #2 on media #1
Backup description: "Set created 10/23/2002 at 1:00 PM"
Backup Type: Normal

Backup started on 10/23/2002 at 1:32 PM.
Warning: The file \Documents and Settings\Administrator\Application
Data\Microsoft\Outlook\outcmd.dat in use - skipped.
Warning: The file \Documents and Settings\Administrator\Application
Data\Microsoft\Templates\Normal.dot in use - skipped.
Warning: The file \Documents and Settings\Administrator\Application
Data\Microsoft\Word\AutoRecovery save of Assault on Christian Island, ver 3.asd in
use - skipped.
Warning: The file \Documents and Settings\Administrator\Application
Data\Microsoft\Word\STARTUP\PDFMaker.dot in use - skipped.
Warning: The file \Documents and Settings\Administrator\Local Settings\Application
Data\Microsoft\Outlook\outlook.pst in use - skipped.
```

Figure L14.9 Viewing the Backup log

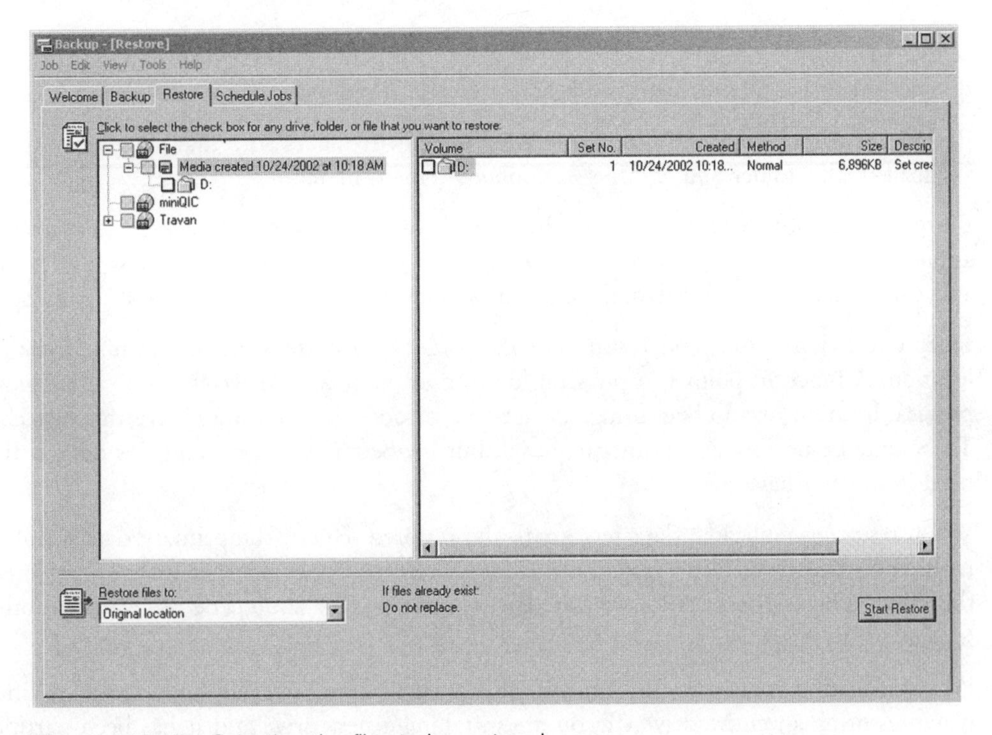

Figure L14.10 Selecting the files to be restored

2. In the Backup utility, click the Restore tab. Click the + next to File and highlight the media set you created in Exercise 2 (**Figure L14.10**).

3. Check the box next to your folder. Make sure that the option Restore files to has Original location selected, and click the Start Restore button. The Confirm Restore screen will appear (**Figure L14.11**) and offer the choice of starting your Restore or selecting Advanced Options.

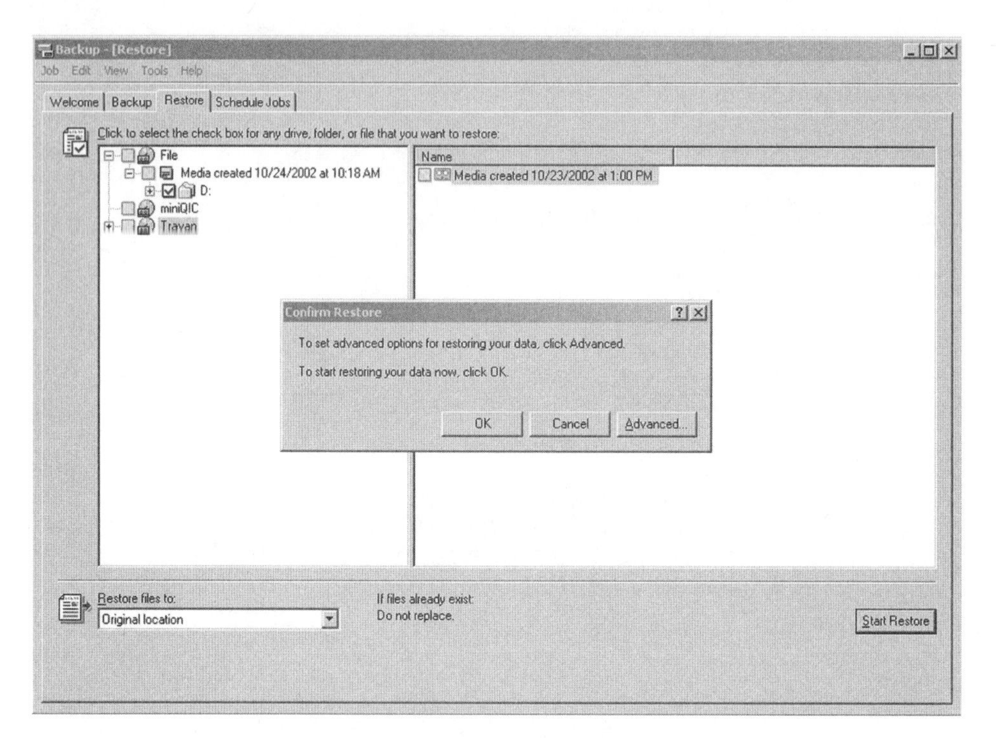

Figure L14.11 The Confirm Restore screen

4. Click the Advanced button. You don't really need to use any of these options, but now is a good time to explore them, since you're here anyway. These options include:

   a. Restore security: This should be checked by default. It makes sure that all permissions assigned to this folder and the files it contains remain intact.

   b. Restore Removable Storage database: Removable Storage is a Windows service that allows applications to access and share resources stored on removable media. Unless you've installed and configured Removable Storage on your system it is not necessary to select this option.

   c. Restore junction points, and restore file and folder data under junction points to the original location: A junction point is a physical location on your hard drive that points to another physical location or another storage device. It's a good idea to always leave this box checked. There may be no junction points required, but it's better to have it and not need it than to need it and not have it.

   d. When restoring replicated data sets, mark the restored data as the primary data for all replicas: This is most likely grayed out on your screen. It ensures that information used by the File Replication service knows whether or not this data should be replicated to other servers on the network.

   e. Preserve existing volume mount points: This particular option really only makes a difference when restoring an entire drive. If you are installing a new drive and it has been partitioned, it is best if this option were not checked. Otherwise, new partitions will be created on the drive.

5. For the purposes of this exercise, none of these options are needed. So click Cancel to get back to the Confirm Restore screen and click OK. You'll be prompted to enter the location of the backup file. C:\backup.bkf should be the default location (**Figure L14.12**). Click OK.

6. You will briefly seen a Restore Progress screen flashing the files as they are restored, and then Backup will settle into the screen shown in **Figure L14.13**. As you can see, it is identical to the

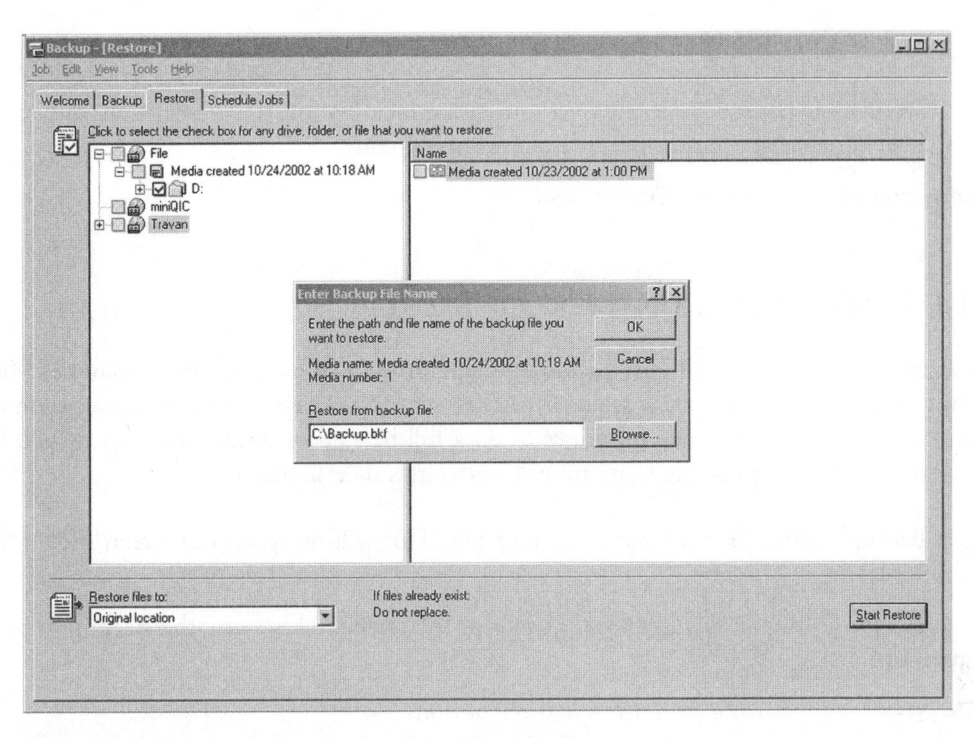

Figure L14.12 Confirming the location of backup files

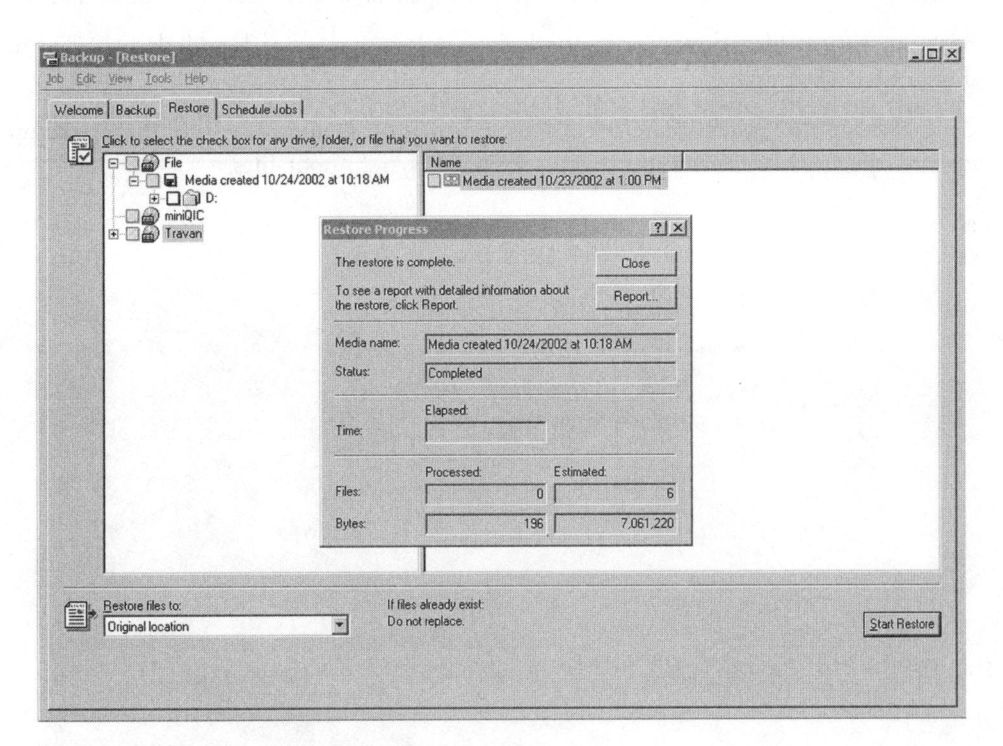

Figure L14.13 The Restore Progress screen

Backup Progress screen you saw in the previous exercise. It, too, offers the option of viewing a report, which will also be identical to the one you looked at in that exercise.

7. Go to Windows Explorer once again. You should be able to browse to your folder and see that all contents are intact.

SUMMARY OF EXERCISE 3

1. One of your users has inadvertently overwritten a critical file on the server. Can you get just that file back, or do you have to restore the whole system?
2. Name some of the advanced options available.

EXERCISE 4: SCHEDULING UNATTENDED BACKUPS

In this area, the Windows Backup utility is a substantial improvement over previous versions of Microsoft's backup utilities. In this exercise, you'll see how you can schedule different backups to occur on different days of the week. You'll set up your machines to do a full backup on Friday evening at 8:00 P.M. and then do incremental backups at the same time Monday through Thursday.

1. In the Backup utility, click the Schedule Jobs tab. This will bring up the screen shown in **Figure L14.14**.
2. Click Add Job in the lower right-hand corner of the screen. This starts the Backup Wizard (**Figure L14.15**).
3. Click Next. The following screen offers three options.
   a. Back up everything on my computer: Does just what it suggests. However, don't put too much faith in what it says. As you saw earlier, open or locked files will not be backed up.
   b. Back up selected files, drives, or network data: Allows you to pick and choose what material should be backed up.
   c. Only back up the System State data: This information includes the files that make up the registry, the COM+ registration database, and all system boot files.

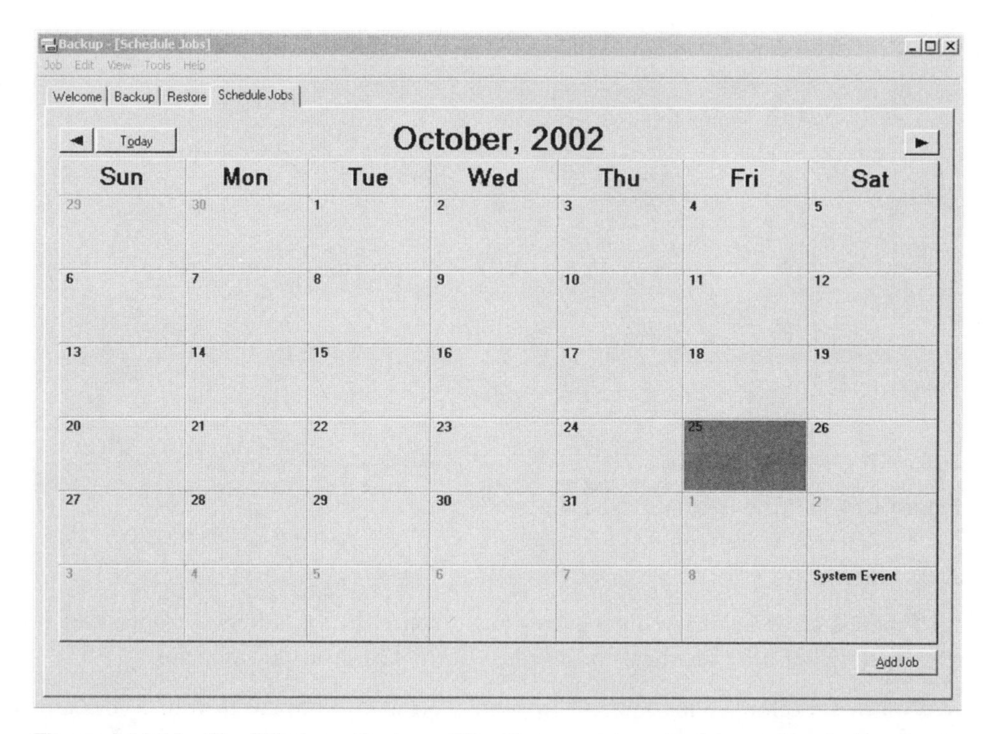

Figure L14.14 The Windows Backup utility allows you to schedule unattended backups.

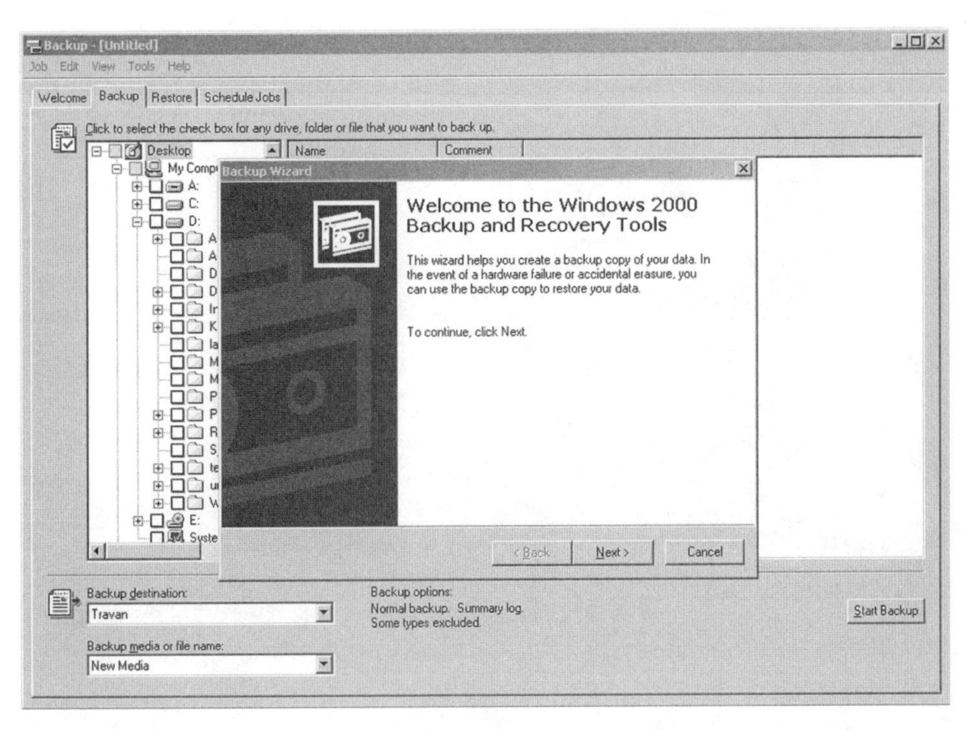

Figure L14.15 Adding a new job to the Backup schedule

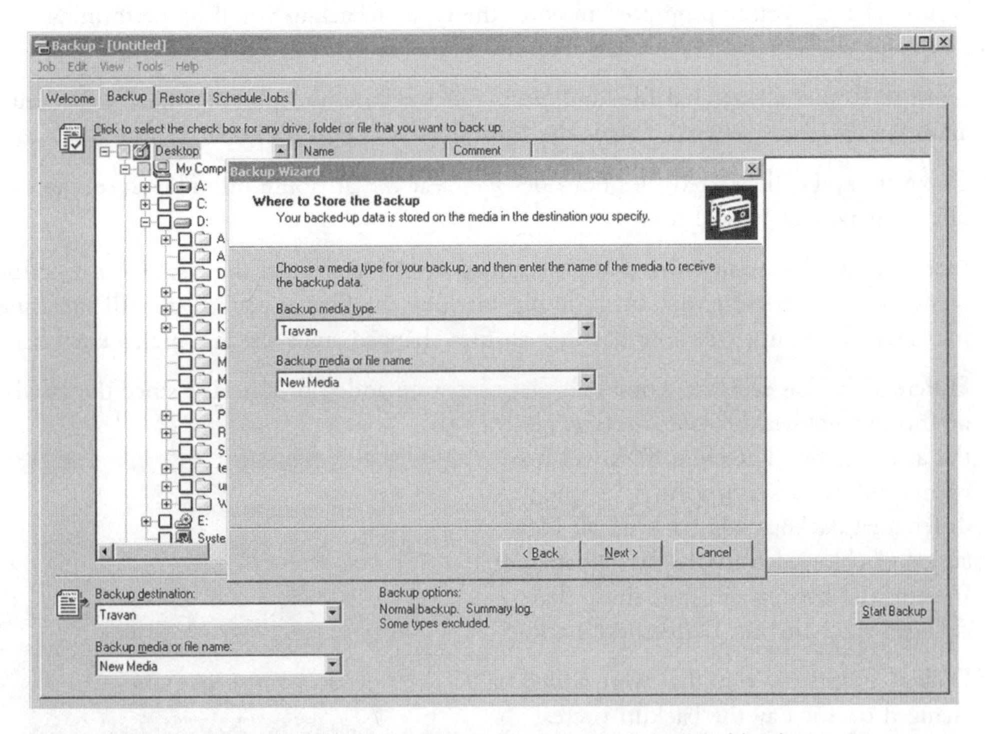

Figure L14.16 Selecting the destination device for your scheduled backups

4. Select Back up everything on my computer and click Next. This brings up the screen in **Figure L14.16**, where you are prompted to select the destination for your backup. In my illustration, I'll select my Travan drive. Depending on your setup, you should either select the tape drive that is available, or select File.

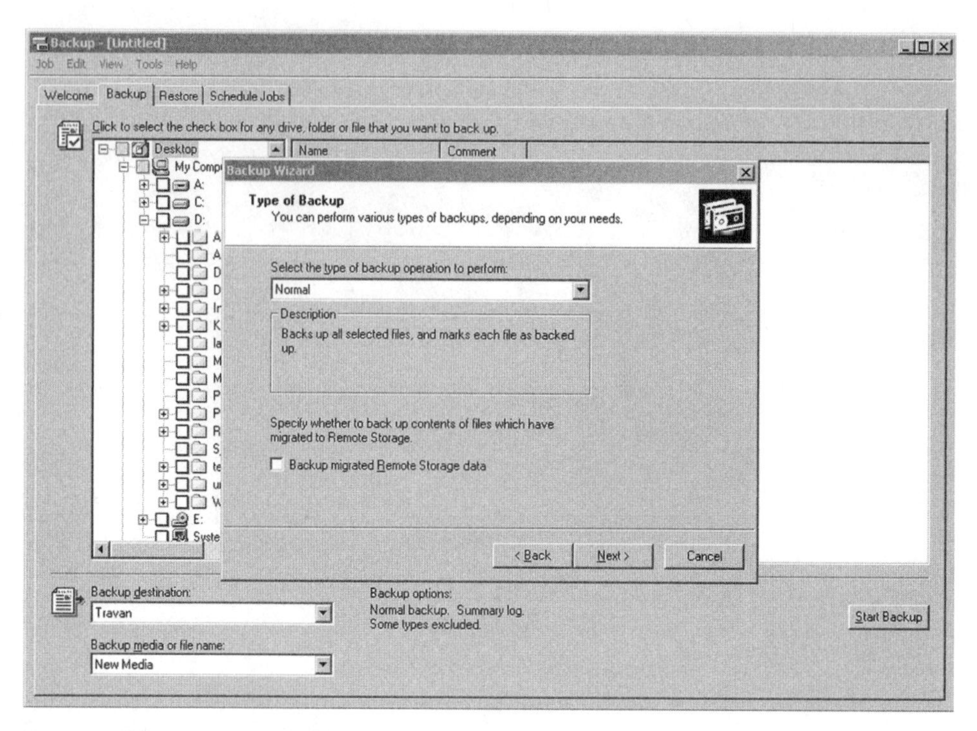

Figure L14.17 Selecting the type of backup to be performed

5. In **Figure L14.17**, you're prompted to enter the type of backup you'll be performing. The options are

   a. Normal: Copies all selected files and clears the attribute bit, marking them as backed up. If an entire drive was selected, this is the equivalent of a Full backup.

   b. Copy: It copies all selected files but does *not* clear the attribute bit. Therefore, the files will not be marked as backed up.

   c. Incremental: Copies any files that were added or changed since the last Normal or Incremental backup. It clears the attribute bit, marking the files as backed up. All subsequent incremental backups will now back up all files changed since the last incremental backup.

   d. Differential: This selection copies all files that were added or changed since the last Normal or Incremental backup, but does *not* clear the attribute bit. Therefore, files will not be marked as backed up. All subsequent differential backups will back up all files added or changed since the last Normal or Incremental backup, but not those that changed since the last Differential backup.

   e. Daily: Copies only files that were added or changed on the day the backup is created. The attribute bit is not cleared.

6. Since you are creating a full backup, select Normal and click Next. The Backup Wizard now asks you how you want to back your data up (**Figure L14.18**). Two independent options are offered.

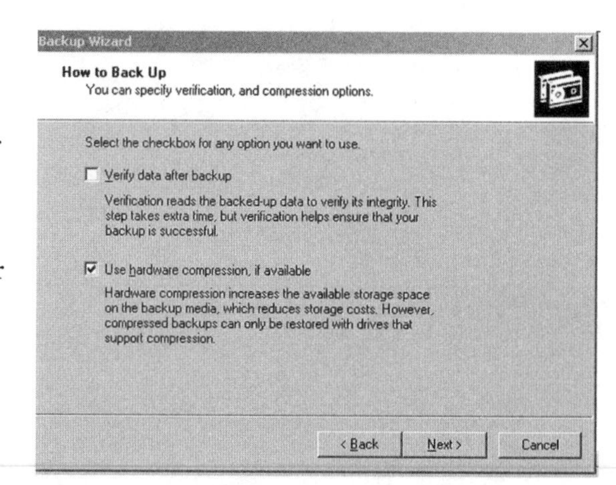

Figure L14.18 Configuring how the backup is to be done

a. Verify data after backup: This option compares each copy of the file to the original when the backup has been completed. This can add a substantial amount of time to the backup but adds security for your data.

b. Use hardware compression, if available: This allows you to pack more data onto a single tape and reduces the amount of time it takes for a backup to be completed.

7. Click Next. You'll be given the Media Options screen (**Figure L14.19**). Normally, you would be using the same tapes over and over again. In that case, you would make sure that the option Replace the data on the media with this backup is selected. If the data is sensitive data, you can add a bit more security by selecting the option Allow only the owner and the Administrator access to the data and to any backup appended to this media. The latter option is not selected by default.

8. The Backup Label screen now appears (**Figure L14.20**). This is the information that you should write onto the label of the tape before storing it. Click Next.

9. Now you'll be prompted to establish when you want your backup to occur (**Figure L14.21**). Select Later and give your job a name. Call it Weekly Full.

10. Now click the Set Schedule button. Under Schedule Task, select Weekly. Under Start Time, select 12:00 A.M. Under Schedule Task Weekly select 1 for Every and click the Friday checkbox, as in **Figure L14.22**. Make sure that all other days are deselected.

11. Click OK and on the Backup Wizard screen click Next. This will bring up the Completing the Backup Wizard screen as shown in **Figure L14.23**. Click Finish and you're done.

12. Now, on the Schedule Jobs calendar, little icons with a blue N (for Normal) will appear on all Fridays from this date forward.

13. To schedule daily differential backups to occur, repeat the preceding procedure except for two key differences. In step 5, where you configured backup type, select differential. In

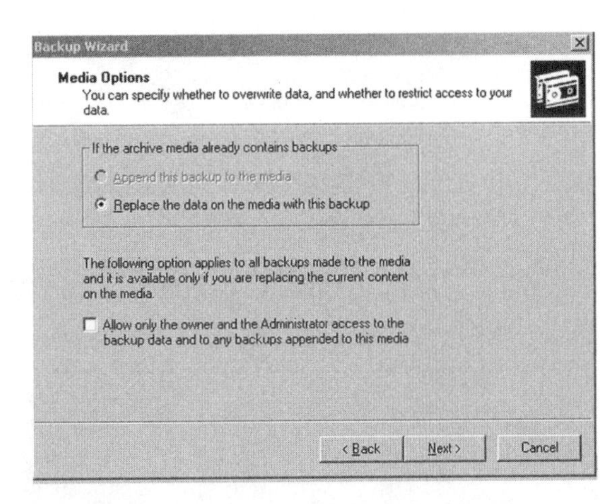

Figure L14.19 You have to tell the Backup utility how media is to be handled.

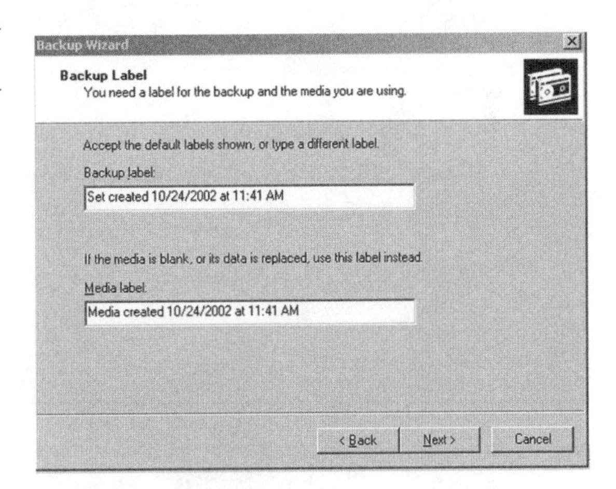

Figure L14.20 The Windows Backup utility is even gracious enough to remind you to label your backup tapes.

Figure L14.21 You must tell the scheduler what time you want these backups to occur. Choose a time when there will be the fewest users on the network.

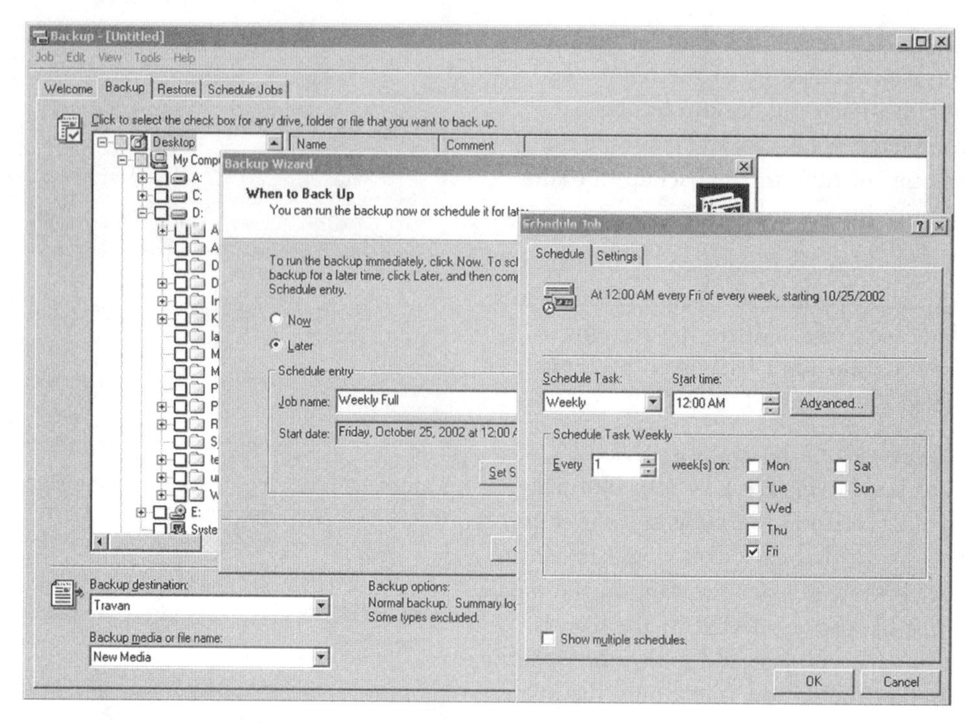

Figure L14.22 Scheduling daily or weekly events

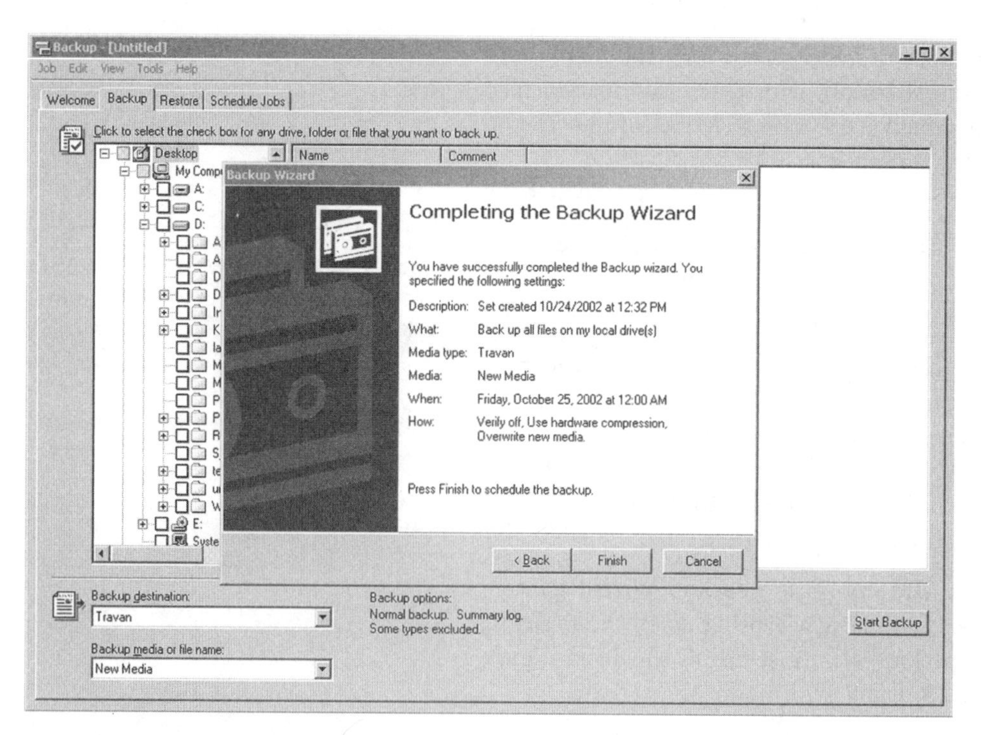

Figure L14.23 Completing the Backup Wizard

step 10, where the events are scheduled, select Weekly as before, but check the boxes for Mon, Tue, Wed, and Thu. Under Job name call it Daily Differential. Finish the Wizard, and now icons will appear on all Mondays through Thursdays with a green D (for differential). Your calendar should now resemble **Figure L14.24**.

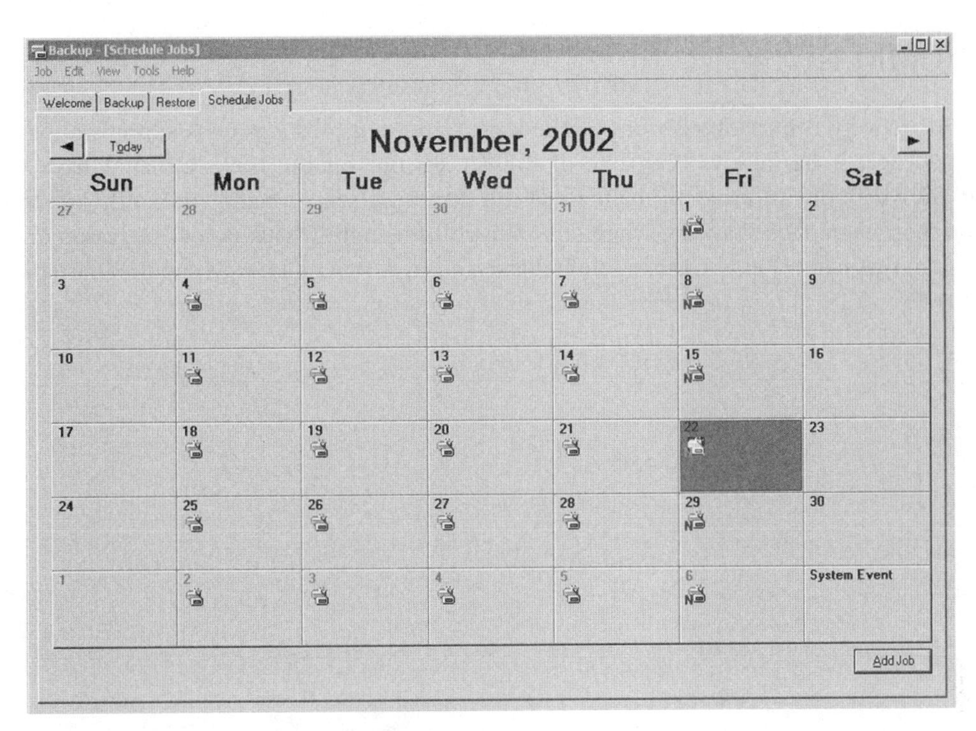

Figure L14.24 A Scheduling Calendar with events in place

14. Now the most important step of all. Make sure there is a tape in the drive for each day an event is scheduled. It may seem like a no-brainer, but an empty tape drive is undoubtedly the most common cause of backup failure there is.

NOTE: You may notice if you look carefully that there is no option in the Backup Scheduler to delete a scheduled event. If you need to delete a scheduled backup for any reason, open Control Panel and double-click Scheduled Tasks. Highlight the job you want to blow away and press the <delete> key on your keyboard. It'll ask you whether you're sure. Click OK and the jobs are gone.

SUMMARY OF EXERCISE 4

1. You want to schedule your server to perform a Full backup every week, starting at 12:00 A.M. on Saturday. But you want your daily backups to be differential backups and to run at 10:00 P.M. every other night. How do you keep these from conflicting?
2. What is the primary cause of backup failure in unattended scheduled backups?
3. You need to delete one or more scheduled backup jobs, but there is no delete function in the Backup utility. How do you delete them?

LAB REVIEW

1. You want to set up a backup routine in which you do a full backup once a week. Then every night for the rest of the week you want to back up only the data that was added or changed that day. Which method do you select for those subsequent days?
2. You have a scheduled backup that you want to remove. Where do you go to do this?

Lab Summary

Backup and recovery is undoubtedly one of the most important jobs a systems administrator does. Yet, in my experience, it has always been one of those tasks put on the back burner. I have worked in organizations where the information maintained was extremely sensitive and vital to the existence of the place. And more than once I saw my "superiors" blow off the nightly backup for one reason or the other. Don't get into that habit. Put together a solid scheme and stick to it. That way, should disaster ever occur, you'll be ready.